BE A TEACHER

—You Can Make a Difference—

by America's Finest Teachers

Edited by
Philip Bigler and Stephanie Bishop

VANDAMERE PRESS
St. Petersburg, Florida

Published by
Vandamere Press
P.O. Box 149
St. Petersburg, FL 33731
USA

ISBN-10: 0-918339-70-7
ISBN-13: 978-0918339-70-6

Table of Contents

Acknowledgements

This book has been truly a collaborative effort, the product of many dedicated and talented teachers. We are indebted to each for their willingness to share some of their collective wisdom with our next generation of American educators. They all have a common belief that quality teachers are vital to insuring the intellectual health and well-being of our nation in the 21st Century.

We would also like to acknowledge the Milken Family Foundation for its commitment to quality public schools and for its recognition of the important role that teachers play in our society. Likewise, the Council of Chief State School Officers (CCSSO) has done much to elevate the teaching profession through its ongoing research and the National Teacher of the Year program. The Virginia Department of Education has been equally supportive and has a steadfast commitment to assist and mentor new educators in making the often difficult transition from the academic world to the realities of the modern classroom. Through the department's generous financial support of the Virginia Teachers of Promise Institute, pre-service teachers from all of the state's 37 teacher accrediting colleges and universities meet annually for a truly unique weekend of celebration and quality in-service instruction.

Of course, this book would never have been possible without the vision of our publisher, Art Brown, at Vandamere Press. Art is committed to publishing significant and meaningful books and for that we will be eternally grateful. Our editor, Pat Berger, was a source of sound advice and much needed direction and we would like to thank her for both her time and patience throughout this process.

We have been privileged to work with two very talented young women at James Madison University—Katie Overstreet and Ashley Connelly. Katie is in the process of finishing graduate school and will soon become an elementary school guidance counselor. For the last three years, she has been a dedicated member of the James Madison

Center and she has assisted in the proof-reading and editing of this entire manuscript. Ashley Connelly is working on completing her certification and licensure in Art Education. She, too, has been invaluable in the production of *Be a Teacher* and has relentlessly worked through countless deadlines and crises without complaint. Both of these young people represent the very best for the future of American education and we know that like you, they will . . . make a difference.

Foreword

Philip Bigler and Stephanie Bishop

If the children . . . are untaught, their ignorance and vices will in future life cost us much dearer in their consequences, than it would have done, in their correction, by a good education. —*Thomas Jefferson*

In Act I of Robert Bolt's classic play, *A Man for All Seasons,* Sir Thomas More is confronted by a confused young man, Richard Rich, who is searching for some meaning in his life. He hopes, through More's intercession, to obtain a position at court that would bring with it both title and great wealth. Sir Thomas, however, was well aware of the temptations, corruption, and moral degradation prevalent in the royal government of Tudor England. He advises Rich to seek something more substantive in his life: "Why not be a teacher?" More asks. "You'd be a fine teacher. Perhaps even a great one...be a teacher."

Thomas More is remembered by history as a man of impeccable character, stellar reputation, and steadfast principles. Even in his day when education was erratic at best, he understood that teaching was an honorable and worthy profession. He also believed that people of great talent could find dignity through their work with students. "Be a teacher"—More's simple yet profound advice still resonates today as we seek an entire new generation of committed educators who will make a positive difference in our schools.

Over the course of our careers, we have been privileged to work with many extraordinary educators. The award-winning teachers, who have kindly contributed to this book, truly represent the best and brightest in American education. Their continuing commitment, enthusiasm, and dedication remain a constant source of inspiration. They have certainly earned the important recognition they have received for their outstanding work in our nation's schools. Each of our authors wants to share some of their experiences and the wisdom they have gained from their years in public education. They hope to help new and aspiring teachers bridge the unavoidable gap (even chasm) between the academic world and the daily realities of our modern classrooms.

Today's new teachers are facing numerous challenges and obstacles. Indeed, the attrition rate for novice teachers is appalling, but much of this attrition is caused by a sense of isolation or a perceived sense of inadequacy. It is our fondest hope that this book will serve as a source of inspiration and guidance and that it will help new educators become great teachers. We have created a website (www.great-teaching.com) to supplement the chapters in this book. It will serve as a resource where you will find additional materials that will assist you as you begin your career journey as a classroom teacher.

Our ultimate goal in writing *Be a Teacher* is to celebrate and elevate the teaching profession. It is important that our society recognize the great service that teachers perform, but it is likewise essential that teachers conduct themselves as true professionals and worthy role models for their students. We honestly believe that you can make a difference through teaching.

Be sure to visit our website often.
We will post regular updates, contact information,
multi-media files, lesson plans and other materials that
will help you on your path to becoming a great teacher.
www.great-teaching.com

Chapter One

A Call to Teach: Excellence for a Lifetime

Jo Lynne DeMary

Former Superintendent of Public Instruction
Commonwealth of Virginia

Teaching is leaving a vestige of one's self in the development of another. And surely the student is a bank where you can deposit your most precious treasures.
　　　　　　　　　　　　　　　　　　　　　　—Eugene P. Bertin

I smoothed down the red and blue plaid dress that my mother had bought me for the first day of school. The colors were vibrant, and the fabric felt luxuriously new to the touch. My mother had carefully saved money from her grocery budget so that I would have a new dress to wear when I began third grade in a new school. I was proud of the dress and eager to show it off to Barbara, my first friend, in my new neighborhood in the small village of Highland Springs, Virginia.

As I squirmed on the tall kitchen stool and kept a lookout for Barbara, mother tied matching, freshly ironed red ribbons into my hair. She kissed me and said that she knew I would make lots of new friends in my new school. Barbara arrived, and together we set off for Highland Springs Elementary School. Thank goodness my family had moved to our new house during the summer in time for me to make friends before school started. Imagine walking to a new school all alone!

After a block's walk, Barbara and I met up with our mutual friend, Carolyn, and together, the three of us giggled our way to the brick, two-story elementary school. We so hoped we would be in the same classroom. As we approached the school, I was overwhelmed by new-student "jitters" and prayed that I would have a "nice" teacher.

1

Mrs. Lipscomb, the principal, sternly directed the arriving students to the large gymnasium, a benefit of our building's prior service as a high school. There were a lot of students crammed into the gym, but they settled down as Mrs. Lipscomb began speaking into a portable megaphone. Her welcome was brief and to the point: "You are here to learn and I expect you to be of good behavior and to do your very best every day." She made it clear that she was there for those who chose to do differently. I resolved then and there to see very little of her.

The teachers, beginning with the first grade, then read the names of the children on their class rosters. It was important to listen carefully so as not to have to wait until the very end and realize that you had missed your name. All of a sudden, I was seized by the fear that my name was not on any of the third-grade teachers' lists since I had just moved to the community. I wanted to run home to the security of my mother's smile or even all the way back to the tobacco farm in North Carolina, where we lived three houses from the school and everyone went to the same church and knew each other by name. I was drawn out of my panic by the quiet but strong voice of Miss Pugh as she called "Jo Lynne Stancil." I quickly fell in line behind my new classmates as Miss Pugh finished her list of 35 names. With her finger over her lips, she led us quietly out of the gym. Little did I know that my life would be changed forever under the tutelage of this demanding but caring teacher.

Miss Ruby Pugh was tall and slender. She wore flowered dresses and smelled of lilac powder. Her dark black hair was neatly swirled into a bun on the back of her head. She wasn't particularly attractive by today's standards, but she had engaging brown eyes that looked directly into yours so you knew she was speaking just to you. I didn't know how old she was, but I knew she wasn't young or inexperienced.

Miss Pugh's classroom was full of desks, crowded by today's standards, but with the big, tall windows thrown open, it seemed spacious and airy. The attractive bulletin boards advertised the content we would learn that year, and Miss Pugh was quick to put us right to

Jo Lynne DeMary is one of Virginia's most popular state school superintendents. DeMary helped mold the once-reviled Standards of Learning while serving as assistant superintendent in the mid-1990s. She believed strongly that a statewide testing program would expose flaws and drive improvement in educational quality. As superintendent she won over critics with genuine concern about the problems imposed by the tests on teachers and students. Her efforts to clarify instructional demands, combined with willingness to adjust unreasonable requirements, helped turn an unpopular program into a broadly accepted one.

DeMary was the first woman to hold the post, but her greatest achievement was in bridging a poisonous political divide. She was appointed to the post by former GOP Gov. Jim Gilmore in 2000 and retained by Democratic Gov. Mark Warner in 2002. The progress of Virginia schools during DeMary's tenure is much noted; scores on both state and federal achievement tests improved substantially. Challenges remain: an unacceptable achievement gap in minority achievement, a need to improve teacher retention, a perplexing dropout rate.

In each area, however, DeMary made improvements. Success may be attributable, in part, to the fact that she never lost sight of her underlying purpose. In a 2002 interview, she noted that her aim was to walk in the footsteps of Miss Ruby Pugh, her third grade teacher, who had "the most amazing ability to look at each child and envision such wonderful potential and she thought she was responsible for helping them reach it." As a prize pupil retires, Miss Pugh might say, "Well done."

—*The Virginian-Pilot*
September 9, 2005

work. When she wasn't "teaching in the front of the room," Miss Pugh was moving about, monitoring our work with sharp eyes that seemed to immediately detect a problem or pupil in need of her attention. If a student experienced difficulty, Miss Pugh knew that she needed to do better as a teacher. I never heard her blame a student for failing to learn. There were no special classes, after-school tutorials, reading specialists, or Title I teachers; there were just 35 students and Miss Ruby Pugh.

While all of the children in the class were white, and most of us were from blue collar homes, we came in different ages and sizes with different cognitive abilities and levels of home support. Miss Pugh accepted us as we were. She visited the homes of students suspected of playing hooky, she stayed after school to help struggling students who needed more time, and she quietly slipped bags of clothes to students who needed them. It was obvious that the showers of this former high school building were used on more than one occasion by students who came to school in need of a bath. Most importantly, she encouraged each of us to do our best, a standard that she set. When a student turned in a paper, she always asked if it was his or her best effort before accepting it. How I labored over my work to make sure it met Miss Pugh's high expectations.

If a student finished an assignment before the others, he or she was expected to read. "Read, read, read," Miss Pugh would repeat. "You can go anywhere or be anything you want to be through books." She introduced me to the *Bobbsey Twins* series, and with my friends, we started a collection.

By the end of the year, as I looked around the room at this odd assortment of boys and girls, I realized what a magic year it had been for each of us. We were prolific readers, we had mastered cursive handwriting, we loved to write and act out stories, we knew our number facts, we had experienced foods and cultures far away from our little village of Highland Springs, and we had explored the wonders of science through experiments and projects. More importantly for me, I knew in my heart that I wanted to be a teacher, but not just any teacher: I wanted to be a third-grade teacher just like Miss Ruby Pugh.

It was that vision that kept me focused and goal-oriented during the remainder of elementary school, into a brand new junior high school, and onto my beloved Highland Springs High School. I never wavered from my desire to be just like my third-grade teacher and to one day make an impact on the lives of young people like she had on me. As my school years went by, I carefully watched each of my teachers, measuring them against the daunting standard set by Miss Pugh.

My parents were not college educated and they didn't talk to me about going to college. But they did encourage me to dream about what I wanted to be when I grew up. My mother and father wanted their children to receive a quality education, and they understood the power of education to elevate individuals and families.

While Highland Springs High School provided the guidance I needed to pursue college, I was discouraged from applying to my first choice, the College of William and Mary in Williamsburg. I fell in love with this historic institution during my first visit, but few students from Highland Springs High School attended William and Mary. We had good, but not great, course offerings in our school. William and Mary was viewed as much too competitive for students from rural eastern Henrico County. This discouragement set a fire under me to achieve my personal best. I studied the college catalog, I read all the literature available regarding the characteristics of students who were accepted by William and Mary, and I mapped out a plan to gain admission.

I took the most rigorous courses Highland Springs had to offer and set out to be the valedictorian of my class. I became an active member, and ultimately a leader, in numerous clubs and organizations to demonstrate that, as a student, I could give as well as receive. There were so many details and deadlines to follow for college applications. While my parents were supportive, it usually fell on my shoulders to get everything completed and submitted on time.

While waiting to learn whether I would be accepted by William and Mary, I worked with my counselor on financing my college education. To this day, it is difficult for me to talk about the sacrifices that my parents made to help pay for my education. Their sacrifices were supplemented by community scholarships and a state-funded Virginia Teaching Scholarship. Repayment of this scholarship would be through teaching in the classrooms of the Commonwealth's public schools.

I stood by the mailbox on April 1, 1964, waiting for news from the William and Mary admissions office. Acceptances from other schools had been placed on hold as I waited for this one last piece of correspondence. It was a joyous occasion for my entire family when the mail finally arrived on that spring day, and we learned that I was going to the College of William and Mary to become a teacher.

The four years of college flew by. I struggled with the academics initially, but after the freshman year, I understood better the expectations of my professors. As a psychology minor, I began to understand the relationship between expectations and academic achievement. Then, in my junior year, I began my education courses. I was assigned to student teach in the third-grade class of Mrs. Nimmo at Matthew Whaley Elementary School in Williamsburg. I was her nineteenth student teacher. Mrs. Nimmo was such an outstanding teacher that the college pleaded with the school district to assign a William and Mary student teacher every year to her classroom, even in the face of grumbling by other teachers.

Mrs. Nimmo's classroom reflected the changes that had taken place in public education since I was a pupil in Miss Ruby Pugh's class. Class sizes were now closely monitored, a reading specialist and other support personnel were available for students, individualized instruction within the classroom was common and expected, and the potential of computers to enhance instruction was becoming a topic of conversation in the teachers' lounge! But one thing had not changed: Just like Miss Pugh, Mrs. Nimmo believed that all children are capable of learning and that it is the solemn responsibility of every teacher to unlock that potential.

Graduation on the lawn of William and Mary's historic Wren Building is a special occasion for any family, but for mine it was history making. Not only was I the first member of my family to graduate from college, but also, I was an example to neighbors and friends in Highland Springs of how a dream can lead young people through the challenges, detours, and obstacles on the way to realizing their potential.

Fairfax County seemed a long way from the security of my small college campus and the semirural village of my childhood. Thank goodness my college sweetheart was now my new husband and was going with me to start my career in this booming suburb of Washington, D.C. I was pleased to get a job in Fairfax County as the salary for beginning teachers, $6,400 a year, was the highest in Virginia. I had been tentatively assigned to Ravensworth Elementary School, and the only thing standing between me and my first full-time teaching assignment was an interview with the principal, Ron

Carpenter. He explained to me that he actually had two vacancies to fill, one in the third grade, and the other in a fifth-grade classroom. Before I could remember that I was the interviewee, I blurted out, "Oh, no, I'm a third-grade teacher, not a fifth-grade teacher." I said it so passionately that he stood up, concluded the interview, and extended his hand to his new third-grade teacher.

So it was that a new plaque engraved with "Mrs. DeMary" was hung outside the door of Room 15 at Ravensworth Elementary School. I was now a real third-grade teacher with my very own classroom. I remember walking into that empty, undecorated room after the interview and praying that I could transform it into the magical environment fostered by the memory of Miss Ruby Pugh. I also prayed that I could teach and inspire each of the children who came through the door, just as Mrs. Pugh had done for me and my classmates fourteen years earlier.

It was a crazy but extremely rewarding year. I never realized a person could actually work so many hours. I had 32 students who all lived in nice houses in the Ravensworth Farms subdivision. The children were like sponges, quickly soaking up the content embedded in my lessons and asking questions and questions and more questions. Thank goodness the school library was well-stocked with resource materials and encyclopedias, which I labored over much more than my students. Our very active PTA provided extra money for teachers to spend on classroom activities and materials, and I was constantly looking for more funds as my class produced outstanding projects and experiments. I struggled to replenish my classroom library as my students clamored for more books.

At the end of the year, I was struck by how much more my students had learned than the students in the other third-grade classes. I could only attribute this to my outstanding teaching abilities. I was content, perhaps even a little bit smug, as my students took most of the academic and citizenship awards at the end of year assembly. I learned several years later, long after I left Fairfax County, that Mr. Carpenter grouped classes by ability and always gave the "top" class to his newest teacher. As it turned out, I would need every ounce of

Mrs. Jo Lynne DeMary proudly stands with her second grade class at Varina Elementary School, November 1969.

confidence, well-founded or not, as I began my next teaching assignment.

Family issues cut short my promising career in Fairfax County. My husband and I had to move to Richmond to be closer to my mother. I immediately contacted Henrico County to see if any mid-summer teaching vacancies existed. The county graciously offered me a contract and assured me that an assignment would be forthcoming. In early August, I was assigned to a new second-grade class at Varina Elementary School. I knew that Varina was a rural area that shared little in common with the affluent Northern Virginia suburbs I was leaving behind, but my success at Ravensworth had convinced me I was ready for any challenge. Second grade? Bring it on. I would have my students performing like third graders by December.

Mr. Cook, the principal of Varina Elementary School, allowed his three veteran second-grade teachers to identify eight children from each of their rosters for assignment to the new class. As loath as

I am to speak ill of any teacher, I have to tell you that those three teachers did not select the children they deemed to be the brightest and best for the roster of their new colleague.

These 24 children put my belief system to the test. It was easy to see the potential of my students in Fairfax County. They came to school ready to learn with a well-developed sense of their own value. Assuming responsibility for their achievement carried little risk. But these hand-picked students in eastern Henrico County were very different. Every suspicious look and blank stare challenged the confidence I had gained so easily during my first assignment. Did I really have what it took to be a teacher in the mold of Miss Ruby Pugh?

Georgia was a heavy-set, over-aged girl in my first class at Varina. She was almost my size, and somewhere along the way, her teachers had come to accept her poor attendance, which year after year caused her to fall farther and farther behind her peers. I knew I couldn't teach her if she didn't come to school. How could she stay in second grade indefinitely? I went to her home. Georgia had older siblings who had long since dropped out of school. Her parents were elderly and seemed to have lost the energy required to get young children organized and off to school. It wasn't a bad home, but Georgia was pretty much on her own in deciding whether she attended school. I remembered similar families from my own childhood in eastern Henrico County. I knew that little would be accomplished by threatening these parents with legal action if Georgia didn't attend school.

So I turned to Georgia. She had little idea of what she wanted to do when she grew up. We talked about different careers, and we looked at magazines so she could see grown-ups in venues beyond her realm of experiences. She liked playing office and soon decided she wanted to be a secretary. I bought an alarm clock for her and told her that she would get points for each day she came to school. She had to catch the bus as there was no other way for her to get there. She would also get bonus points for consecutive days of attendance.

I cautiously approached the office manager, Mrs. Edwards, to see if she would allow Georgia to work in the office one hour a week as a reward for improved attendance. I was nervous about approaching Mrs. Edwards because she ruled the office with an iron fist, but she readily agreed to give Georgia a taste of office work under her watchful eye. Mrs. Edwards taught me that everyone employed in a public school can be an educator and make a difference in the life of a child.

Georgia became my constant classroom companion. She followed me everywhere, ate with me at lunch, and begged to stay and help me after school so I could take her home. More importantly, she was mastering the second-grade curriculum more quickly than anyone, including me, expected. I began to expose her to third-grade material that I had used the previous year in Fairfax County. I told her that she was so smart that I needed to give her different materials than the other students. She thrived. She took workbooks home and brought them back completed the next day. It was then that this inexperienced teacher took an even bigger risk. I went to the principal to propose a bargain. If Georgia could demonstrate that she knew the third-grade content by the end of the year, would he promote her to the fourth grade? I shared with him the drop-out research I had from the College of William and Mary about how retentions put children at significant risk for dropping out, especially when older siblings had already shown the way. I pleaded with Mr. Cook to increase Georgia's chances for success. He expressed concerns about the fancy ideas I had brought with me from Northern Virginia but accepted my proposal. He said he didn't want word getting around the county that we were doing things like this, but to his great credit, he conceded that it might be best for Georgia to move on. I was so excited I almost grabbed his neck and hugged him, but I maintained my reserve, and after thanking him, hurried back to my classroom.

Then there was Patti, a quiet African-American girl who was also over-aged for second grade. This was the year that Henrico County first integrated its public schools, and Patti seemed particularly anxious about being in Varina, an area of the county where some white students still sport Confederate emblems on clothing and vehicles. She was one of dozens of African-American children with the same last name in our school, and they all lived on the same property on Ruffin Road. Patti often wore the same clothes to school for a week at a time, but she loved books and was eager to read well. I dug into the cardboard boxes stored in our attic to retrieve a book we had used at William and Mary in my teaching of reading class. In college, the content was academic; in Fairfax County, it wasn't needed; but now I scanned the pages looking for a nugget that would help me tap Patti's potential and develop the reading skills she craved. I made vocabulary flash cards for her and put her in double reading groups so I could spend more time on her reading skills. Soon she was reading fluently. Her quick smile told me she was as proud of herself as I was of her.

I shall never forget the day I was standing at the library door waiting to escort my class back to their room. I smiled as I watched Patti sitting on a tall stool in the corner of the large room reading a book. Then a terrible thing happened. I heard the librarian shout, "Patti, what are you doing with those dirty hands on my new books!"

For a moment I was frozen in horror for this child, and then I headed down the hall and right into the open door of Mr. Cook's office. I described the incident in an elevated voice. "Since when did the books in this school belong to the librarian and not the children," I asked indignantly. "If this is the case, then you need to buy some books for the children to read!" I told him how hard Patti had worked to become a good reader and how I had visited the ramshackle home where she lived, and how there were no books there for her to read. I demanded that he accompany me to the library to pick up my children and said that, if he didn't, I might march down the hall and take on the librarian myself. Mr. Cook complied with my request, and we headed toward the library. I don't know if he ever reprimanded the librarian, but from that point forward, my children always washed their hands before going to the library, and I never left my students alone in the library again.

When I noticed that my usually cheerful Samantha hadn't smiled for a couple of days, I decided to go by her house after school. I discovered that her woodcutter father had cut his hand severely and that he could not work because of the injury. Consequently, the family now had no income. While a wonderful mother and housewife, Samantha's mother had no marketable skills. The family needed help. The school social worker said she could get some clothes and food from social services but that there was no source of funds for bills. I knew I was getting far more deeply involved in Samantha's family than a teacher should be, but I knew they needed help. After doing some research, I took the father to apply for welfare. Social services did not take appointments, so applicants had to just sit and wait until their names were called. I was treated with the same disdain as the other embarrassed folks sitting in the cramped waiting room. Finally, Samantha's father's name was called, and we entered a small interview room. I introduced Samantha's father to the case worker and said that I was the injured man's advocate! It took us forever to fill out the form. Even as a William and Mary graduate, I had difficulty understanding many of the questions. The level of documentation required bordered on the absurd. But while I had the confidence to ask for explanations and clarifications, I realized that had Samantha's father been alone, he would have eventually walked out, defeated by the insensitivity and bureaucracy of the process. The power of education became even more evident to me as a result of my experience trying to help this proud man, and I grew even more determined to make sure that my students were empowered with the education they needed to lead quality lives.

My experiences at Varina Elementary School inspired me to see if I could have an impact on young people beyond what is possible as a single teacher in a single classroom. I went back to school for additional formal education and eventually left the classroom to assume broader responsibilities, first as a principal, then as a director of special education and as an assistant superintendent. Despite these new titles, I remained a teacher at heart. I stayed focused on the students and never lost sight of my calling.

In 1994, I surprised everyone, including myself, by leaving Henrico County after 25 years, and going to the Virginia Department of Education to assume similar duties on a statewide basis. I went there in part to continue to work for my former superintendent, William Bosher, who had been appointed state superintendent by the Commonwealth's newly elected governor, George Allen, a Republican who had campaigned on the need to raise academic standards and hold schools accountable for student achievement. When Dr. Bosher announced he was leaving the state department, I was sad to see him go, but I realized that I had a new commitment. It wasn't to a single person; it was to 1.2 million children in thousands of classrooms across the Commonwealth of Virginia. If Virginia was to prosper and grow in an increasingly competitive global marketplace, then we needed to raise the bar for all of our children, regardless of their race or socioeconomic status. We needed to create classrooms like Miss Ruby Pugh's in every school in Virginia.

I quickly learned that not all Virginians shared the beliefs at the core of the Commonwealth's fledgling reform movement. As an assistant superintendent, I participated in public hearings all over the state as the department attempted to determine what knowledge and skills Virginia students needed to possess as they advanced from grade to grade and eventually graduated from our public schools. I left many of these hearings troubled by the testimony I heard. It was not about content; passionate debates about content were expected. I was troubled by comments by some educators that "these children" should not be held to high standards and that, as their teachers, neither should they. Who were "these children?" Certainly not the third-grade students I remembered from Ravensworth Elementary School. I knew they meant children like Georgia, Patti, and Samantha, and for that matter, students like me and my classmates in Miss Ruby Pugh's room. Each comment about "these children" strengthened my resolve to see Virginia's reform through to the end. In 1995, after considerable debate and compromise, the Virginia Board of Education adopted new academic standards for the public schools of the Commonwealth. These new "Standards of Learning" quickly became known, and reviled in many quarters, as the "SOLs."

The adoption of the SOLs was just the beginning. The Board's intent was to use the content embedded in the standards to drive a statewide assessment system that would verify that the expected learning had taken place for each child. For the first time, school accreditation would be based on student achievement.

Even though it took three years from the adoption of the standards to the administration of the first test, there were only a handful of school divisions across Virginia that seemed to truly embrace this culture change and accept the concept of accountability for student achievement. When the results of the first year of testing were announced, only 2 percent of Virginia's 1,800 schools could claim to have met what would be the eventual standard for state accreditation. No one, including me, believed that only 2 percent of our schools were doing a good job with students, but it was a wake-up call for all of us that our focus needed to be on each child if we were going to be successful. The backlash from the field was considerable, and I was concerned that parents and other stakeholders would not tolerate repeated negative reports about the performance of the Commonwealth's schools, especially in communities that had always taken pride in the quality of their schools.

In December of 1999, the state superintendent of public instruction resigned, and I was appointed by Governor James Gilmore to serve as interim state superintendent. Quite honestly, I was anxious for Governor Gilmore to find a permanent replacement so I could get back to my work as assistant superintendent for instruction. But after three months as acting chief, I began to realize what a critical role the state superintendent played in shaping the educational policy of the Commonwealth. I enjoyed the interaction with the Board of Education, the Governor's office, and key members of the state legislature. With a lot of support from the professional educational organizations, I threw my hat into the ring for state superintendent.

On June 2, 2000, Governor Gilmore appointed me superintendent of public instruction, and I became the first woman to lead the Commonwealth's public school system. What a wonderful day it was when Secretary of the Commonwealth, Anne Petera, presided over my swearing-in ceremony. I moved into the office on the 25th

Dr. Jo Lynne DeMary congratulates National Milken Educator, Mark Ingerson, at a reception in his honor at Salem High School.

floor of the James Monroe Building in Richmond. The large windows of my office overlooked the James River, and on especially clear days, I could make out the faint outlines of the Blue Ridge Mountains on the western horizon. Every day while I was superintendent, I looked out those windows and thought about the 1.2 million children entrusted to the public schools of Virginia. When visiting schools around the state, I liked to tell the students that I could see them from the windows of my office. Wide-eyed elementary students would squeal or gasp in amazement, middle school kids would smile, as if to say, "Right lady, you expect us to believe that?" but the high school students seemed to understand what I was trying to say, that their needs were always at the center of our discussions in Richmond.

As more and more school districts embraced the challenge of accountability, and the state department of education provided additional resources and technical assistance for principals and teachers, the once despised SOLs gained at least grudging acceptance. Newspapers that were once filled with headlines proclaiming failure and dissent now celebrated the success of schools that had passed the SOLs and earned full accreditation.

I put thousands of miles on my state car during my six years as state superintendent. It was such a joy to visit schools and classrooms where children were learning and thriving in environments where expectations for achievement were high. Gifted educators all over Virginia were leaving no stones unturned as they worked tireless hours to make sure students were meeting with success. There were no silver bullets, just hard work, and a laser-like focus on the needs of individual students.

The opportunity to acknowledge our outstanding teachers in Virginia was one of my great joys as state superintendent. I delighted in the surprise announcements each October of the Virginia Milken educators as I accompanied representatives of the Milken Family Foundation to schools in affluent suburbs, inner-city neighborhoods, and rural counties famous for moonshine and bluegrass music. I could only imagine what it is like for these unsuspecting teachers to hear that they were the recipients of $25,000.

What fun it was to interrupt the classes of Virginia's regional teachers of the year by walking in with balloons and flowers and announcing to the students that their teacher was among the best of the best. I never wanted to lose sight of the fact that I was a teacher, and I relished our efforts to acknowledge the Commonwealth's outstanding teachers. As we recognized these incredible teachers, we lifted our entire profession. The Milken Educators, the state teachers of the year, the National Board Certified teachers, and Virginia's presidential scholars began to play a more important role in shaping our thinking and actions at the state level. Connecting these teachers through a formal network and gathering them together to discuss ways to elevate the profession also gave me a platform to talk about my own calling.

While Virginia's reform was gaining increasing acceptance, there was a great apprehension as the Commonwealth approached the watershed year of 2004. This was the first year that students would have to demonstrate competency on certain SOL tests in order to graduate. It is one thing to talk about accountability; it is something else to actually experience it with real students.

By then, Virginia had a new governor. Democrat Mark Warner had said little about the SOLs on the campaign trail. It was important to me to know that he was going to stay the course that had been set by his two predecessors. A meeting to discuss the SOLs and the diploma requirements that would become effective on his watch was one of the few times that Governor Warner and I met without the other members of his educational team. I remember saying to him that it was important to signal now to the schools and districts if he was going to change course, and if not, he needed to make sure they were clear on that as well. He said, "You're right, I need to do that." But he didn't say what he was going to do. The suspense was almost unbearable as I waited for Governor Warner to signal his intentions. I had devoted the crowning years of my career to the SOLs, and I was desperate to know whether the reform would continue, or if the Commonwealth's public schools would be asked to lurch in yet another new direction.

The next day, Governor Warner spoke to a standing-room-only audience at the annual conference of the Virginia Association of School Superintendents. About midway through his speech, as he talked about the importance of high standards for our students, he affirmed his desire to stay the course, and he pledged his commitment to "walk the extra mile" with any student who wanted and needed extra help to meet the new diploma requirements. His statement reassured me that the reform we had begun a decade before would live itself out in the lives of millions of Virginia's children, and that the culture change we had sought for our schools would come to full fruition.

The progress made by the public schools of Virginia's great seaport, Norfolk, demonstrated the potential of standards-based reform to change lives. I was honored to be in Washington, D.C., on the day that Norfolk Public Schools were awarded the prestigious Broad

Prize for Urban Education. Here was an urban school system that refused to accept the excuses that were often made by leaders of urban districts for low student achievement. The entire Norfolk community set to work to improve its schools by adopting a common vision: no excuses, and all means all. Norfolk made education a priority for all students, and the results were evident in the increased achievement of students in all subgroups. Norfolk showed districts across the state that all students, regardless of race and family income, could meet higher standards for learning.

I recently was invited to speak to eighth graders who were leaving the middle school I attended to go on to Highland Springs High School. I felt obligated to do this because of what these schools meant in my own life. When I arrived, the parking lot was packed, and there was an air of excitement and expectation. As I approached the gymnasium, I saw hundreds of middle schoolers waiting for their moment to march inside. As the first students entered to the strains of "Pomp and Circumstance," my eyes filled with tears and chills tingled down my spine.

The students walked in sporting the best clothing their parents could provide. Mothers, fathers, grandparents, siblings, and other relatives strained to see their loved ones turn the corner. The students were tall and short, slim and stout, black and white. Regardless of their success at middle school, they were full of anticipation for the future, just as I had been as a rising freshman in this same building 46 years earlier.

I shook each of their hands as they came across the stage to receive their certificates of promotion, and as I did, I prayed with all my heart that they would have teachers during the next stage of their journey who would see in them the tremendous potential that I saw that night. I realized how fragile many of them were and how easy it would be for them to become discouraged by the rigors of high school or distracted by activities that often compete with our goals for them. But I also knew that a single caring teacher could make all the difference in each of their young lives.

You might be that teacher. The United States recently reached a major milestone—a population of more than 300 million. An increasing percentage of the children who will fill the nation's public schools will live in urban centers. Many will be from poor families and many will be recent immigrants, or the children of recent immigrants, with little or no command of English. There is a good chance that you will find yourself teaching in a school attended by these students. Don't ever lose sight of the power you possess to plant dreams and sow hope. Tell your students everyday that you know they can do it, and more importantly, that you will not give up on them. Refuse to label your students "at-risk." Instead, look for their strengths and interests and start there. They are only "at-risk" if you cannot see the gem within each of them.

Dementi Studios

About the author:
Jo Lynne DeMary retired from state service January 1, 2006, after 37 years as an educator. She was recently recognized by the YWCA as the Outstanding Woman of the Year in Education. Dr. DeMary currently serves as a professor at Virginia Commonwealth University where she savors the opportunity to prepare the next generation of Virginia educators.

Former Virginia State Superintendent of Public Instruction, Jo Lynne DeMary.

Chapter Two

A Legacy of Excellence: My Great Teacher

Wade Whitehead

2000 National Milken Educator,
National Board Certified Teacher (NBCT)

A teacher effects eternity; he can never tell where his influence stops.
—Henry B. Adams

I will always remember the summer before I started kindergarten. For the most part, it was an idyllic time, typical of life in rural Virginia. My parents were both elementary school classroom teachers, so they were at home nearly every day. My younger brother, Scott, and I split time between the backyard, the local swimming pool, and the occasional trip to visit family and friends. We even stayed up until dark most nights, which was well past our official, but temporarily unregulated, bedtime.

That summer was filled with anticipation of my first year in school, which moved closer with every passing day. In every sense of the word, I was an excited student-to-be. As a preschooler, I had spent time at countless school events and in my parents' classrooms. I had a good idea, thanks to them, of what attending school would be like. I knew about recess. I had heard all about school lunches. I even knew about school bus rules and expectations. But the thing that excited me the most about starting school was the possibility that I might end up in Miss Sandy Chapman's class.

Simply put, Miss Chapman was the best teacher at High Point Elementary School. Whether she knew it or not, she was head and shoulders above everyone with whom she worked. The older kids who lived nearby were always saying things to me like: "You'll want to be in Miss Chapman's class" and "Nobody is as fun as Miss Chapman." She was, it seemed, the dream teacher. This was reinforced on a regular basis, as friends and neighbors grew to school age and reported back this indisputable truth to the rest of us preschoolers.

So, as summer progressed, I wondered more intently about whose class I would end up in, and what school would be like. I anxiously pondered the reality of sitting quietly in a carefully positioned row of desks. I considered the prospect of standing in an orderly line of five-year-olds, and I wondered how many kids would laugh at my funny sounding last name.

Kindergarten wasn't to be my first taste of learning, however. As a youngster, I had already been exposed to incredible instruction. As the son of two true master teachers, I was blessed by a home that was full of learning opportunities. From measuring ingredients in the kitchen and creating original board games to going on family adventures at the local lake and conducting Indiana Jones type archaeological digs in the sandbox, my parents never let a teachable moment slip by. But, even as a five-year-old, I instinctively predicted that school couldn't possibly provide the individual attention I had received at home. I somehow knew school would be different.

Just a day or two into August, an envelope with my name on it arrived in the mail. It was from Mr. Guessner Musick, who had been principal at High Point School for many years. Officially addressed to "PARENTS OF EDGAR WHITEHEAD, JR.," his letter reported that my vaccination records were complete. It stated that my academic prescreening had gone satisfactorily. However, most importantly, he announced that I had been assigned to Miss Chapman's homeroom class. Either the planets had aligned or I was just plain lucky; in either event, I knew right then that kindergarten would be a great year.

Now, in hindsight, I can say that I was right. Kindergarten, it turns out, was full of excitement. We learned the letters of the alphabet. We talked about policemen and firefighters and rescue workers. We studied weather and magnets and plants and even addition.

To step into Wade Whitehead's classroom is to immediately understand his commitment to education. Wade's classroom is very different from the average teacher's. Visitors are struck by the innovation and creativity abundant in his teacher-created lessons and the enthusiasm with which his students engage in learning. Wade, systematically, and with purposeful intent, creates a learning environment where failure is not an option, and success is a given. The curriculum he creates to teach the Virginia Standards of Learning is a delicate construction of complex concepts, principles, generalizations, and skills that provide his students with the conceptual foundations necessary to retain material over time. So often, teachers in today's society lament this era of standards and high stakes testing, but one never hears Wade complain. He infuses his lessons with creativity and discovery teaching, letting his classroom make statements about the importance of teacher quality in meeting and exceeding state standards. Wade measures success not by where a student starts, but by where he finishes, and he uses many varied assessments to lead each student to the desired goals. Students move forward from their unique entry points because he meticulously fine tunes his instruction to meet their needs. They develop an immediate rapport with him, which begins a strong relationship where students move heaven and earth to meet his high expectations. His knowledge of his students working in tandem with this high quality curriculum provides the observer with a glimpse into delicate educational choreography. Truly, one can take a register of current best practices in education into Wade's classroom and use it as an observation checklist.

Wade Whitehead is a man of integrity. He is by far one of the most innovative and creative teachers with whom I've had the pleasure of working and his efforts have merited local, state, and national recognition. However, his true gift for teaching, and the most significant rewards of his work lie not in the knowledge he imparts, but in his ability to inspire….not only his students, but his colleagues as well. Through his professional development initiatives, Wade's influence grows far beyond his classroom. Indeed, his work with teachers impacts the education of young people he will never even see or directly teach. Wade Whitehead is the most talented teacher with whom I've had the pleasure of working. In 23 years of classroom teaching and school administration, I have never met a teacher who knows his students and their unique qualities more intimately than Wade. I am very fortunate to have had the opportunity to work with him for the past ten years. I have learned from him and grown as an educator, and I am forever changed as a result.

—Michele H. Dahlquist, Two-time National Board Certified Teacher

Wade Whitehead (circled front right) in Miss Sandy Chapman's kindergarten class, 1977-78.

There was no shortage of concepts to explore or activities to try. Many of us who were ready, learned to decode words and began to emerge as readers. We attended school programs, practiced fire drills, and even had a class party or two. Just as my older friends had predicted, and as I expected, there was never a dull moment in Miss Chapman's class.

Everything I had heard about her turned out to be true. She was smiling every morning when I arrived at school. She was organized and clean and neat. She hugged me every afternoon before I went home. She always put her own personal twist on everything we learned in her classroom.

In September, Miss Chapman announced that the time had come for us to learn about Native Americans. Just like that, our classroom was transformed into an Indian camp. We gathered materials for a teepee and built one. We mixed paint and used it to reproduce symbols on the teepee cover. We constructed headdresses, cooked Indian food, and listened to authentic myths and stories. We practiced simple computation using pieces of corn. We collected feathers both for scientific analysis and to accent the headdresses we were making. We even filled a wooden box with dirt from the schoolyard and planted vegetable seeds in it.

The excitement didn't end there. In October, Andrea Ormundt (who lived just across the street) and I were selected as cowinners of the much anticipated High Point Elementary Halloween costume contest. As a first prize, we were invited to stand in the school trophy case. There, Mr. Musick handed us a paper cat to share as a reward. Our photograph ran in the county newspaper and was posted prominently behind Miss Chapman's desk. Even the fourth and fifth graders recognized me as a minor celebrity in the hallways after that.

Two months later, as if things couldn't get any better, I auditioned for, and received, the part of a snowflake in the school Christmas play. My costume consisted of tights, a turtleneck, and tinsel pulled straight from our family tree. There were three performances of the play, including one at night, which my parents and brother attended.

But the biggest event of the year involved Miss Chapman. Right in the middle of my kindergarten year, the Washington County Education Association chose her as their Teacher of the Year. Out of every teacher in every grade at every school, she was picked as the best. As such, she advanced to the state competition, where she eventually finished in second place. She narrowly missed winning a brand new set of *Encyclopedia Britannica*. Of course, at school, she never made a big deal out of this well-deserved recognition. She was modest about her accomplishments, and I only found out through my parents, who heard from their colleagues about her honor.

Then, as suddenly as it began, kindergarten abruptly ended, and we all went home for summer vacation. The next year, I did well in first grade. I flew through second, and then third, and fourth, and so on, until I moved to John S. Battle High School in the eighth grade.

Wade Whitehead as "Batman" stands in the High Point Elementary School trophy case with Andrea Ormundt, the angel, receiving a paper cat for the "Best Halloween Costumes" reward.

I can still name every teacher I had in every grade I attended. Most of them were good—and many were outstanding—but I never forgot Miss Chapman. She was, and still is, the best teacher I ever had.

Now years later, I am myself a veteran classroom teacher. Over the years, I have learned all the things good teachers are supposed to know. My professors in the School of Education at the College of William and Mary taught me how to plan a unit of study. They demonstrated how to properly write lesson plans. They modeled team-teaching and emphasized use of current technology. We learned detailed processes for preparing and implementing an effective lesson. They exposed me to the indispensable, fundamental tenets of the education paradigm, which contribute to quality teaching and collectively play a role in effective classroom instruction.

Over the years, I have attended countless conferences, summits, and conventions, all ostensibly geared toward improving classroom teaching. At these events I have listened intently as other skilled educators have outlined what teachers should know and do, and explained what is necessary to create a positive classroom learning environment. As well, I have taken graduate courses and have read more education-centered books than I can name, all in an attempt to uncover exactly what quality teaching is made of.

All of this has given me an interesting perspective on my own teachers that I had while growing up. I now know, from my own experiences as a professional teacher, that Miss Chapman managed her classroom in a way that would stand up to any modern criteria for "best practice," and undoubtedly would meet any official criteria for top-notch instruction. As I now look back at her teaching through the "high quality" lens, I finally have realized how effective she actually was.

What's interesting, however, is that I knew nothing about the educational jargon of good teaching when I made my first judgment about Miss Chapman and her teaching methods. At the age of five, with literally no knowledge of educational theory or pedagogy, I knew she was excellent. How? I knew that I learned when I was around her. I did not know, and honestly would not have cared, whether her lesson plans were written in a specific format. I had no idea whether her instructional calendar was organized in the manner mandated by the school district. I simply knew she was a great teacher, because she was.

What was it, then, that made Miss Chapman such an incredible educator? For starters, she was a professional, and she was totally committed to student learning. She prepared her lessons carefully and creatively she maintained an organized, colorful classroom. Each day was a new adventure and a time of magical discovery. We were in awe as she secretly covered every academic requirement.

But now, as I think back on it, I realize something significant about many of her professional attributes and qualities. As special as they may sound, many of them are simply routine things that good teachers do. They are, essentially, measures of competency. The truth is that teachers everywhere adhere to scope and sequence charts, implement units of study, and hold parent conferences just like Miss Chapman did. These things are important to maintaining an environment for learning and are what all teachers do. Still, they will not make an educator exceptional nor do they define what set Miss Chapman apart from her peers. Indeed, great teachers do far more. They embrace an entire arena of values, skills, philosophies, and behaviors that are critical in our schools. Too often, though, these traits are overlooked in formal performance evaluations and contemporary dialogue about standards, assessment and progress. Yet, these crucial characteristics separated Miss Chapman from those around her. They have, in my mind, come to represent what great teaching is and what great teaching can be.

Why is it important to consider these qualities in the first place? In an age of quantifying education, we have created multistep processes and curriculum guides. We have produced unprecedented funding for technology and reduced class size. Yet we still have to ask: Are school systems, higher education centers, and state and federal departments creating the highest caliber of teacher through existing training and professional development activities? Moreover, is it realistic to expect master teachers in every classroom or should we settle for simple competency?

These questions should be asked, but they must be considered with one overriding issue in mind. We now know, thanks to recent research, what a difference teacher quality makes on student learning. The difference between instructional mediocrity and teaching excellence has a profound and lasting impact on student achievement and success. Indeed, recent studies recall that teacher quality is the single most important variable in student learning. It makes more difference than school demographics, class size, or numbers of computers or instructional models. It makes more of an impact than what time school starts or even what learning materials are available. In the world of learning, teacher quality is everything. Thanks to one teacher, my friends and I knew this fact at age five, and contemporary research has finally confirmed it.

What is it, then, that great teachers do? What traits do they possess? What do they value? The answers, which are surprisingly simple yet incredibly profound, are universally true regardless of grade level or subject or location.

Great Teachers Believe that Every Child Has Talents, Intelligences, and Gifts to Offer

For decades, our schools were configured to fit a single type of learner: the one who readily sits still and learns best in a passive, adult-centered environment. Desks were neatly arranged in rows and students faced forward. Teachers expected students to conform to fit their delivery style. Those students who were unable or unwilling to do so met with few successes.

Today's teachers, however, are the beneficiaries of an unprecedented amount of research on brain function and child development. Thanks to scholars from psychology, biology, and neurology, we are able to consider empirically how children think, learn, and share. Children have their own individual constellations of strengths, abilities, and experiences that guide their every move. Renowned educational theorists, like Howard Gardner, have helped to demolish the notion that intelligence should be measured in just one way.[1] This epiphany has paved the way for a new breed of modern educator who functions on the assumption that every child is gifted in some way, and who believes that every child can, in fact, learn.

As a result, great teachers are able to capitalize on an astounding array of individual student talents and abilities. The best teachers maintain classrooms full of perspectives, experiences, and achievements that might have otherwise never surfaced. They maintain appreciation for the individual strengths of each of their students and are energized by their differences.

The simple act of acknowledging and celebrating individual intelligences has a reformative effect on classrooms. Several years ago, I stood by the door of my third grade classroom and welcomed each of my students on the first day of school. As expected, "Robert" came to school that day, but he was hesitant about his newly assigned teacher, me. He was initially polite, but reticent, and he hid, quite well, the stuttering problem that had plagued him since age two.

His struggle with speaking had been well documented. I had conferenced with his mother, his pathologist, and former teachers about what they had done to help him. I read every book and article I could find on the subject. Sure enough, as days turned into weeks, Robert's speech remained a steady obstacle between his thoughts and the people around him. On his best days, his peers and I could decipher most of what he said; on the worst, a single word wouldn't come out.

A couple of months into the school year, my class studied plants. We learned the usuals, including plant structure, functions, and types. After my students had mastered the basic standards, I designed an independent plant experiment for each student to undertake. They would, I hoped, make some new and exciting discovery about plants and would expand upon their newfound knowledge by taking on a more meaningful project.

Towards this end, I created a unique assignment for each of my students, based upon the things I already knew about them. This took time, as I worked to match their learning opportunities with their individual personalities, preferences, and learning styles. Creating an assignment for most of my students was fairly easy and straightforward. I asked Oliver to determine how a plant's height is related to its weight because he loved math. Sayveon, on the other hand, created a comic book about taxonomy since he was a budding artist. My goal was simple: to allow each of my students to use an individual strength to increase their understanding of an unfamiliar area (knowledge of plants, in this instance).

A few days before we began our projects, I was researching stuttering to help Robert succeed in this task when I found a study that suggested something very interesting. It revealed that some children who stutter when speaking don't necessarily do so when they sing. It also suggested that stutterers often speak normally in talking to animals. So, as I considered what plant assignment to create for Robert, I decided to test this hypothesis. His speech, after all, had become an obstacle; it had hindered him and his academic achievement during previous years. I decided on a plan that would allow him to achieve. For Robert's plant assignment, I simply asked him to answer the question: "Will a plant grow better if it's sung to?" I typed this on a piece of paper, handed it to him, and stood back. Immediately, with the question in hand, Robert disappeared with a potted plant into the hall where he began his experiment. I tried to stand unobtrusively near the door to observe. At first, he whispered inaudibly to the pot in front of him. As minutes passed, he raised his voice a little, composing lyrics on the spot, making sure the tiny seeds heard his effort. This went generally unnoticed, as my other students were preoccupied with their own discoveries.

So things went that way, every morning for a couple of days. All of my students, including Robert, worked diligently on their projects. He would slip into the empty hallway, plant in hand, where he serenaded his plant in solitude. But on day four, something remarkable happened, and all of us were forever changed.

I was standing at the door observing Robert, when I noticed that my entire classroom had fallen silent (an unusual occurrence in itself). The students had collectively paused at their work and were intently listening. Robert was singing to his plant in the hallway, unaware (or unconcerned) that everyone could hear him. He was singing, and remarkably, he was enunciating each word perfectly. He didn't stutter once.

I don't think my classroom has ever been as quiet as it was that day. It wasn't so much that my students and I couldn't believe what was happening. It was that the moment we all were waiting for had finally arrived, the time when Robert's impediment was miraculously lifted, and he was free to shine. Robert was using his love for science to improve his speech. His unique constellation of abilities and interests had come to the forefront, all because of a simple classroom assignment.

I have never been able to find a federal or state mandate that requires teachers to celebrate individual student preferences, experiences, and strengths. Thanks to Robert, I'll never need one.

Great Teachers Find Something Likeable in Every Child

The diversity in today's classrooms is truly astounding. Great teachers use this as an asset and always manage to discover something unique and exciting about every child. This connection can be academic, and it can take a variety of forms. Teachers who are caring and open with their students, and who take an active interest in their lives, will form more meaningful relationships. It is impossible, I believe, to overestimate the power of enjoying life-based, casual conversations with a student. The rewards go both ways and contribute to the experience of both teacher and learner.

Frank Charles Winstead [see Chapter Three], a former principal and now a lecturer on excellence in America's classrooms, says that great teachers are willing to go the extra mile at the schoolhouse, both inside and outside the classroom walls. Hidden in his brilliant advice is the assumption that a great teacher finds a way to like every student and searches for at least one meaningful connection.

What's the effect of this sort of attitude about kids? I always thought I was Miss Chapman's favorite student, but now I realize that she probably made every child feel exactly the same way simply by liking us. Miss Chapman may not have ever decided who was her favorite student, yet every one of us thought we were that person.

The power of liking every child doesn't stop with just developing a positive teacher-student relationship. That sort of attitude assumes a life of its own and causes students to change their perspectives about one another as well. Recently, my wife shared a story about a young teacher who was struggling with a disruptive class. She felt that she wasn't making a personal connection with anyone and that her students were unmotivated, disinterested, and unruly. There were many ways she could have chosen to deal with the situation, but she chose an unusual one. One day, she asked each of her students to write his or her name at the top of a piece of paper. Then, over the course of several days, these papers were passed around the room. Each student would write one complimentary sentence about the person whose name appeared at the top. Then, the page would be passed along.

After a few days, each student ended up with two new and positive experiences. First, each child had communicated something positive about each one of their peers. Equally significant, each child in the class was now the proud owner of a list that was full of constructive and encouraging opinions from others. At the bottom was a personal note from the teacher herself.

Many years later, that same teacher attended the funeral of one of her students from that particular class. On display during the memorial service, among other personal and family items, was the wrinkled piece of paper from that simple long-ago classroom activity. Carefully preserved in a frame were many upbeat and positive comments from others. Later that night, the teacher encountered several other students from that same class, all of whom remembered the activity and one who actually had his own page in his wallet.

Initially, the teacher had sought to solve a classroom problem by finding something likeable in each of her students. In the end, she helped to build relationships and enhance her students' self-esteem in a way that had lifelong consequences.

Great Teachers Listen to Their Students as Often as They Speak

In the not-so-distant past, teachers were regarded as absolute dispensers of knowledge. They were considered to be the ultimate resource, upon which students were expected to call, and with whom no one could question or argue. Lecture was king and nothing a teacher said was disputable (or, as I recall from high school, interruptible).

Today, information moves at the speed of light, and students can frequently know more about some particular subject than a teacher. Great teachers know when to hit the pause button, sit back, and take in new knowledge, whether it's from a colleague, an outside expert, or even a student. In fact, the best teachers intentionally establish learning environments in which the official line between teacher and learner is quite blurry. They frequently explore and learn alongside their students. French moralist Joseph Joubert accurately observed: "To teach is to learn twice."[2] It truly is.

Of course, listening to their students also provides great teachers with background information, opinions, and curiosities that can become lost in one-way interaction. Armed with such data, great teachers can personalize the school experience in otherwise impossible ways.

Great Teachers Make the Student (Not the Teacher and Not Standards) the Center of the Classroom

A teacher may well construct and maintain the background elements of any classroom. They may plan lessons and possess vast content knowledge and even have the final say when it comes to decision-making at a school. But this does not mean that the teacher should be the center of the learning that takes place in a classroom. Great teachers know that learning is child-centered and kid-focused. They invent scenarios through which kids direct themselves, and ones which build on juvenile interests and priorities. This is not to say that great teachers allow their students to take over their classrooms, do whatever they want, or decide when to work. Rather, great teachers combine direct and indirect instruction to produce a child-centered environment for exploration. This type of learning environment may be messy, noisy, and unpredictable, but the great teachers relish this possibility.

Of course, this child-centered thinking is nothing new. Miss Chapman always seemed nearby when I needed help but never seemed to bother me when I was in the middle of my work. From trying to figure out how to tie the poles of our teepee together and measuring water for our indoor garden to adding the finishing touches to my facepaint and painting a mural-sized bison background, I cannot conjure a single memory of her discouraging a possible solution. She never corrected my thinking even though I'm sure my "answers" weren't exactly 100 percent correct.

Great Teachers Know that It Takes a "Fleet"

Teachers and students must work together if learning is to be maximized. Schools must also work to involve families, churches, synagogues, and neighborhoods if students' true potential is to be fully met. It is important to remember that many parents of school-aged youngsters had less than positive school experiences themselves. For parents of particularly disruptive or high-needs students, years may have passed without positive interaction with teachers and staff. Often, the only communication they receive from school arises from problems or difficult situations. This atmosphere contributes to an unhealthy, or altogether absent, relationship between teacher and family. That's why great teachers leverage a student's accomplishments against the void that can exist between school and home.

When I was a new teacher, I received the following advice: If a teacher's first contact with a parent is negative, the teacher has made an adversary forever. This statement couldn't be truer. The best educators proactively reach out to parents and become their allies. Together, they identify their mutual goals and align their hopes and expectations. The success of the child is the shared, number one priority. Establishing such meaningful relationships among school, student, and home can be quite difficult, but is absolutely essential. It makes a critical, long-term difference for student success.

Peter and Paul Reynolds, who happen to be twin brothers, have been friends of mine for some time. Years ago, they envisioned this school-family-child relationship as a fleet of ships, dependent on one another and headed for a common destination. Their poem, "It Takes a Fleet," sums up exactly what great teachers believe about the school-home connection.

It Takes a Fleet
by Peter and Paul Reynolds

I had a dream
I saw three ships

At the beginning of a voyage
Three ships huddled in the harbor
A misty sea stretched out before them.
In my dream upon a cliff
I could see that two ships were large
and one was small.

Upon the smaller I saw a child,
Wide-eyed, wind-touseled hair.
A lantern on the bow glowed
lighting a few feet ahead
in the murky harbor.

On either side of the child's ship
Nestled the two large ships.
Upon one a Family gathered on starboard side
On the other, a Teacher standing on port side
Ready to guide the child on the journey ahead.

One ship captained by the Teacher
Was filled with precious cargo:
Books, music, stories, art, and more;
The other ship—skippered by the Family,
Carried compassion, love and guidance.

In my dream,
The Journey took many days and nights,
And weeks and months and years,
Along the way there were brilliant views
And others of murky fog.
There were doldrums and mighty storms.

One night the two large ships lost sight of the smaller,
Rushing to starboard and to port,

Searching in vain through the fog,
"Where has the small ship gone?"

"Wandered off course," they thought,
"Too curious? Or perhaps fallen asleep at the
wheel?"
But when the smaller ship reappeared,
It had treasure in its hold!
Not gold or spices but rather wisdom.
Wisdom about the stars.
Discovery of a unique constellation.
The ability to read it and be guided
The power to navigate on its own.

The ships signaled one another in celebration –
Each captain agreed that the voyage
Would have been far more difficult
If voyaging alone.

They had voyaged as a Fleet,
Teacher sailing alongside Family...
School voyaging together with Home...

It takes a Fleet,
Dreamy and hopeful,
Ready for oceanic challenges,
It takes a Fleet,
Attentive and loving
To prepare for
The Lifelong Voyage.

I believe it is impossible to overestimate the impact a positive teacher-family relationship has on a child's achievement. Forging this sort of interaction takes effort, but it can be the single biggest factor in whether a child's family invests in that child's school experience. This investment pays great dividends, and makes all the difference in the world.

Great Teachers Realize that One Size Fits Few

Historically, school has been a "one size fits all" proposition for many students. Learning environments are frequently inflexible, predetermined, and standardized. However, as we continue to solve the puzzle of how the human brain works and how it constructs new knowledge, one idea is reinforced repeatedly—that different people learn in different ways. Great teachers have always known this, and they have used it as the main ingredient in every one of their instructional recipes.

There are many ways to accommodate varying learning styles, preferences, and modalities in school settings. The classrooms of the best educators are full of choices and opportunities for their students. Some teachers elect to differentiate the material or content each of their students is learning. Other times, teachers may alter the process through which each student discovers new ideas. At other points, changing how a student shares that which is being learned is appropriate. In all three scenarios, great teachers change their educational methods to fit kids, instead of always asking their students to change to fit a learning environment. The result of changing the learning environment in these ways is predictable. Children become more interested. They feel more comfortable. They try harder. And, most importantly, they learn more.

Great teachers create a customized school experience for every one of their learners. They differentiate instruction. They alter schedules. They provide personalized enrichment and remediation. Most importantly, they look at each child as a unique individual with gifts, curiosities, abilities, and potential. They see the development of

Miss Chapman, now Dr. Sandra Birchfield, with her former student, Wade Whitehead, at Wise Primary School in Wise, Virginia, 2006.

those strengths as their duty, and they apply themselves exclusively toward it.

The tradition of great teaching has been around as long as teaching itself. Great teachers, like Miss Chapman, will continue to shape the boundaries of the profession and will always push the envelope of achievement. Some have received credit for their efforts, but most have worked for years without any recognition whatsoever. All have been part of a legacy of excellence that manifests itself in a dynamic mix of imagination, discovery, and sharing.

Why do I teach? I have the opportunity to add to the rich legacy built by my parents and the great teachers before me. I have the potential to create, out of the elements around me, that which did not exist before. By acknowledging the great teachers of our time, I hope to ultimately impact the lives of thousands of learners and, possibly, make my own unique contribution to the paradigm of teaching and learning. This is the least I can do, because this is what great teachers, like Miss Chapman, did for me.

Author's Personal Collection

Milken National Educator, Wade Whitehead

About the Author:
Wade Whitehead, (www.wadewhitehead.com) teaches fifth graders at Crystal Spring School in Roanoke, Virginia. A product of Washington County, Virginia Public Schools, he graduated with majors in Anthropology and Elementary Education from the College of William and Mary in 1994. In 1999, he earned certification from the National Board for Professional Teaching Standards. He has received a number of recognitions and awards, including the Milken Family Foundation National Educator Award and the McGlothlin Foundation Award for Teaching Excellence. He is a former member of the USA Today ALL-USA Teacher Team and is a former Roanoke City Public Schools Teacher of the Year. Wade has worked extensively with FableVision Animation Studios to develop the North Star Approach to Teaching and Learning, which serves as the cornerstone of his classroom today.

Chapter Three

Wayside Teaching:
In a Place Called School

Frank Winstead

Master Teacher/Principal/Lecturer
Advocate for Excellence in America's Classrooms

One rarely becomes a 'significant other' on the basis of actions when formally instructing. It is in relationships developed in wayside teaching that one is most likely to influence the lives of others.

—John H. Lounsbury

Teaching for me has been a joyful and rewarding career filled with many heartwarming experiences, the kinds I would not have encountered in any other career. Let me share with you some of the events that have made teaching so rewarding, interspersed with varied comments. First, a recent event: The often-delayed rewards of teaching came home to me in a special way the night of March 18, 2005. I was at James Madison University preparing to present the keynote for the Teachers of Promise Institute. I was reviewing my notes when the phone rang. It was my wife, Christina Ann, calling from Magnolia, Texas. She asked, "Do you remember a former student named David Queen? He just called from Villa Rica, Georgia."

"Yes," I replied without the slightest hesitation. "I taught David Queen world history in 1965 when he was in the tenth grade at Pebblebrook High School." Chris responded, "How in the world can you remember that level of detail from so many years ago?" I chuckled and assured her, "If you had ever taught David Queen, you

David Queen and Becky Skinner at Pebblebrook High School in Mableton, Georgia, during the 1965–1966 school year.

would remember him."

"David Queen! My goodness," I exclaimed. "Tell me, what did he want?"

Chris replied, "David told me that you had been on his mind for several months and that he had decided to try to find you on the Internet. He wanted to thank you for all that you had done for him so many years ago. He said you were his favorite teacher."

I am not ashamed to tell you, a tear rolled down my cheek.

David Queen! When he walked through the door, he lit up the classroom. He was bright and funny. I still remember his caustic wit. My mother would have called him a "live wire."

I recall readily the day when he turned his wit on an elderly math teacher. In her early 70s, this teacher was energetic, stern, competent, and demanding. However, humor was not a part of her temperament. (For the reader to connect with this story, it is important to know that a cult movie, popular with teenagers in those days, was

Mr. Winstead, your visit in 1992 to the classroom at Emory University where I was teaching brought back memories for your former student of the sweltering days at Hawthorne Elementary in the summer of 1966. When you rose to speak, I remembered why you had been my favorite teacher and how your example inspired a twelve-year-old boy's love for history and teaching. Then when you put your hand on my shoulder, I felt twelve again and wished that I could express verbally all that was welling up in my heart.
—Casey Patrick Cochran, Ph.D, lecturer, Emory University. Formerly he was a student taught by Frank Charles Winstead in Cobb County, Georgia's first Program for Gifted and Talented Students in the summer of 1966.

a 1959 release entitled, *The Attack of the Killer Shrews.*)

This veteran teacher, highly irritated and under a full head of steam, came roaring into my classroom. She demanded that I point out David Queen. I did, and she proceeded to level a blistering attack on him. She accused him and a few tenth-grade conspirators of hiding the pasteboard box that she kept under her desk. (She was particularly sensitive to drafts as her feet were perpetually cold; so, during the day, she sat at her desk with her feet wrapped in a blanket in that box.)

Finally, after this teacher had vented her wrath, she made a stormy exit. When she was a safe distance down the hall, David breathed an exaggerated sigh of relief. He turned toward me and, to the delight of his classmates, remarked, "Hey, 'Teach,' I thought the last showing of *The Attack of the Killer Shrews* was last week."

That was David! A nonconformist, he challenged, questioned, pushed, pressed, and probed. I found him delightful, one of the crown jewels in the student body. I know this, too: He made me a better teacher.

One of the challenges of teaching is that, as teachers, much of the time, we don't know if we are doing any good or not. My father reinforced that nagging doubt when I was a beginning teacher. Every time I came home to Mississippi on a visit, he would always ask the same troubling question, "Son, you doin' any good at the schoolhouse?"

Admittedly, from time to time, teachers get positive feedback.

However, there is far too little positive public reinforcement, given the importance of what teachers do. The story that follows illustrates that one teacher had to wait far too long before she learned whether she had "done any good" at the schoolhouse.

Dr. William L. Stidger, a physician in Tucker, Georgia, wrote a letter of thanks to a schoolteacher for the encouragement she had given him when he had been in her class 30 years before. The following week, Dr. Stidger received a reply from his teacher. The message was written in a very shaky hand. I can close my eyes and visualize this elderly, long-retired schoolteacher as she struggles with poor eyesight and trembling fingers to compose a response to her former student, the distinguished Dr. William L. Stidger. Here is her letter as reprinted in the *Tucker Times:*

> My Dear Willie: I want you to know what your note meant to me. I am an old lady in my eighties, living alone in a small room, cooking my own meals, lonely, and seeming like the last leaf on the tree. You will be interested to know, Willie, that I taught school for 50 years, and in all that time, yours is the first letter of appreciation I have ever received. It came on a cold, blue morning and cheered my lonely old heart as nothing has cheered me in many years.[4]

When I taught David Queen, I was 24 years of age. He was a lad of 15. Forty years later, when he was 55 years of age, David called to thank me for what I had done for him during the 1965-1966 school year. He cheered my heart!

Interestingly, while I have not seen or talked to David Queen during the past 40 years, I have carried for the past 16 years a photograph of David and his classmate Becky Skinner in my traveling exhibit. The vintage photograph reminds me that, as teachers, every once in a while, we enjoy bright and shining moments with students that last a lifetime.

Later I called David to express my appreciation for his continuing interest in me. I look forward to the time when I will again see David Queen—now a grandfather—who crossed my path when he was an adolescent. I want to thank him face-to-face for the joy and creativity he brought to the classroom and for keeping this novice teacher on his toes.

I have reflected many times on the circumstances that prompted David's call and on his warmth and kindness during our conversation. Since students forget about 80 percent of the material we teach them within a year, he was certainly not calling to express fond memories of studying the Punic Wars, the Ottoman Empire, the French Revolution, or the Treaty of Brest-Litovsk. David was calling to thank me for providing a classroom experience that featured humor, interaction, warmth, and academic rigor. Many of our students, if only in later years, remember teachers who demanded self-discipline, commitment, and quality workmanship. However, I have come to believe that the lasting influences of a teacher are outgrowths of the culture and caring made evident in meaningful relationships and personal attention.

As a young teacher, I did not have a name or term to identify the kind of teaching that helped me create a joyful but productive learning environment. However, even in my youth I had enough wisdom to understand that successful teaching was rooted in building relationships.

Finally, seven years before my retirement, I discovered a term for, and a definition of, the kind of teaching that I have always believed to be the essence of teaching, that is, getting in touch with the student's heart as well as his or her mind. I picked up a copy of the May 1987 *Middle School Journal,* and there it was in black and white, the descriptor I had been searching for: "Wayside Teaching." The editor of the journal, John H. Lounsbury, whom I had known as a colleague in the middle school movement, authored a monthly column entitled "As I See It." His essay for May was entitled, "Wayside Teaching," and, there, I found the term I had been searching for. That essay is printed below in full. I urge teachers to keep it a close companion and reflect on it often. "Wayside Teaching" will make you a better teacher. Remember, while written for an audience of middle-level educators, "Wayside Teaching" is applicable prekindergarten through college. So, wherever you see "middle level" or "middle school" in the text, simply substitute your grade level or school.

Wayside Teaching

Formal, organized instruction is, and ought to be, the major component of the educational process. It deserves our best attention and our most thoughtful planning. The important place that planned instruction has in the school day is highly evident; bells signal the beginning and the endings of time allotments established for its occurrence and the school day is almost completely given over to it.

While not seeking to deprecate this formal teaching or diminish its primary place in the educational enterprise, I believe there is much more to middle-level education than organized instruction. The more influential aspect of middle-school education is often what might be called wayside teaching. By wayside teaching, I mean the teaching that is done between classes, i.e., when walking in the halls, after school, and in dozens and dozens of one-on-one encounters, however brief. For principals it is usually the main means of teaching.

When all is said and done, what is said informally and casually may have more impact on a person's behavior than what is said formally while instructing a class or conducting a faculty meeting. A response to a student's non-academic question, given spontaneously and without particular fore-

thought, can have great impact. In terms of affect-
ing behavior, such a response may be the most
influential act a teacher performs all day. Wayside
utterances are often heard at a deeper level than
classroom pronouncements.

Fortunately, middle-level teachers do not think of
themselves as "on duty" only when standing in
front of a class. The casual walk with a student or
two on the way to a student council meeting is recognized as an opportunity to develop the kind of
personal relationship that underlies true excellence
in middle-level education. The unplanned after-
school encounter with a discouraged student is
seized as an occasion to express caring and offer a
reassuring word. Even a surprise meeting in the
mall on a Saturday is seen as a chance to communicate a genuine interest in a student as a worthy
person.

Wayside teaching, however, is neither as casual nor
as completely accidental as it may appear.
Preparation of the heart as well as the mind has to
precede it. If teachers have credence with pupils,
they will often seek opportunities to engage students in conversation, and vice versa.

While the occasion may come up suddenly and
unexpectedly, the quality of the relationship pre-
ceding the conversation will reflect a bent of the
heart and spirit that usually was a long time in the
making.

As middle-level educators we cannot evade the
responsibility that is inherent in our personal

example—and we shouldn't try to. We may not dwell on it a great deal—that would seem self-righteous, even egotistical—but we need to be sensitive to the effect our behavior has on students and faculty.

Our conscious influence, when we are on dress parade, instructing a group, playing the role of teacher, may be relatively small compared to the impact of our wayside teaching. The silent, subtle radiation of one's personality, the effects on one's spontaneous words and unplanned deeds apart from those times when one is in front of the class have great impact. One rarely becomes a "significant other" on the basis of actions when formally instructing. It is in the relationships developed in wayside teaching that one is most likely to influence the lives of others.[5]

Teachers, hold on to this concept throughout your career. Do not allow the regulated conditions of teaching, as difficult as they may be, to cause you to abandon what so many students desperately need—a teacher who listens and provides a habitat for meaningful learning in the classroom. Furthermore, never minimize the importance of those opportunities that arise on the school campus for dialogue as John Lounsbury says "between classes, when walking in the halls, after school, and in dozens and dozens of one-on-one encounters, however brief. . . ."

Haim Ginott, an imminent child psychologist and author of the best-selling book: *Teacher and Child: A Book for Parents and Teachers,* wrote, "While parents possess the original key to their offspring's experience, teachers have a spare key. They too can open or close the minds and hearts of children."[6] It is through "Wayside Teaching" that we as teachers most often employ that "spare key" and make a difference in the lives of young people.

Teaching is often difficult, always complex, and frequently stressful. As Rodney Dangerfield would say, teachers "don't get no respect." The challenge of teaching is compounded by the fact that today's teachers have to live with a myth that, if we just had good schools like we did in the 1950s, we could solve all the problems of society. This common message is clear: Schools and teachers of today do not measure up to the excellence and high standards of the past. Perhaps Will Rogers had it right when he commented, "Schools ain't nowhere as good as they used to be—and they never wuz."

The October 16, 1950, cover of *Life Magazine* is emblazoned with this headline: "Our Schools Face a Crisis." In an essay in that publication, Bernard Iddings Bell writes, "Thoughtful parents—often aghast at what is being done and not being done—organize, agitate, protest, and petition. Leaders of business and industry commonly deplore the ignorance, laxness, and gaucherie of the products that tumble by the thousands each year from our educational assembly line. Teachers themselves voice embittered disillusion. . . . Most Americans today [1950] can only with sweat and tears read anything more difficult than a tabloid newspaper or a comic strip."[7]

Ahh . . . yes. If we could just return to the '50s, the so-called "Golden Age of Education." Unfortunately, we have far too many failing schools but our good schools are better than they have ever been. Despite greater responsibility, with less moral support, and a significantly more diverse student body, America's public schools are doing a remarkably good job. *Houston Chronicle* columnist, Rick Casey, reminds the detractors of public education that "For all the criticism of public schools, the good schools are better than ever. They produce increasing numbers of students who . . . are prepared to go to top colleges."[8] All schools, including the "good schools," must, of course, be committed to continuous improvement in order to provide students with a level of skill and technical know-how never before imagined.

Journey back in time with me to the year 1957. That ought to take us far enough back on the calendar to arrive at a time when teachers were admired and respected and, according to people my age and older, we had really good schools. Look carefully at the lyrics from "The Class of '57" by the Statler Brothers. This tune is a reflection on the membership of the high school class of 1957. Admittedly, country music is always overstated and a bit outrageous, but it is popular, in large measure, because it is rooted in truth. With that in mind, note carefully the line about the schoolteacher.

The Class of '57

Tommy's selling used cars
Nancy's fixin' hair
Harvey runs a grocery store
And Margaret doesn't care
Jerry drives a truck for Sears
And Charlotte's on the make
And Paul sells life insurance
And part-time real estate

Helen is a hostess
Frank works at the mill
Janet teaches grade school
And prob'ly always will
Bob works for the city
And Jack's in lab research
And Peggy plays organ at the Presbyterian
Church

And the class of '57 had its dreams
We all thought we'd change the world
By our great works and deeds
Or maybe we just thought the world would change to fit our needs
The class of '57 had its dreams

Betty runs a trailer park
Jan sells Tupperware
Randy's on an insane ward
Mary's on welfare
Charlie took a job with Ford
Joe took Freddie's wife
Charlotte took a millionaire
And Freddie took his life

Johnny's big in cattle
Ray is deep in debt
Where Mavis finally wound up
Is anybody's bet
Linda married Sonny
Brenda married me
And the class of all of us
Is just part of history

And the class of '57 had its dreams
But livin' life day to day is never like it seems
Things get complicated
When you get past eighteen
But the class of '57 had its dreams
Ah, the class of '57 had its dreams[9]

(Used with permission, House of Cash, Inc.)

Think about it. Out of all the occupations identified in that
depressing little ditty—from running a trailer park to working for the
city—only one job was demeaned. "Janet teaches grade school and
prob'ly always will." However, isn't it ironic that Janet is the only person identified in the class of '57 who can actually help the children of
her classmates have a more productive and fulfilled life? In the real
world, the classroom becomes the bridge to a dream for so many of
our students. Dreams become realities because schoolteachers, at all

levels are preparing students for the future—one year at a time. That preparation is critical because: "Things get complicated when you get past eighteen." But, oh, how the social, economic, and cultural landscape has changed since the kids in the class of 1957 walked across the stage some five decades ago to receive their diplomas. Today, for many of our kids, things get complicated in the first grade.

I would like to share with you a composition entitled, "My Special Christmas Wish." This piece, written by a seven-year-old child, was given to me many years ago by a school librarian.

My Special Christmas Wish

There are many kinds of wishes. There are wishes for clothes and food. Most kids wish for toys but I wish for my dad's problem. He's very sick right now. He has a problem with drinking and drugs. So Saturday, I'm moving. I wish he would get well really, really, really soon! But not everything you wish for comes true you know. But I hope this one comes true. Cause it really hurts to know that you have an alcoholic for a parent. Please don't tell a lot of people cause I don't want people making fun of me. Cause like I said, it really does hurt. So please, don't hang it outside in the hall.

By Heather, age 7

An observation by journalist and lecturer, Jim Trelease is apropos here: "Each day millions of children arrive in American classrooms in search of more than reading and math skills." Trelease is not soft on reading and math, and we must always keep the main thing, student learning, in mind. Trelease continues, "They (the students) are looking for a light in the darkness of their lives, a Good Samaritan who will stop and bandage a bruised heart or ego."[10] The message is clear: While teachers are delivering the content, they must recognize that they have a substantial number of students who are struggling and looking for "a light in the darkness" and a "Good

Samaritan" who will help them through the day. In many of these children, the lights have gone out in their eyes. They need someone to turn the lights back on. If that transformation is going to happen, in most cases, it will be because a teacher makes the decision to get involved and engage in "Wayside Teaching."

As a classroom teacher, my top annual salary was $6,000. The most I ever earned as a principal was $19,500. During the last ten years that I worked, my earnings did increase substantially, but the truth is, I worked two-thirds of my career for next to nothing. However, if I could turn back the clock and become 22 years old again coming out of Mississippi State University, I would walk down that same path and become a teacher. I love teachers. I adore students, and I am fascinated by this craft called teaching. I have always believed, even as a young teacher, that teaching is the most important job in the universe.

The landscape has changed dramatically, however, since I started teaching. Because of the changes that have taken place, I have come to understand that today there are more reasons than ever why teaching is the most important job in the world. When those of us over 50 years of age went to school, three institutions supported most of us: The home, the church or synagogue, and the school.

Today, for a great many students, the best hope they have for acquiring a sure footing in life is rooted in what happens in our classrooms. For some of these youngsters, the schoolhouse offers the only avenue of escape from dysfunctional homes, deteriorating neighborhoods, and dead-end jobs. The good news is that out of these dismal environments can come what Harvard Professor Dr. Daniel Goleman defines as resilient children, children who have grown up in chaotic homes under the worst circumstances imaginable, and yet have made something out of themselves. How is that possible? Goleman believes that, in many cases, it is because "one caring adult really got involved in their lives and helped them out. And oftentimes that person is a teacher."[11] For those students fortunate enough to have a teacher who builds relationships by engaging in "Wayside Teaching," the school truly becomes a bridge to a dream.

Some readers may be thinking that we don't have kids like that in our school. I certainly don't want to leave you with the impression that it is only the children from disadvantaged homes who need caring "Wayside" teachers in their lives. Some of our most dysfunctional students come from the most affluent backgrounds. Syndicated columnist Clarence Page noted, ". . . it is becoming more common for kids in better-off neighborhoods to come from broken homes with overworked parents and other difficulties typically associated with the less fortunate."[12] Many of these students may be getting good grades in school; yet, they too often feel alone, angry, isolated, alienated, and unable to connect. Many are in desperate need of the guidance that comes with "Wayside Teaching." They, like the economically disadvantaged children, need a "Good Samaritan" in their lives. Unfortunately, I have found that for many affluent parents, their interest in schooling is limited to the accumulating of good grades so their kids can get in the most prestigious schools. As teachers, we have an added responsibility to impart to these parents the wisdom of Walker Percy: "You can get all 'A's' and still flunk life."[13]

In 1989, at the 94th Annual Meeting of the Southern Association of Colleges and Schools in Atlanta, Georgia, the keynote speaker was the late Ernest Boyer, one of the outstanding educators of the 20th century. I found the audiotape in my archives and transcribed a piece of it, included here, to share with you. Boyer said, "George Steiner, the contemporary British philosopher, reminded us that a man who is intellectually advanced can, at the same time, be morally bankrupt. We now know that such a man can listen to Bach and Schubert at sundown, read Goethe in the evening, and the next day go to his daily work at the concentration camp to gas his fellowman. What grows up inside literate civilization that seems to prepare it for barbarism?" Boyer responded by saying, "What grows up, of course, is information without knowledge, knowledge without wisdom, and competence without conscience." He continued, "We must give priority to moral education and help our students see a connection between what they learn and how they live."[14]

How do we help students see the connection between what we

teach in school and how they live? We do so, in large measure, with "Wayside Teaching." Following a presentation in Guatemala City, Nancy Larsen, a teacher of English at *Escuela Americana* in El Salvador, came out of the audience and handed me a paper on which she had jotted down a poem from memory. "Originally," she explained, "the title was 'Sermons We See.' However, I have modified the text and call it 'The Lesson.'" It is a slight adaptation of Edgar Guest's well-known poem that makes its point as only simple verse can.

The Lesson

I'd rather see a lesson than hear one any day.
I'd rather one should walk with me than merely show the way.
For the eye is a better pupil and more willing than the ear.
Fine counsel is confusing, but examples are always clear.
And the best of all the teachers are the ones who live their creeds.
For to see the good in action is what everybody needs.
I can soon learn how to do it if you'll let me see it done.
I can watch your hands in action, but your tongue too fast may run.
And the lectures you deliver may be very wise and true,
but I'd rather get my lessons by observing what you do.
For I may misunderstand you and the high advice you give,
but there's no misunderstanding how you act and how you live.[15]

This poem reminds me of statements made by Karl Menninger and L. Thomas Hopkins. Menninger said, "What the teacher is, is more important than what he teaches."[16] L. Thomas Hopkins put it simply, "What a teacher really teaches is himself."

Again, some readers may be thinking: "Has this guy never heard of high stakes testing?" Others may be saying to themselves, "'Wayside Teaching' may be appropriate for some schools, but I will be in a school with a rigorous college preparatory program or in a school where the faculty is struggling just to meet Adequate Yearly Progress (AYP)."

"Wayside Teaching" is, in fact, directly related to improved student achievement. Teachers who have high expectations use it as a tool to push students to reach their potential. Child psychiatrist James Comer, said, "No significant learning occurs without a significant relationship."[17] For all of you who will be teaching at the secondary level, remember, too, the words of wisdom from education reformers, Ted Sizer and Ernie Boyer. Sizer tells us, "Personalization is the single most important factor that keeps kids in school." Boyer said, "One of the reasons so many kids drop out of high school is that no one notices when they drop in."[18] For those who will labor in high-poverty districts, remember the words of former principal and author, Ruby Payne, "The key to student achievement from students from poverty is in creating relationships with them."[19]

Remember, it is in "Wayside Teaching" that we use fully our potential as persons who have the awesome opportunity to make a real difference in the learning and lives of young people. Teachers may have little control over most of what goes on at the schoolhouse, but they have complete control over the most important factor in the teaching/learning process: The climate in the classroom. Haim Ginott wrote, "I've come to the frightening conclusion I am the decisive element in the classroom. It is my personal approach that creates the climate. It is my daily mood that makes the weather."[20] The climate in your classroom is as distinctive as your fingerprint. It is whatever you choose to make it. When the climate is inviting, warm, and safe, incredible things happen. Every once in a while, there will come that rewarding and humbling moment when you look into the face of a student, and you will see the lights in his or her eyes turn on—all because of something you said or did!

The 1950-51 school year was the worst of my life. I failed the fourth grade. I have reflected often on leading educator John Goodlad's evocative question: "Is one's fate in school virtually determined by, or in, the fourth grade?"[21] As an adult, I have wondered how Theodore Roethke could have written his poem, "My Poppa's Waltz" with such stunning accuracy without having lived in the house with me in Meridian, Mississippi. When I hear the opening lines of that poem, I am always transported back in time to the fourth grade.

> The whiskey on your breath
> Could make a small boy dizzy;
> But I hung on like death,
> Such waltzing was not easy.[22]

Daddy, a survivor of pellagra, became an alcoholic at an early age. He was twenty-one when he married my mother. She was fourteen. Together, armed with six years of schooling, they faced the Great Flood of 1927 and the Great Depression. My daddy was wonderful in many ways, and I loved him very much. Daddy instilled in me a strong work ethic. My mother was responsible for my moral compass.

One night during that miserable 1950-51 school year, my mother asked me to set the table. In those days we had a set of cheap dishes, and one dinner plate was out-of-round. When touched with a fork, that plate would wobble about and walk across the table. By mistake, I gave my father that plate. He was drinking and when he touched that plate with his fork, the plate wobbled. For some reason this imperfect plate infuriated my father. He jumped up, picked up a broomstick, and beat everything on the top of the table into a million pieces. As the crockery, utensils, and glassware rattled around on the linoleum floor, my mother said to me, "Son, you need to go to your room and study."

Not long after the incident at the supper table, my teacher, as was customary in those days, called out my name and my grade on a math paper. I had made the lowest grade in the class. As I trudged to the front of the room between my snickering classmates, my embarrassment turned to dismay. My teacher, who treated me worse than a redheaded stepchild, looked over her glasses and snarled, "You need to get this paper signed by your mother and father." My heart sank. I'm thinking, "Signed? I'm nine years old. How am I going to get this paper signed and survive?"

I got on the school bus that afternoon depressed, with hot tears in my eyes. As the bus came closer to Route 2, Box 46, I suddenly started to feel better about my dilemma. After all, I was a good kid. I had been brought up in the church. Indeed, I attended a church in Mississippi that was, theologically speaking, considerably to the right of Southern Baptists. I have no regrets about that rigorous upbringing. Well, to be totally honest, I do have one tiny lingering regret: Someday, I hope to learn how to dance.

Among other things, I had been taught to believe that the Lord is aware when the sparrow falls to the ground. He knows the number of hairs in my head. Ask and ye shall receive. Also, with the faith of a mustard seed, one can move mountains. Teachers, I didn't want God to move any mountains. All I wanted from God was a grade change. Compared to moving mountains, that request seemed like small potatoes to me. I jumped off that school bus with my spirit renewed. With my paper in one hand, I ran toward the storage shed next to the chicken house. In that building, my father had a 55-gallon drum in which he stored the laying mash for his chickens. With my free hand, I lifted the lid and placed my math paper on top of that pungent, mustard-colored laying mash, and said a prayer. My prayer 56 years ago, with an apology to Judy Blume,[23] probably sounded something like this, "Are you there, God? It's me, Frank Charles. I made an F in school today, God. And that ain't good. I don't want you to change my grade to an A or B, God. If you could just change it to a C or D, I'll do better next time. I want you to be proud of me. Thank you." I put the lid back on the drum and the weight of the world lifted from my shoulders. The next morning at 7:00 A.M., I raced out of the house and, before the screen door on the back porch had slammed shut, I lifted the lid on that drum to view my personal miracle. There, on the laying mash, rested my paper with the grade—unchanged! That was my first theological experience in life, and at age 65, I have not yet fully recovered.

If the fourth grade was the worst year of my life, the fifth grade was the best year of my life. The only thing that had changed was my teacher. In the fifth grade at Stevenson Elementary, students had two choices for a teacher: The screamer and Miss Mary Ann Bonney. Through the luck of the draw, I was assigned to the classroom of Mary Ann Bonney. We adored her. She was 24 years old and absolutely brilliant—Phi Beta Kappa, double major, University of Alabama. She would get so excited teaching social studies that she would talk 100 miles an hour with gusts up to 300. Out of her own pocket, she purchased the first raised relief map that any of us had ever seen. It was breathtakingly beautiful. It was about six feet wide and suspended with two large rings from an aluminum framework. She let a small group of us stay in from recess for about a week to fondle the mountains and caress the valleys. Miss Bonney was strikingly attractive, and she wore the most beautiful clothes. When she would pass by my desk, the scent of her perfume would hang in the air like peach blossoms blowing in a soft wind. Every day, she wore high-heeled shoes to school, even on the playground. She had class!

I don't remember much of what Miss Bonney taught me because students forget most of what they learn in school. However, as long as I live, I will always remember how this teacher treated me. In one year under Miss Bonney, who was a "Wayside" teacher par excellence, I went from a zero to a star. The light in my eyes had gone out in 1949 when the only grandparent I ever knew died. This picture of me with my beloved Granny Patterson was taken the day we took my grandmother home to die. It contrasts with the second picture: What I looked like when Miss Bonney brought me new life.

In the archives at the Meridian, Mississippi, Public Library, I

Author's Personal Collection

Frank Charles Winstead with his grandmother, Losia Blanche Patterson, in 1949 (left), and as a fifth grader in teacher Mary Ann Bonney's class (right).

discovered Miss Bonney's personal formula for success in the class-room in an old school scrapbook from Stevenson Elementary School. From that vintage collection of memorabilia dated 1951-1952, here is that formula: Children + Books + Charts + Globes + Pictures + Maps + Handwork + Time + Happy Situation = Learning. I am certain that the component in that formula that made the biggest difference in my life was: "Happy Situation." Today, we would call that a positive classroom climate.

In my early forties, it came to me one day that the good life I have enjoyed I owed, in large measure, to a handful of teachers who saw a lot more in me than I could see in myself. This revelation came to me strongly while I was reading the introduction to *What Teachers Need to Know*. Ernest Boyer wrote the introduction to this book. What he said there opened my eyes. "When I was Commissioner of Education I called together twenty high school seniors from around the country. We spent the day talking about their schools and about their teachers. At the conclusion of our conversation, I asked, 'How

many of you have ever had a teacher who's changed your life?' Every
hand went up. And then I asked, 'How many of you have ever
thanked a teacher?' Not one hand was raised."[24] That passage
weighed heavily on me. I was troubled and embarrassed.

About the same time that I was reading *What Teachers Need to
Know,* my dear friend and professional colleague, Ray Bruce from the
University of Georgia, sent me an audiotape of a presentation by
Dean Birkley from Indiana University. In a note, Ray said, "You need
to listen to this tape. It will make you feel better." I needed to feel
better. My colleagues and I were still suffering with the fallout from
the 1983 federal report, *A Nation at Risk.*[25] Driving down the road, I
heard Birkley's gravelly voice boom forth as he announced the title of
his keynote, "It Ain't All Bad!" Then, in his message, Birkley said
something that touched my heart: "Teaching is an art, and you constantly search for ways to light up people's faces. And, you do that.
That's why, unknown to you, someplace, somewhere, somebody
envies you because you work in a productive kind of environment
and because you work in that kind of arena in which once in a while
somebody says, 'I've got it! That's it! And that's why you belong in
somebody's hall of fame somewhere, and that ain't all bad.'"[26]

With Birkley's tape playing in my head and with Boyer's introduction in my hands, I conceived the idea for my hall of fame. The
special people featured in the portraits in my collection of memorabilia are the people who helped me make it in this life. They are all
teachers. Three of them did not have teaching certificates or portfolios. They were my mother, my neighbor, and my minister. However,
all of these teachers had one common characteristic. They were all
terrific "Wayside" teachers.

In the display of my hall of fame, six of the portraits are identified with green tabs. Every year, I honor these teachers by funding six
$1,000.00 scholarships at the junior college I attended from 1959 to
1961 in Meridian, Mississippi. The scholarships are for students who
plan to become teachers. Those teachers who touched my life in very
special ways were Miss Mary Ann Bonney, my fifth-grade teacher in
1951; Mrs. Maude Reid (deceased), who taught me World History

in 1956 in the tenth grade and European History in 1959 at Meridian Junior College; Mr. Eli Pacetti (deceased), my high school band director from 1957 to 1959; Mr. Jack Shank, the camera club sponsor at Meridian High School/Meridian Junior College from 1959-1961; Miss Reva Breckenridge (deceased), who taught me Botany and Zoology at Meridian Junior College from 1959 to 1961; and Miss Marguerite Jenkins (deceased), my English teacher at Meridian Junior College in 1959.

Some may feel that "Wayside Teaching" is really applicable only at the elementary school level. Not so. Come with me back in time to 1959 to Meridian Junior College (MJC). I want you to meet Mr. Jack Shank, one of the most wonderful "Wayside" teachers on this planet. This World War II veteran, now in his eighties, is in my hall of fame. He is the teacher who made it possible for me to remain in the teaching profession. He taught me the craft of photography in the camera club at MJC. These glowing comments were written about Mr. Shank in the 1960 annual: ". . . no teacher on campus of MJC is any busier with the common interests of the school than is he. No teacher devotes more time or energy to promote all phases of school life." Like all master teachers, Mr. Shank looked beyond the walls of his classroom and asked, "What can I do to make this a better school?" He sponsored the *Quill and Scroll,* the student newspaper, the camera club, and served as the school photographer. Also, he was an absolutely marvelous history teacher.

He taught me photography with patience and with generous amounts of "Wayside Teaching." The first photograph I ever

Author's Personal Collection

First place award-winning picture of "Lady Sue," 1959.

Author's Personal Collection

Majorette Janet Rainer as photographed by Frank Charles Winstead, 1960.

entered into competition was a portrait of my dog. This print won first place. I was so proud! I walked around the college boasting about my "salon print." Trust me, that photograph will never make it into any gallery or museum. However, when you are eighteen years of age and you see such a print developing in a tray in a darkroom, you believe that it is a salon print. That is what is important. My next entry of a high school majorette was also a first-place winner, but you will certainly note a dramatic change in interest in my subject matter—dog to majorette.

When I graduated from Mississippi State University in 1963, I was offered a job in my home state that paid $3,000.00 a year. For that same salary, I also had to agree to drive one of the school buses. So I signed a contract to teach in Cobb County, Georgia, for $4,265.00. When I crossed the Mississippi/Alabama line on the way to Georgia, I thought I was in tall cotton. When I received my first paycheck, the reality of life as a schoolteacher settled in on me.

Since I don't throw away anything, I still have the stub from that paycheck. Reading from that stub, I can tell you that after working for one month in the fall of 1963, my take-home pay after deductions was $264.48. My rent was $60.00 a month. The place should have been condemned by the fire marshal. My car note was $68.00 a month. When those two obligations were paid, I was left with $136.00 and some change for food, clothing, and related necessities. If I wanted to remain a schoolteacher, it was obvious I had to get a second job. For seven years, I made my living on the weekends out of a camera bag. The work I did for the Cobb County School System could be best described as "community service," but I was able to remain in the profession that I loved because Mr. Jack Shank taught me the craft of photography. What enormous power lies in the hands of teachers! At the time he was sponsoring the camera club (1959-1961), I am certain Mr. Shank had no idea that he was "doing any good at the schoolhouse" with one Frank Charles Winstead.

I end this chapter by sharing my favorite story. It was a significant event in my life as an educator. While it is about a sixth-grade student and her young principal, it is more than that. It is a story in praise of all those educators who day after day and year after year go the second mile without praise or recognition.

I became a principal at an early age, having been an assistant principal only one year. I knew just enough to be dangerous. I had been on the job only a few weeks when the 12 teachers from the sixth-grade school and the two counselors came to me with a proposal: They wanted to take the sixth-grade class to Camp Tremont in Tennessee. Our school was located in the Atlanta metro area. Those teachers wanted to put some 300 kids on contracted school buses, drive through the mountains of north Georgia, cross the Tennessee state line, and then travel deep into the Appalachian Mountains to an environmental education center called Camp Tremont.

My mentor, Mr. Tom Mathis, who incidentally is in my hall of fame, taught me the year we were together as principal and assistant principal that part of my job was to allow good things to happen. So I announced to that excited group, "You work out the details, and we will send those kids to Tremont." They floated out of my office ready to make it all happen.

A couple of weeks later, the buses arrived before dawn. After they were loaded, I went back to my office, parted the blinds, and watched those buses drive off into the sunrise. I was so proud of those teachers and counselors—and myself because I had allowed this event to happen.

About 20 minutes later the school secretary appeared in the doorway to my office. Trembling and with the color drained from her body, she gasped, "We have a big problem. You need to go to the lobby immediately!" I rushed out of my office. When I reached the lobby, I saw a solitary figure gazing in my direction—a frail, poorly dressed, little girl. As I got closer, I recognized her. It was Rhonda—sixth-grade, special education Rhonda!

Before I could speak, she greeted me with sparkling enthusiasm, "Hi, Mister Win--tead, I'm weady to go to Tweemont." She had not a clue. My heart sank. "Rhonda," I said, "the buses are gone. You missed the bus! I don't have any way to get you to Tremont." This little girl looked up at me with very large eyes and announced, "Mr. Win--tead, you wook at me, I paid my money!" And I said, "Rhonda, you look at me. I know you paid your money, but the buses are gone." Rhonda, thin, pale, and trembling, stood in front of me with pleading eyes. Without words she conveyed to me this clear message, "Mr. Win--tead, surely you can find a way to get me to Tremont. After all you are the principal."

I remember that she had bright orange-red hair, and on one side of her head, her hair was a matted mass of tangles and knots where she had slept on it. She looked like the wrath of God. There was not a place on her face that was not covered with a freckle. She also had a yellow snot-dripping cold. Every time she breathed, she bubbled. That child was hard to love.

Finally, it settled in on Rhonda that she was not going to Tremont. The biggest tears you have ever seen started to form. The tears rolled down both sides of her nose, collected on her little chin, and dropped softly on the carpet below. I admit I am soft. When little girls or big girls cry, I go to pieces, which come to think about it is not a bad title for a country music tune.

"Now, Rhonda," I said, "get your things together and go to Mr. Winstead's office." Totally dejected, she walked down the hall pulling a rope attached to an olive drab duffle bag that appeared to be a survivor of the Korean War. About half of her stuff was hanging out of the pockets. It was clear she had packed in a hurry.

When I got back to my office, Rhonda was sitting directly in front of my desk sobbing quietly. I sat down behind my desk and put my fingers over my face and watched her through the cracks in my fingers. My strategy was to wait until she got herself together, and then I would do what most principals of that day probably would have done, that is, send her to the library for three days.

While I was looking at her through the cracks in my fingers, she said to me in a remarkably strong voice, "Mr. Win-tead, Mr. Win-tead, wook at me! We got a big problem. Whut we gonna do?" I said to myself, "This child is not special ed. This child is gifted."

"Rhonda, listen to me," I said. "I don't have any way to get you to Tremont." Immediately, the tears started to flow, her tiny body shook as if she were about to have a convulsion. Every time she exhaled, she bubbled. "Hold on, Rhonda." I called the school secretary. "Get the highway patrol on the telephone." The conversation went something like this, "This is the Georgia Highway Patrol, how can we 'hep' you, buddy?" I said, "Stop those damned school buses." He said, "We 'be' glad to stop 'them' buses, 'whut' highway they on?" What highway they on! I'm a first year principal. I didn't realize I was supposed to file a flight plan. I had no idea what highway those buses were on. I rushed up to the library to find a road map. Looking at the map, my heart sank. Every road leading out of north Atlanta goes to Tremont.

I came downstairs, and Rhonda was bawling her eyes out. "Rhonda," I said, "hush! Get your stuff together and put it in Mr. Winstead's car. We will go catch the school buses." I didn't know what highway those buses were on, but, trust me, that was a minor point in the drama that was rapidly unfolding. We got into my car, a 1960 green Datsun that had been totaled in a wreck and rebuilt. The eighth-grade boys called it the "bondo buggy." It used a quart of oil every 60 miles. I put in two quarts of oil, and we took off. Immediately, Rhonda went to sleep and she bubbled every time she breathed. I was miserable. To illustrate my lack of readiness to be a principal, I didn't even have enough sense to call the county office and say, "Hey, folks, I'm leaving school grounds with an 11-year-old child. In fact, I'm about to cross the state line with her."

Every time I got to the top of a hill, I just knew I would see those school buses. I never did, and for a good reason—they were on a different road. Outside of the little town of Blue Ridge, I saw something that caused my heart to jump up into my throat. There was, as I would have said in Mississippi in 1950, a "PO-lice-man" leaning against the side of his cruiser, and he was flagging me down. I looked over at a snoring and bubbling Rhonda, and I said, "Rhonda, for God's sake, wake up and smile." The policeman ambled up to my car and gave to me that legendary greeting from the southland, "Lemme' see 'yo drivin' license, boy." I was terrified! They don't allow policemen built like this fellow on the force today. He dressed out about 385 pounds. He stood about five foot three inches tall. He looked like a human bowling ball with a Hermann Goering Luftwaffe-style hat pulled down low on his forehead and cocked to one side. He was wearing a badly stained clip-on tie that came to an abrupt end six inches above his belt. Here was the stereotypical officer of the law from the Deep South. He loved to stop people for traffic violations. This was especially true for people from up "nawth" because he did not believe that the Civil War was over yet. It was commonplace for this type of policeman to stop people from the north, walk up to the car and ask, "Where you people from anyhow and where you headed?" When told, "Officer, we are from Chicago, and we are going to Miami," this lawman was often totally confused. A common response was, "Well, if y'all from Chicago, how come you got one of 'em 'ILL-I- Noise' license plates?"

The policeman gave back my license, stuck his head in my car, and said, "You and 'yo' daughter have a good day now—you 'heah.'" As he waddled back to his cruiser, Rhonda blurted, "Mr. Win-tead, I'm not your daughter." By this time I had completely lost my composure, and through trembling lips I shouted, "Just hush! At this moment, you are my daughter!"

We got to Tremont about 25 minutes after the caravan of buses arrived. In fact, the kids were still unloading. Rhonda immediately jumped out of my car, opened the hatchback to retrieve her duffle bag and quickly melted into the crowd. The kids never figured out that she had missed the bus. She never said thank you or looked back. Rhonda's parents never even called me. Even so, taking that child to Tremont was about the best thing I ever did for a child in my career.

Driving back to the school that afternoon my car broke down, so I did not arrive at the school until 10:00 P.M. I wondered if I still had a job. When I opened the door to my office and flipped on the lights, the first thing that caught my eye was a display on my desk. A lump formed in my throat and tears came to my eyes. During the day, some of those wonderful faculty members had gone out and bought a toy school bus and a little green car. They tied the two together with a yellow string. This rolling stock was pointed north on my desk and was surrounded by notes and cards, all thanking me for going the second mile.

That day, so many years ago when Rhonda came to me looking for a "Good Samaritan" who would provide that "light in the darkness," I was, at first, too distracted; but then, the voice of my mentor, Mr. Tom Mathis, spoke to me; and I remembered what he had taught all the members of the staff at Griffin Middle School when he was the principal. "In this school we go the second mile for all of our kids." In the end, I could not turn my back on what I had been taught. So, I went the second mile that day. Actually, I went about 290 miles!

I share this story with you not to portray myself in some heroic way, but just to remind you that doing the right thing sometimes means taking a chance, that is, trusting your instincts and putting the wonderful children we are privileged to serve in first place and that is where they belong.

Teachers are going to have some bad days at the schoolhouse. That goes with the territory. When you are having one of those bad days and you are down and blue about our noble profession, I want you to remember that when you engage in "Wayside Teaching" and go the second mile, regularly bright and shining moments will emerge. Sometimes that transformation in a child may require no more on your part than the glance of an eye. When you look into the vacant face of a child and you see those eyes brighten up, and when you see a smile on a face that has never smiled in your classroom, you will know that teaching is the most rewarding and important job in the world.

A final footnote, please. Now that this chapter is complete, I'm not certain about you, but Frank Charles feels a lot better knowing that "Janet (from the class of '57) teaches grade school and probably always will."

Frank Charles Winstead with his Hall of Fame and related memorabilia in Lake Charles, Louisiana.

Author's Personal Collection

About the Author:
Frank Charles Winstead (www.advocateforexcellence.com) is convinced that teaching is the most important job in the world. This former Outstanding Young Educator for the State of Georgia, Georgia STAR Teacher, and Georgia's Outstanding Principal focuses his professional endeavors on creating positive learning environments and supporting instructional excellence. He wraps substance about school climate, teaching, and learning with humor.

Winstead has a great sense of humor, is well-read, and is a master storyteller. To illustrate the power and importance of teaching in the new millennium, he highlights exemplary teachers from his past as he artfully weaves numerous anecdotes into his presentation with research from contemporary scholars. Winstead reinforces all key points with visual images and memorabilia. This approach to teaching makes his presentations memorable. Winstead entertains, but he is not an entertainer; rather, he is a gifted teacher and communicator whose messages are genuine, powerful, uplifting, and often poignant.

Chapter Four

Forever an Optimist: Changing the World One Child at a Time

Philip Bigler

1998 National Teacher of the Year

The great teachers fill you up with hope and shower you with a thousand reasons to embrace all aspects of life. —Pat Conroy

I became a teacher at precisely 8:00 A.M. September 2, 1975. I was just 23 years old. As my new students entered the cramped confines of room 141 at Oakton High School in Fairfax County, Virginia, I nervously handed each one of them an aromatic welcoming letter, still soaking wet from fresh ditto fluid. On the reverse side was a meticulously prepared and detailed course syllabus that outlined my goals, objectives, and hopes for their state-mandated junior-level United States/Virginia History class. When all of the students were finally seated, I stood before a sea of anxious faces while instinctively clutching my attendance sheet and notebook full of untried lesson plans for protection, hoping desperately to disguise my profound sense of inadequacy.

It had been just five years—1,825 days—since I had graduated from this very same high school. I still retained my youthful appearance. Without the slacks and tie, I was virtually indistinguishable from the more mature senior boys. Yet a chasm now existed because I was a "teacher," some mythological figure—the possessor of wisdom, the keeper of knowledge, the all-powerful evaluator of student progress. Thank heavens the students didn't know the truth. I was

Your tools have changed over the years—textbooks have been updated, slates have given way to computers. But the most important tools—the heart and soul and compassion—are still the same. The passion for opening young minds to knowledge; the unshakable faith in the potential and possibility of every child; the commitment every now and then to stay after class to help a struggling student; the vigilance to answer every child's discouraged "I can't" with a determined, "Yes, you can."

Our national honoree, Philip Bigler, brings all these gifts to his history classes at, appropriately, Thomas Jefferson High School for Science and Technology in Virginia. For more than 20 years, his students haven't just studied history; they have lived it. He's transformed his classroom into a virtual time machine, challenging students to debating each other as members of rival ancient Greek city states: As lawyers before the Supreme Court as presidential candidates named Thomas Jefferson and John Adams.

Through these historic simulations, his students have learned lessons about democracy and the meaning of citizenship, lessons that will last a lifetime—lessons we want every American to know.

We need more teachers like Philip Bigler and all our other honorees in every classroom in America today. For it is they who can make our schools the best in the world. It is they who can guarantee that America will have another American Century in the 21st century.   —President Bill Clinton

scared to death, haunted by my recurring nightmares of being unable to control a classroom full of adolescents.

I had been shocked by how much the high school had changed during my brief absence. It seemed as if the entire American educational system had undergone a metamorphosis. Beginning with the Supreme Court decision (*Tinker v. Des Moines Independent Community School District*) that declared that "students... [do not] shed their constitutional rights to freedom of speech or expression at the schoolhouse gate," students had been liberated from many of the arbitrary rules and restrictions of the past. Gone forever were the much-despised dress codes so that the students in my classes were free to wear the era's most fashionable attire, which, in the 1970s, included polyester bell bottoms, leisure suits, puffy silk shirts, earth shoes, medallions, and mood rings. Throughout the overcrowded hallways of Oakton High School, young people could be found in every corner, sometime in amorous embrace while others were gathered together listening to the music of Barry Manilow, the Bee Gees, the Captain and Tennille, Tony Orlando and Dawn, and Chicago on 8-track or cassette tape players.

The new, laid-back atmosphere in the public schools had become something of a national phenomenon. Tradition had been discarded as old-fashioned, and rules and regulations were reduced to the bare minimum. Some school districts experimented with abolishing tardy bells while others radically altered their "repressive" truancy policies. High schools even went so far as to accommodate their nicotine-addicted students by designating special smoking courtyards for such activity between classes and during lunch. Meanwhile, the country's more innovative jurisdictions were spending millions of taxpayer dollars constructing open space classrooms, euphemistically referred to as "schools without walls," to give a physical representation to this era's new sense of freedom.

Inevitably, our collective insanity intruded into the academic curricula where there was a concerted effort to make all courses socially "relevant." All of the Social Studies teachers in my department, for instance, were expected to require the students to read the daily *Washington Post,* as if this mundane exercise would miraculously stimulate some latent and repressed interest in history. Regular current event activities punctuated all of our lesson plans, but these exercises often came at the expense of historical context, in-depth study, and reasoned judgment. We spent countless hours of valuable instruction time mired in endless and pointless arguments about modern public policy but struggled to progress chronologically beyond World War II in our courses. Incredibly, the Cold War, Civil Rights movement, Vietnam, and Watergate would never be part of these students' academic experience. This bordered upon educational malpractice. Our English department colleagues faced similar curricular challenges. For the sake of relevancy, they had miraculously managed to morph the music of Simon and Garfunkel and the "poetry" of Jim Morrison into instruction on Shakespeare and Mark Twain. Other nonconventional teachers abandoned traditional content altogether and were instead trying out techniques designed to help teenagers clarify their own personal values by posing esoteric and unrealistic ethical dilemmas for purposes unknown. *Happy Days* and *Saturday Night Live* were among the nation's most popular television programs; Gerald Ford was the accidental President of the United States; rampant, double-digit inflation was ravaging the nation's economy; and Philip Bigler was alone, without help or a mentor, trying to figure out how to survive and become an effective teacher.

Rather than try to develop my own personal style of teaching, I instead mimicked my own teachers from high school. I stood rigidly anchored to my podium and lectured every day for 45 minutes to the students, sometimes with the assistance of a handwritten transparency displayed on an overhead projector. Periodically, I would break this monotony by showing a 35-mm film from the county's centralized media repository. On schedule every Friday, I would administer a 25-question, easy-to-grade multiple choice quiz on the material I had covered. I was content competent, but I was merely conveying information rather than actually teaching. My classes were uninspired and boring; they had become an endurance trial for everybody involved. Fortunately, I quickly realized that something had better change and soon.

I have since forgiven myself for this lamentable start because I know that you can learn a lot from mistakes and failure. At this early point in my career, I certainly was not a good teacher, but I was astute enough to know when things were not working. I had reduced history to a litany of facts and dates without any real context or insight. Yet, I knew it was supposed to be something magical and inspiring. As Tony Hendra writes in his book, *Father Joe:* "…history was not simply a catalog of the dead and buried and benighted, but rather a vast new world to be pioneered; that if you approached the past generously, so to speak—its people as humans not facts, as modern in their times as we were in ours, who thought and felt as we do, the dead would live again, our equals, not our old-fashioned, hopelessly unenlightened, and backward inferiors."[27] Somehow I had to convince my students that my beloved subject was worth studying,

Students in Phil Bigler's humanities class conduct a simulation on the 1960 Presidential campaign between John F. Kennedy and Richard Nixon.

not necessarily as an oracle of future events but rather as a source of important lessons on how to live a good, productive, and ethical life. These students were now my professional responsibility, and it was my obligation to teach and inspire them.

One late autumn afternoon after everyone had gone home, I was browsing through the dozens of Social Studies catalogs that were scattered throughout the teacher's workroom in hopes of coming up with some new ideas. I saw an intriguing advertisement in one magazine for a historical simulation entitled, Grand Illusion, which purported to dramatize the events surrounding the outbreak of World War I. It cost a staggering $50 but came complete with a series of detailed lesson plans, a collection of primary source materials, a laminated map of 1914 Europe, and a long-playing record to introduce each class period. It seemed innovative and exciting, so the next morning I submitted a purchase order for the simulation. It was routinely rejected by the finance officer on the grounds that the school's strict budget allotted no funds for the purchase of curriculum materials for individual teachers. Frustrated but undeterred, I personally wrote a check to cover the cost out of my own pauper's salary of $9,500.

When the simulation arrived a few weeks later, I eagerly read each page of the extensive teacher's manual and then spent the weekend decorating, rearranging, and transforming my classroom to create a realistic atmosphere for a mythical international peace conference to be held in Geneva, Switzerland, during the critical summer months of 1914. I purchased several small desk flags for all of the involved countries. (I was forced to adapt modern flags for countries that no longer existed substituting the Austrian flag for Austria-Hungary, the Soviet flag for Imperial Russia, the Yugoslavian flag for Serbia, etc.) I also made special desktop nameplates for each of the students and prepared portfolios full of secret information outlining the group's goals, objectives, and national aspirations.

On Monday, something astonishing happened. For the first time, my students became enthused and excited about learning history and were totally captivated by their roles. History had become something real, not just meaningless words confined to the pages of a stale textbook or notes to be transcribed from a lecture. Soon, the German delegation became belligerent and angry with the British over naval supremacy in the Baltic Sea; the Russians were simultaneously asserting their unwavering support for the Serbs, their Slavic kin in the Balkans. The Austrian-Hungarian diplomats pompously issued ultimatums while openly mourning the death of their assassinated archduke, Franz Ferdinand. The French coveted their long, lost territory of Alsace-Lorraine while the Italians hoped to annex the disputed Tretino region located along their northern border. The Ottoman Turks, meanwhile, sulked and cursed their ignoble status as "the Sickman of Europe," and the Americans steadfastly remained neutral "...in thought as well as deed." Before long, secret discussions and negotiations were taking place before class in the hallways and at lunch where passionate arguments erupted without warning. The more powerful nations repeatedly threatened military action unless their nationalistic demands were met and began to mobilize and amass their troops along their national borders. Before long, the entire world had stumbled into war just as it had in reality. It was an amazing couple of weeks. The students were finally learning history and understanding its many intricacies while I had discovered an exciting, powerful, new methodology. By taking a risk and trying something new, I had become a better teacher. It was an epiphany, and it proved to be a major turning point in my career.

My Social Studies classroom was transformed into what President Clinton would later call "a virtual time machine." The students were reliving history and experiencing it first hand. One of my favorite projects was our annual field trip to the Soldiers' and Airmen's home in Washington, D.C. With the aid of cassette tape recorders, the students conducted oral history interviews with the World War II veterans who were in residence. They personally met survivors of the Bataan death march, liberators of the Nazi concentration camps, Pearl Harbor survivors—the real "Private Ryan's" before modern Hollywood ever discovered the great generation.

On one trip, there was a very elderly soldier who was dressed smartly in his navy blue blazer and veteran's cap but was sound asleep in his wheelchair. Initially, we were reluctant to disturb him, but the director assured us that it would be perfectly fine and that George was looking forward to meeting the students. Jason Goodale, one of my most gifted and brilliant history students, volunteered immediately to interview George and before long the two were engaged in an intense conversation. Jason soon discovered that George was not only a veteran of World War II but also was one of our nation's last surviving World War I soldiers; he had, in fact, been seriously injured during a chemical gas attack in 1918.

Shortly after we returned to school, my teaching partner, Sheri Maeda, had the students transform their notes and tapes into one-act plays dramatizing the lives of these amazing people. These plays were

Philip Bigler

Jason Goodale interviews a World War I and II veteran at the U.S. Soldier's and Airmen's Home in Washington, D.C.

then performed for the soldiers during an assembly near the Memorial Day holiday while a World War II era 48-star flag flew proudly over the school in their honor.

Jason continued to correspond with George after our visit. In one letter, he wrote: "Words cannot describe how thankful I am for your talking to me. Your words were so fascinating, and yet they only break the surface as to what a remarkable and important life you have led. . . . I will never forget the hour I spent with you. I can only hope that fate draws us together again some day. You are an American hero to me. If you don't remember anything else about me in the future, remember that for one hour you touched my heart, and for this I will always keep your spirit alive in my heart and mind." Sadly, this incredible man passed away a few months later having lived a long, distinguished and heroic life. Little did I imagine that a few years later, Jason himself would answer our nation's call to duty after the attacks of 9-11 and would serve two tours of duty with the United States Marine Corps in Iraq. Some history lessons are so profound that they last a lifetime.

In truth, over the 23 years that I was a high school teacher, there were many ups and downs—good days and some bad—yet I somehow managed to learn something new about the craft of teaching each day. I certainly got better with time and experience, but I also slowly began to appreciate what is required to become a truly great teacher. These important "lessons" came from observing and working with literally hundreds of talented teachers in a variety of academic settings. Regardless of what subject or grade level they taught, I found that there are some common characteristics of great teachers, a few universal truths, and a couple of commandments.

Rule Number 1: Thou Shall Change

One of the greatest ironies in our current educational system is that the expectations and responsibilities for a novice teacher are essentially the same as those for a veteran educator who may have been in the classroom for over 30 years. That statement is not to imply that the two are in any way comparable in terms of quality, content, or pedagogy; but it is clear that during your teaching career, you can either choose to change and become a better teacher or you can stagnate and eventually burn out. Yet, too many of our teachers seem to be fearful of innovation and new ideas. They seem perfectly content with mediocrity, sheltered within the privacy of their own classrooms, teaching the same subject with the same lesson plans for decades, oblivious to modern progress. It seems to me that life for such individuals must be a perpetual purgatory because they never attempt something different, risk anything new, or dare to be great. Each day is routine and indistinguishable from the next, marked only by the change of the calendar.

The best teachers in our schools have little time or patience for such individuals. Instead, as committed, lifelong learners, they are always seeking new ideas, trying the latest innovations, and looking for creative ways to help motivate and inspire their students. They practice their beliefs by constantly learning, reading, and updating their lesson plans all the while retaining their enthusiasm and commitment to the teaching profession.

During my career as a high school teacher, I taught 22 different Social Studies courses, including modern European History, Economics, World History, Political Science, Government, American History, Russian History, Geography, and Middle Eastern History. I was hardly an "expert" in each of these subject areas and frequently found myself out of my comfort zone, but I was anxious to learn. I knew that teaching these classes would be intellectually challenging and would help me be a better and more flexible teacher. Today, for instance, if someone asked me to teach a class on feudal Japan or the age of Peter the Great or the Constitutional principles of the Electoral College or virtually any other Social Studies topic, I already have a file full of ideas and lesson plans.

The need for change and innovation is particularly apparent in adapting modern technology effectively for classroom instruction. Today's students were born after 1982 and are sometimes referred to as the "millennial generation." They have grown up wholly during the age of computers; the information revolution has been a daily part of their lives. They have a right to expect technology to be transforming classroom instruction. Indeed, right now is the most exciting time in history to be a teacher because there are limitless opportunities for innovation and creativity. Likewise, there are incredible curricular resources available online to assist teachers in preparing lesson plans and in dealing with routine classroom difficulties. Inexplicably, though, there remains a general reluctance among far too many educators to incorporate the digital revolution into their classrooms. Others use it poorly and waste time by assigning students rote assignments and meaningless (not to mention potentially dangerous) tasks, such as blind Internet searches and unsupervised computer lab time. Whether deterred by techno-phobia or just plain cynicism, a teacher's inability to adapt to modern times hinders his effectiveness, especially in dealing with our current techno-savvy, iPod generation. As one student succinctly observed, the best teachers ". . . know that it is not 1970." Indeed, the most effective educators are those who embrace innovation as a tool of instruction and work continually to grow and improve professionally.

As astonishing as it may sound now, the first major technological invention that changed me forever as a teacher was the introduction of the pocket calculator. During my early career, the entire faculty was expected to do our quarterly grades for report cards in the school's library. We would sit quietly together for hours like cloistered monks in an ancient abbey, laboring over columns of long addition tables, carefully calculating and transcribing the numerical averages for each of our 150 students. Unfortunately, our accuracy rate began to decline with the tedium of each passing hour and our mistakes multiplied incrementally. Once the report cards were finally issued, the next few days were devoted to calming angry parents and horrified teenagers whose grades had been radically lowered by a simple arithmetic error. (For some reason those who mistakenly received higher grades than they deserved never seemed to complain.) When I purchased my first calculator at a cost of over $100, I felt liberated, convinced that this incredible new technological device would transform American public education. It immediately saved me countless hours of time (still a teacher's most precious commodity) and freed me from the boredom of repetitive arithmetic while correspondingly improving my accuracy rate. I had instantaneously become a better teacher through the use of the latest technology.

The next major advance occurred just a few years later when our school's ditto machine was miraculously replaced by a modern Xerox copier. Previously, every single document generated by the high school had to be precisely typed on special carbon-backed "ditto masters." When you made the dreaded and inevitable typographic error, you had to remove the stencil from the typewriter carriage to correct the mistake, and carefully scrape off the reverse carbon impression with a razor blade. Then the ditto was reinserted back into the typewriter and you would retype the offending letter. After a few such mistakes, simple sanity dictated that any hope of producing a pristine document had to be abandoned. Instead, the materials everyone distributed to our students were full of crossouts, type-overs, and handwritten corrections. To make matters even worse, the highest quality ditto master could produce only about 100 clear, legible copies before slowly fading away into invisibility. Of course, all teachers had far more students than that number, so the handouts reproduced for the late afternoon classes were barely readable. Further exacerbating the situation was the fact that the paper retained the wondrous smell of ditto fluid. As soon as the students received their assignments and handouts, their first instinct was to smother their faces in the paper in order to inhale its fragrant smells. So much for the effectiveness of our antidrug policies, but regardless of content, it was certainly true that our lessons never smelled better than during this era.

When the first Xerox machine finally arrived and was unpacked and installed at our school, the faculty was in collective awe. For the first time, it was possible to use correction tape and whiteout to correct our typing errors so the quality of our handouts, worksheets, and tests quickly improved. Moreover, I was finally able to replicate for my Social Studies classes political cartoons, maps, charts, and graphs that required students to use higher-order thinking skills and sophisticated analysis. Modern technology, once again, had improved my teaching.

Despite all evidence to the contrary, society and the media continue to romanticize the past, the so-called "good old days" of American education. In truth, these times exist only in the myth of memory, and I am astonished about how primitive our materials and resources actually were when I first began teaching. In my media and methods class at Madison College, preservice teachers were taught such things as how to use a filmstrip and the procedure for threading a 35-mm movie projector. More advanced students created their own instructional slide show and our class constructed a battery powered light-board for quiz review. These were state-of-the-art skills by the standards of the day, and we were anxious to apply the latest innovations in our "modern" classrooms. Today, these skills are as obsolete as a record player.

Showing a 16-mm educational film was once considered to be a creative way to increase student interest and motivation. In Fairfax County, our district maintained a massive, centralized film repository and distribution system, which was designed to serve the entire county's many schools. In practical terms, that meant that every single Social Studies teacher was in competition for the exact same audiovisual resources, which would be allocated on a rigid first-come, first-served basis. Thus, on the first workday after summer vacation, I would forsake the traditional PTA provided "welcome back" coffee and donuts in order to rush down to the school's library to begin to fill out an entire year's worth of film requests. I desperately tried to anticipate a film's likely availability, the school's academic calendar, and my own curricular needs in an effort to schedule the right movies at the appropriate instructional time. It proved to be an impossible task since there was no way to anticipate the routine interruptions to the school year, which included sports assemblies, pep rallies, holiday concerts, field trips, and snow days. It seemed that by January, I would already be behind my carefully envisioned schedule. We would be studying something like the causes of the American Civil War when I would receive a notice from the school's library that the film, *Teddy Roosevelt and the Progressives,* had arrived. I was forced to stop instruction, explain the relevance of the film, and give a brief overview of the period so that it could be returned in a timely manner. The movie, no matter how good, was horribly out of context. I knew, however, that it would be the only opportunity I would have to use this valuable audiovisual resource regardless of how little sense the scheduling made educationally.

With the advent of the Reagan administration and the onset of the 1980s, videotape technology became increasingly available and soon every school library was converted into a media resource center. They established and maintained their own individual film archives full of first-rate educational documentaries. These incredible resources were easily available so that they could be used at the perfect time to enhance instruction and supplement course content.

Today, DVDs have supplanted videotape as a superior technology, and once again, the tools that teachers can use to enhance instruction are improving.

Computers, smartboards, digital photography, podcasting, class webpages, online journals, the Internet, and wireless technology are the immediate future of American education and have the potential for transforming our schools into true learning centers. Textbook manufacturers are investigating ways to deliver electronic versions of chapters, maps, and supplementary resources, while tablet PCs and electronic personal planners make note-taking and organization simple. The Internet has thrown open the doors of the archives, museums, and libraries of the world for student research, while word processing programs have removed the tedium from spelling, editing, and rewriting. But to be a truly great teacher, you must first be willing to embrace these exciting innovations in order to maximize student learning.

Rule Number 2: Thou Shall Take Pride in Your Profession

Teachers are, for the most part, dedicated, hard-working, and modest people. Much of this character is due to the caring nature of the profession since the best educators are eternal optimists and unrepentant idealists who honestly believe that their work with children will make a positive difference for the future. Teachers receive their greatest job satisfaction and joy not from personal aggrandizement and individual laurels, but rather from seeing the intellectual growth, personal accomplishments, and successes of their students.

In our current political climate, though, teachers often feel besieged and have developed a fortress mentality to shield themselves from a seemingly unending barrage of unjust criticism. Virtually every societal problem and national ill, from teen pregnancy to drug abuse, is reduced by politicians and demagogues to an issue that can be miraculously and instantly solved somehow through more education. The media are also culpable. Motivated by the impossible demands of the new 24-hour news cycle and an insatiable appetite for the sensational, the press will appear in force at a school at the first sign of trouble. Their gigantic communication trucks with their specially designed satellite booms are capable of beaming negative news stories nationwide in an instant. It is perfectly understandable that to the general public Columbine and Mary Kay Letourneau have become some of the biggest educational news stories in recent years rather than the anomalies and perversions they actually are. Still, in our tabloid-driven society, one well-publicized bad news story can easily negate a school's entire year of progress and success. The routine good works that occur daily in our schools are rarely reported; there is, for instance, no press coverage of the third-grade spelling bee, the fall drama production of *Antigone,* or the senior class trip to the U.S. Capitol. Academic achievements are rarely celebrated in print and certainly do not make "good" television, yet the news media chronicles in exquisite detail every sports victory, varsity touchdown, basketball dunk, and homerun as if these feats of athletic prowess were truly consequential. Faced with such stark realities, it is little wonder that educators seek comfort and refuge within the relatively safe confines of their foxhole classrooms. Some will spend their entire careers desperately trying to avoid the harsh public spotlight.

In our complex modern world, it is no longer good enough to be "just" a competent classroom teacher—instead, we each must take responsibility for our profession and celebrate and elevate teaching as a career. Collectively, we have a professional obligation to keep parents and the community informed and apprised of what is truly happening in our classrooms and in our schools. That means that teachers must serve as positive role models for their students, and we need to realize that it takes an enormous amount of skill and talent to be a teacher. Indeed, to captivate, motivate, and inspire young people is hard and creative work and, in truth, few people can do this on a daily basis. I have personally seen $400 per hour K-Street lawyers, who are comfortable debating the most intricate and obscure point of law before their peers, quiver in fear in front of a group of 16-year-old students. As Roger Mudd observed in a commentary for the PBS documentary, *Learning in America:* "From sunup to sundown, the school teachers you have seen tonight work harder than you do—no matter what you do. No calling in our society is more demanding than teaching. No calling in our society is more selfless than teaching. No calling in our society is more central to the vitality of a democracy than teaching."

American culture associates success and status with high salaries, personal wealth, and fame. On a recent vacation to Hawaii, I observed a large, boisterous group of young, ambitious salesmen and corporate executives enjoying an exotic sunset *luau* on a beach. They were being treated to a luxurious, all-expense-paid vacation, and the champagne and mai tais were flowing freely. Their CEO took the podium and proudly boasted about their company's booming sales and profitable earnings while urging all of them to work hard to "win" another trip next year. As I watched the unfolding festivities, I actually felt a sense of pity for them because they were devoting their lives to making deals and earning money while we teachers were actually engaged in transforming lives and making a difference. Lee Iacocca, the former chairman of the Chrysler Corporation, astutely observed: "In a completely rational society, the best of us would be teachers and the rest of us would have to settle for something less."

Rule Number 3: Thou Shall Have Passion

It is easy to identify the great teachers in any given school. They are well-respected and have earned a solid reputation for excellence. These gifted teachers' classrooms are dynamic learning centers with the walls and bulletin boards filled with colorful posters and decorated with dazzling displays of student work. Motivational sayings are often strategically placed to provide daily wisdom and encouragement, but most importantly, their students are engaged and enthused about learning. There is always a high level of energy, activity, and excitement. Poor socioeconomic conditions or unfortunate demographics are never accepted as excuses or justification for failure because these extraordinary teachers are engaged in the serious business of learning. They retain a common passion for what they are doing and a commitment to their students' well-being.

Countless educational studies, scholarly reports, and expensive government grants have confirmed the obvious—that a dedicated, high-quality teacher remains the single most important factor in determining overall student success. The impact of a great teacher will last a lifetime, and most students will come to love or hate a subject based solely upon the quality of their teacher.

It is important to understand that in our diverse educational system, there can be many different teaching styles, dramatically diverse pedagogical approaches, and varying teaching philosophies. This fact is true even in an era of standards-based education and growing accountability. The best teachers, though, all share a universal belief that what they are doing is important and vital to the health and well-being of our society. They have a common passion for teaching and they respect one another.

For novice teachers, it is important to recognize that a child's education is a collaborative effort, the collective work of many people including those who labor outside of the classroom. When you begin your teaching career, you should first make a concerted effort to introduce yourself to the school's secretary. She is the single person in the building who knows all of the administrative procedures and bureaucratic minutiae that is necessary for running a modern school. Moreover, good secretaries are a building's best and most cherished institutional memory; their tenure usually surpasses that of principals, counselors and teachers. Next, it is important to meet the school's cafeteria manager. Her vital role is to provide students with healthy and nutritious meals so that they are physically ready and able to learn in your classroom. Likewise, you should become friends with the school's custodians because they, too, are critical members of the school-community. They work day and night, without complaint or recognition, to clean the building so that it is a comfortable and conducive place for learning. We also should honor and respect the efforts of our bus drivers, parent volunteers, counselors, the school nurse, the crossing guards, and police officers.

Unfortunately, in virtually every school there are a few teachers who are full of negativity and who take joy in denigrating the efforts of others. They are usually found hibernating in the teacher's lounge plotting, drinking coffee, and trading harmful stories about students and their fellow colleagues. For whatever reasons, they are burned out and can quickly poison a school's climate and destroy staff morale. These "teachers" must be avoided at all cost because they have lost their sense of mission and should be seeking employment elsewhere where they can do less harm. Instead, it is important to associate with those hard-working, busy educators who have little time or patience for such nonsense and who retain their essential optimism and hope for the future.

Rule Number 4: Do What Is Best for Kids

Every year, I took my American history classes on a field trip to the Gettysburg battlefield in Pennsylvania. It was such a popular activity that the students from other classes wanted to go along, so it soon grew and evolved to include virtually the entire junior class.

A quality field trip is an outstanding teaching tool, but it also requires weeks of detailed planning and is quite a logistical operation. It certainly is not a "free day" out of school, but rather an integral part of a course curriculum. In my classes, the students were required to read Michael Shaara's outstanding historical novel, *The Killer Angels,* in advance preparation for the trip since the book would serve as the focal point of our visit.[28] On site, we would carefully analyze Shaara's accuracy in his detailed portrayal of the battle, and we would try to determine whether his protagonist, Colonel Joshua Chamberlain of the 20th Maine, was the true hero of the battle. Likewise, it would be a great opportunity for the students to look at historical fiction as an entire genre, one that now includes Hollywood movies (*The New World, Amistad, Pearl Harbor, The Gangs of New York, JFK,* et al.). The students also needed to understand the importance of separating the historically accurate from an author's vivid imagination.

The students eagerly arrived at school a full hour before the regularly scheduled classes were to begin, and they were served a continental breakfast consisting of bagels and juice in the school's cafeteria. The food was generously donated each year by a local restaurant. At precisely 8:00 A.M. with the help of our numerous parental volunteers, we boarded privately rented buses, which were clearly identified by Union corps badges, each honoring an individual unit that had actually fought at Gettysburg in 1863. Despite the Washington, D.C., area's legendary rush hour traffic, it took only two hours to arrive at the battlefield visitor's center and there, specially trained guides awaited. Each assumed command of an entire bus and immediately began to teach our students about an incredible event that transformed the nation forever. They pointed out Gettysburg's unique topography and how it shaped the course of the battle; they chronicled the major troop movements of both the Union and Confederate forces; and they assessed the competency of the military leadership of the armies. At regular intervals, the guides ordered the students off the buses. They were quickly organized into companies and taught how to march, drill, maneuver in open fields, and form lines of battles. They also learned the intricacies of how to fire a Civil War cannon and were humbled when they discovered its devastating, destructive power. Finally, at Little Round Top, the students replicated the exhausting charge of the 15th Alabama on the hot summer day of July 2, 1863, which was ultimately repelled because of the singular bravery and courage of the Union soldiers under the command of Joshua Chamberlain. There was, indeed, a great deal of truth in Michael Shaara's novel. Realistically, in 50 years these same students will recall little about their day-to-day high school experience. They certainly won't remember the intimate details of their individual classes, and they will have even forgotten many of their teachers' names without the aid of their antique yearbook. But I have full confidence that they will never forget their field trip to the Gettysburg battlefield and what they learned on that singular day.

Still, despite the obvious value of this activity, every year as the date for our field trip approached, I received a nasty note from a teacher in a different department complaining that the students were missing his class lecture for the day. It was unprofessional behavior, especially since I had gone through all of the bureaucratic requirements for the field trip and had received approval from all of the appropriate authorities including the department chairman, the principal, and county transportation officials, but sometimes, teachers can be our own worst enemies. Yet as much as I hated this annual confrontation, I remained undeterred because I knew that what I was doing was in the best interest of my students. As a classroom teacher, their welfare is my primary concern and my most important responsibility. In truth, far too many decisions involving our nation's schools are made for reasons other than sound educational objectives. I have developed little patience for meetings, committees, and initiatives that fail to address the needs of our individual students. Indeed, every lesson plan that I write is motivated first and foremost by my desire to help students learn and achieve.

Rule Number 5: Don't Sweat the Small Stuff

February is undoubtedly the worst month for school teachers. The weather is awful, the days are short, and all the students have runny noses and are seriously contagious. Spring seems a long way off. This is a treacherous time because all of the petty hassles and routine inconveniences of the year have piled up, and the smallest thing can quickly escalate into a big problem. A nasty email, a broken copier, or an irritable colleague can be the catalyst that sends a teacher over the edge. During such periods, it is important that we remind ourselves that whatever happens, it is not our students' fault and that we must not take our frustrations out on them. A harsh word or a single moment's indiscretion can have a lifelong impact on a child.

Most of the things that frustrate us as teachers really aren't that important. As the First Century stoic philosopher, Epictetus, once astutely observed: "There is only one way to happiness, and that is to cease worrying about things which are beyond the power of our will." In truth, no matter how much we try, we cannot control everything and we must never lose our sense of perspective: we are teaching kids.

I never dreamed that one day I would be nationally recognized for my work as a classroom teacher. I worked long hours and tried each day to live by my educational philosophy, but I didn't really think anyone really noticed except, of course, my students. I was deeply honored and pleasantly surprised when the McLean High School faculty selected me as their Teacher of the Year. I was recognized at a special dinner at the chamber of commerce, and subsequently, I became the Fairfax County and Virginia Teacher of the Year. In 1998, during a Rose Garden Ceremony at the White House hosted by President Bill Clinton, I was officially named the National Teacher of the Year. Five of my students were able to accompany me that day, and each had the incredible opportunity to meet the President of the United States.

The next year, I was given a sabbatical and served as a spokesman for teachers. I had numerous opportunities to speak to various groups about what I called the "good news" in public education. My travels that year took me to over 30 states, and I even had the opportunity to visit Japan and Germany.

One of the highlights was my appearance on the *Late Show with David Letterman*. I must admit that it was an extremely intimidating venue, and I was scared to death, but Letterman proved to be a gracious and appropriately funny host. It was obvious to me that he honestly admired teachers and truly cared about our nation's schools and children. After I finished my interview, I left the stage during the brief commercial break feeling relieved and pretty good about how things had gone. When Letterman returned to the air, he paused and looked over to his band director, Paul Shaffer, and said: "Wouldn't it be nice to know that each day when you went to work you were making a positive difference in the lives of people." He said that to every single teacher in America because that is exactly what we do every day of our lives. The students are our ultimate legacy, and I am proud to be a classroom teacher.

Official White House Photo

Philip Bigler is honored at a Rose Garden ceremony as the 1998 National Teacher of the Year by President Bill Clinton and Secretary of Education Richard Riley.

About the Author:

Philip Bigler was named the 1998 National Teacher of the Year during a Rose Garden Ceremony hosted by President Bill Clinton. Mr. Bigler taught history and humanities in the Washington, D.C. metro area for 23 years and was widely recognized for his innovative instruction. He has received numerous teaching honors including the Milken National Education Award and the Disney American Teacher Award. He is the author of five books including *In Honored Glory: Arlington National Cemetery, the Final Post* and *Hostile Fire: The Life and Death of Lt. Sharon A. Lane.*[29] Mr. Bigler is currently the director of the James Madison Center at James Madison University and continues to teach in the History and American Studies departments.

Chapter Five

Following the Yellow Brick Road: A Teacher's Journey to Success

Stephanie Bishop

2001 Milken National Educator

The highest reward for a person's work is not what they get for it, but what they become by it.
— John Rushkin

I was in second grade when I watched *The Wizard of Oz* for the first time. I could not sit close enough to the television. The colors were mesmerizing and the characters were magical. Judy Garland's rendition of "Somewhere Over the Rainbow" became my own personal theme song, and Dorothy was my new hero. In third grade, my mom gave me just enough money to buy one book at the annual school book fair, and I had my sights and total net worth of $2.75 set on a hard back version of L. Frank Baum's classic. Imagine my surprise and disappointment when the book did not mirror the movie. Dorothy was supposed to have ruby slippers but Baum had written that they were silver shoes. How could this be?

In fourth grade, a miracle seemingly happened—our assistant principal announced that she would be directing *The Wizard of Oz* for our annual school play. Rehearsing voraciously for the audition paid off and I got the part of Dorothy. The fact that my grandmother was willing to make the traditional blue gingham costume may also have given me a slight edge on winning the role.

In college, my professors at Virginia Tech tainted my rose-col-

Stephanie Bishop, as Dorothy from the Wizard of Oz, in her fourth grade play.

ored view of *The Wizard of Oz* by expounding on the underlying themes and theories about the text and its characters. In a history class, we read Henry Littlefield's creative essay, "The Wizard of Oz: Parable on Populism," which used the story as a political allegory and a way to teach students about the political and economic issues of the era.[30] In Sociology, we analyzed Dorothy in terms of representing the typical adolescent who left home when she did not get her way; in Women's Studies, we hailed Dorothy as the female version of the male-dominated notion of the archetypal hero.

My beloved *Wizard of Oz* morphed from a fantastic childhood fairy tale into something far more—a metaphor for life.

During my junior year in college, I was walking across the Tech campus after a less than stimulating Sociology class contemplating my future when I made a decision. I wish I could say that I had been researching various career options, carefully weighing one against another, but the truth is the decision to teach was sudden and spontaneous. I changed direction and headed to the College of Education to pick up an application, and I was swept up like Dorothy in the tornado that started my remarkable journey. Unlike Dorothy's cinematic tornado, which lasted a mere three minutes and featured a swirling, grey funnel with a mooing cow, a spinning house, and a witch cackling, "I'll get you, my pretty," my own personal tornado was destined to last three years.

I was a double major in Theatre Arts and English. After being accepted into the College of Education, I started working on a

A few of us are lucky enough to have a truly exceptional educator, who betters not only the quality of our school experience, but who also makes it possible for us to live our best lives. These people are not only teachers; they are fortunetellers—predicting who we might be and giving us the tools and confidence to live up to it.

In my life, none compares to Stephanie Bishop. While others have taught me things I still think about, no one has so clearly taught me how to think. Ms. Bishop possesses intelligence, kindness, compassion, presence, discipline, and creativity. These qualities are expertly blended and topped off with an earnest humble attitude and a sort of magic I can't put my finger on.

My first year of high school was Bishop's first year teaching theatre in our system. Throughout the next four years, I got to watch as her excitement and investment took roots in everyone around her. She awoke in me the confidence to perform, write, and teach. At the end of a day of rehearsal, the lessons her students took home weren't limited to the stage. At the end of my high school education, I realized that Ms. Bishop had cleverly been teaching us "life" instead of theatre. Ms. Bishop is a person who could have been the best at anything she picked, from acting to corporate law. But I'm sure hundreds of students would join me in celebrating her choice. She chose us!
—Vanessa Hope Ragland-Irwin, Prince George High School, Class of 2000

Master's degree in Curriculum and Instruction that would lead to certification and licensure. In 1996, I received my student teaching assignment at Patrick Henry High School in nearby Roanoke. I got up each morning at 5:00 A.M. to finalize my new lesson plans and get ready for school. My fellow college classmates remained oblivious to the rising sun and would blissfully slumber until their first classes began sometime around noon.

Why did everything seem so different? I was myself just five years removed from high school and things swirled around me in a funnel, but instead of mooing cows and a swirling house, I saw passing students and mounting lesson plans. I had a dual student teaching assignment in Theatre and English. I worked tirelessly to make my lessons relevant to "today's" students, but the more I tried to be relevant, the less effective I was. I got so wrapped up in linking pop culture to the curriculum and getting students to talk and write about personal experiences that I lost sight of my content objectives. My lessons went in circles with no clear destination or end.

My student teaching slowly lost momentum and speed as my eight-week assignment came to an end. Almost immediately, I joined all the other prospective teachers looking for their first grown-up jobs in the real world. I discovered that my life's tornado had not carried me to a mythical land of Oz, but rather to Greensville County, Virginia, where I was hired to teach tenth grade English and assigned to coach Forensics. The next phase of my life's journey had begun, and my new teaching career seemed to be a journey down my own yellow brick road. I was committed to following it wherever it would take me on a continuing course of self-discovery to help find what it took to be successful in the classroom.

I was initially skeptical about where that path would take me, but it was as if the munchkins were subconsciously encouraging me to just "follow the yellow brick road." My own munchkins were not the cute characters from the film but rather took the form of high school teenagers. It was my students who prompted me to travel down the road. These adolescents did not sing or skip to get me started, but deep within their eyes, I saw an intense desire to learn. It was often embedded behind a stoic façade that attempted to appear cool and disengaged. It takes a thoughtful eye and a steady heart to see the future of a child, especially on the first day of school when you are carefully balancing adrenaline and butterflies. When each student crossed over the threshold into my classroom, I knew I had made a solemn contract with him or her when I first said, "Welcome."

It is vital that teachers uphold their end of this unwritten commitment, but you cannot expect to walk into class on the first day of school and see students sitting up straight in their seats and hanging on to your every word because they have an "intense desire to learn." The desire may well be there but it is only through your enthusiasm and dedication that the desire to learn will be extrapolated from the sometimes deep recesses within each child. I have found that the harder you work as a teacher, the harder your students will work for you. Just photocopying worksheets created by some textbook company "ain't gonna" cut it in our modern schools. Students see through this type of busy work. It does nothing but destroy their desire to learn.

When you know your students as well as your content, only then will you fully understand your obligation to create meaningful activities that challenge them intellectually. You will then be taking your own crucial steps down the golden path to a successful teaching career.

In my school community in Greensville County, I made choices that often took me down a different path outside of my classroom. When I was asked to serve on the school improvement and Standards of Learning committees, I gladly said yes. In so doing, I began to network with other teachers, administrators, central office staff, and school board members. I discovered that networking is just as important in education as it is in the corporate world. Likewise, signing up to chaperone school activities and attending school-sponsored events increase your perspective on your students and make you a real part of the community you serve. Going that extra mile, both in and out of the classroom, and making connections early in your career will inevitably validate you as a caring teacher.

My childhood heroine, Dorothy, also received additional encouragement from the good witch, Glinda. Dorothy's famous ruby red slippers, Glinda told her, held great powers and she should never take them off while in Oz. Dorothy was skeptical about the magnitude of the power those shoes supposedly possessed, but she listened to the good witch and wore the shoes because she instinctively trusted this new person to help guide her through this strange and unfamiliar environment. Glinda gave Dorothy advice but did not provide her with all of the answers. Just like any good mentor, she knew that Dorothy was setting out on her own journey of personal self-discovery, a difficult path that all teachers must likewise take. It is imperative for all teachers to find their very own Glinda, especially during that difficult first year. An ideal mentor freely shares materials and strategies and encourages a passion for teaching by listening and providing much needed wisdom. Mr. Ray Sasser was my salvation. He inspired me on my path and gave me my very own metaphorical ruby slippers. He showed me the routine things, such as the location of the copier and snack machines, but he also became my own teacher and inspiration. Ray shared everything, gave me teaching materials and advice, but just as importantly, he listened. On one particular day my teaching life was not so good. I felt like the time when Dorothy ran into the forest and the trees came to life and chucked apples at her. I was very defeated when a particular lesson on *Julius Caesar* did not go as planned and I took the defeat personally, a harsh indictment of me as a teacher. Mr. Sasser stopped me in the hall because, like any good mentor, he could tell that I desperately needed to talk. I told him about my abject failure. He looked me straight in the eyes and calmly explained, "There will be some days in this profession when you have to leave this building with the understanding that you merely did your job. If you leave every day with that mentality, there is a serious problem, but on bad days like this one, it is a job." He went on to say that I would have a clearer head for self-analysis once I got past the personal feeling of failure. His simple advice miraculously helped me and I now know that over the years, there have been many other new teachers who have similarly benefited from Mr. Sasser's patience and wisdom. I did not always fully understand or appreciate the magnitude of Ray Sasser's power, but I trusted him completely. Trust is a critical factor in any successful mentor-teacher relationship. Hopefully you will be paired by your school system with an appropriate mentor, but if not, you must seek out that special person who will help guide you through your early teaching years. If Dorothy did not have Glinda, she would never have had the protection and encouragement that she needed to complete her journey, and new teachers must have similar help and guidance in their careers.

Many times, like the beloved Scarecrow, I have silently crooned, "If I Only Had a Brain." I feel I should know loads of facts and be able to quote historians and philosophers at the snap of a finger. In college, I was a model student. I paid attention, took diligent notes, and put forth maximum effort on all assignments and projects. When I became a teacher and got my own classroom, I found myself using only around 10 percent of the knowledge I had acquired in college. During my first year of teaching, I struggled to learn the new content I was supposed to teach my students, often just before school began, and then pretended that I had known it my entire life. I discovered that using our brains in teaching consists of being masters of our course content and practitioners in the art of self-reflection.

I learned very early that your decisions in school could widen the road and create multiple paths, or conversely make it more difficult to follow. In the classroom, I often took risks. Sometimes they paid off and other times they failed. Even when lessons do not work and your strategies fall short, it is important to analyze where the breakdown occurs and why. Then, you must revisit your initial goals and objectives. In doing so, you are creating a new path. My first cooperative learning activity failed simply because I did not have a proper process for grouping students. Once I learned to do that, the exact same strategy worked wonderfully. Had I merely abandoned cooperative learning and not evaluated my failure, I would never have had access to teamwork activities and critical thought. My students would have suffered.

Good teachers take what they do very seriously. Our relationship with our students is personal and we have a love of our course content. The strategies we use and strive to perfect become part of our self-identity. As a result, we must be careful about what we internalize because it could lead us down a dark, narrow path. Bad teachers never intended to become burned out and ineffective. These teachers, and they are in every school building, are cynical about students and have lost their faith in the future. They are without purpose and have resigned themselves to viewing teaching as a "job," rather than a noble vocation. These bad teachers are full of excuses when they confront a strategy that did not work or students who will not stop talking in class. Their complete lack of honest self-analysis and reflection has led them to a dead end. One slight turn earlier in their lives could have instead led them to a road of endless possibilities.

That 'dead end' mentality leads you straight into the open arms of the Wicked Witch of education—a negative mentality that lurks in the teacher's lounge, hides in the hallways, and even infiltrates the classroom. It can quickly contaminate an entire school's culture, and when it does, it takes far more than a mere pail of water to melt and destroy. It is as dangerous to our students as the winged monkeys who swooped in to prey on the weaknesses of Dorothy and her companions. We must be able to recognize the tell-tale signs of an unhealthy school climate because when it begins to manifest itself in individual teachers, it can soon infect the entire building and destroy the staff's morale.

Dedicated, committed teachers labor far beyond contract hours, making copies, planning tomorrow's lesson plans, grading papers, and completing the endless paperwork, which bulges out of your already overflowing mailbox. The negative teachers, though, can be readily identified because they have already zoomed out of the faculty parking lot well before 3 o'clock. Another obvious sign is that they refuse to take any educational risk or try something new. Rather, they continue to teach in their traditional way, content as long as the students stay passive and quiet. These teachers speak in meaningless clichés, such as: "We don't get paid enough to do this much work" or "Kids these days don't care...they don't pay attention . . . they don't do homework," or the best one—"When I was in school . . ."

How do we combat this pervasive negativity without performing an ancient ritual or casting a magical spell or wearing garlic to ward off the evil spirits? It is actually very simple: We do what is in the best interests of our students. When our mission is clear, we are willing to take risks and we perceive our lessons as exciting learning adventures. We even accept the routine paperwork as a necessary means to an end. We must remain vigilant and steadfast in our quest for student learning and achievement. We also must stay positive about our profession and recognize our awesome impact on the future.

The next leg of my continuing teaching journey along my yellow brick road was inspired by my love for drama. I was hired to be the full-time theatre teacher at Prince George High School in my second year of teaching. Theatre was what I felt was my true calling. I couldn't wait to have the students read and direct Samuel Beckett's *Waiting for Godot* or Luigi Pirandello's *Six Characters in Search of an Author*. I was going to expose my new students to classic theatre, modern theatre, and all movements that shaped the genres of plays. The problem was that I discovered my love for the subject was no more than a shiny, hollow vessel of tin. My heart was in the wrong place since it was initially with my subject rather than with my students. In planning my new lessons,

I was falling prey to the type of teaching that I had been subjected to while I was in college.

When my first theatre students arrived, I hurried through the introductions and the syllabus in order to dive head first into Sophocles' *Oedipus Rex*. I planned to start with the ancient Greeks in September and ultimately end up with the evolution of the modern American musical by June. I was absolutely convinced that everyone would love theatre as much as I did. For three class periods, we read *Oedipus*. I planned a seminar to discuss the major themes as a culmination on the fourth day. The oral reading proved less than stimulating, and the students read the play without emotion as if they were gnawing on stale biscuits with no water. I stopped the exercise periodically and tried to fill in with meaningful epistles. They only showed a glimmer of interest when they finally realized that Oedipus was married to his own mother. They also liked the part where he grotesquely gouged out his own eyes. The seminar was, in fact, better than the oral reading, but on the whole, we were merely scratching the surface of the text. At the end of this first week, I needed to do some serious self-reflection and analysis. There was no way we could spend the rest of the year reading and discussing plays like we had *Oedipus*. I sat in front of my computer one Saturday morning and asked myself, "What are we going to do?" A key word emerged from my question: "Do." My students needed to do theatre, not read about theatre. I began to create a unit for my students on playwriting. The next Monday was completely different from our first day together. After exploring some playwriting strategies and discussing things that worked and didn't work in example scenes, the students began writing their own scenes.

That week sparked a veritable writing frenzy, one that still continues in my theatre classroom over nine years later. Over the years, my students have entered playwriting competitions and have been honored with several statewide first place distinctions. I found that playwriting was something relevant to all students no matter what their cultural origin, social status, or academic label. I spent nearly every weekend during my second year of teaching creating new lessons and innovative activities where students were actually doing theatre. Now, the students

Author's Personal Collection

Stephanie Bishop directs drama students during the Summer Fine Arts academy at Prince George High School.

still read the classics but with newfound focus, especially if they will be, for example, designing costumes for Kate and Petruchio in *The Taming of the Shrew*. With each unit, there is a responsibility and accountability for the teacher that go far beyond simply penciling in a grade in your gradebook. With each project or assignment, there must be personal and creative investment and a work ethic that enables pride and self-confidence. My class soon gained a strong and steady heartbeat. My love for a subject was actually deepened by doing what was best for my students.

I finally had engaged two vital organs into my teaching—my brain and my heart. Another vital ingredient would be added forever during my third year. Along Dorothy's journey down the yellow brick road, she meets a seemingly ferocious lion. He should be the brave "king of the forest," but instead, this lion lacked courage and cowered from challenges and recoiled in fear. A teacher is, in many ways, king (or queen) of the forest, but teaching can also be scary. It takes true courage to do what is best for students. In terms of teaching strategies, there are some ideas that are obviously easier to employ than others. There is probably a 95 percent chance students will become quiet and focus once the classroom lights are dimmed and the overhead projector turned on. It is like a magic button that lulls students into writing mode, but one should be careful. This situation can also anesthetize students into a zone devoid of any real critical thinking. It takes courage to step beyond the relative safety of "sure thing" lessons and risk things that are different. "Different" can mean upsetting the balance and taking you out of your own personal comfort zone—but you must still do it. We are dealing with students who receive their intellectual and emotional stimulation from a variety of resources including I-Pods, video games, "My Space," cell phones, and e-mail. You can be absolutely certain that next year there will be even more gadgets and gizmos that will capture both their cash and attention. It is our professional obligation to make our classrooms and our content as interesting and relevant as possible. We also have to compete against those "fun" activities in which students voluntarily engage during their own time.

Sometimes things occur within the classroom that require courage to handle. Our own "forest" can get a bit restless at times and, when dealing with children, things certainly will happen that you never planned or anticipated. During my early career, there were several instances that occurred that required courage to face. When "Mark" and "Debbie" began exchanging unscripted angry words and expletives during the reading of *Our Town,* as master of the classroom, I had to do something immediately. Had the two of them not been stopped, they would have torn down the walls of my mobile classroom. Then there was also the day "Bill" calmly strolled into my classroom reeking from the stench of marijuana. I could have pretended not to notice and overlooked the situation by taking the easy way out and proceeding with my scheduled activities, but that type of behavior is unacceptable in school. Had I ignored him, it would have been detrimental to Bill and unfair to the rest of my students. Indeed, I would have been sending all the other students a terrible message: There were no adverse consequences for entering my classroom in an altered state. I immediately removed Bill from class, expressed my extreme disappointment in his actions, and turned him over to our school resource officer. Such issues are tough because you frequently second-guess yourself on how well and effectively you handled the situation, but what is most important is that you do handle the situation.

Fortunately, fights and drugs have not been commonplace occurrences in my school, but there are other routine things that still require courage and attention. When a student snickers or says something under his breath while another student is reading aloud, it is absolutely unacceptable behavior and must be corrected immediately. If you fail to effectively address such an incident, you are openly sending a message to your other students that they are not valued or respected. When students do not feel appreciated by their teacher or peers, they will never reach their maximum potential, and we would have failed as educators. By allowing just one snicker or callous comment, you are at risk of losing the offended student for the remainder of the year. Sometimes this adolescent and immature behavior will even be directed toward you. Even the most effective teachers, who stress the importance of respect for self, others, space, and subject, can be victims of an off-handed, disrespectful remark from a student. It is important not to retaliate instinctively; you must have the courage to avoid escalating and complicating the situation. Every incident must be assessed quickly. It is incumbent upon the teacher to determine an appropriate course of action. For some students, a one-on-one talk in the hall will prove most effective. For others, it may take a meeting after school, a phone call to a parent, or a conference with a counselor. It is only when you know your students that you will realize what is best in terms of resolving such unpleasantries.

The halls of a high school can, in fact, seem more like a jungle than a forest. With everything teachers need to carry to their classes, we sometimes look like explorers equipped for a safari. I regularly navigate my own jungle with a cart, three tote bags, and a laptop. Even though I am anxiously scurrying to my next destination, I am always a teacher, even outside the relatively safe confines of the classroom. Although students congregate together in mobs of varying sizes in the halls, they are still kids often in need of adult guidance. As a teacher, you must make your presence known in the hallways. It is important to speak to students—say "good morning"—even when they may not be in your own class. If a student is wearing a hat in violation of the rules, politely ask him to remove it. Avoid hostile confrontations with students because you will not win. When you are polite and respectful though, students in return will be courteous to you. They may even offer to carry one of your heavy tote bags.

It is always important to communicate regularly and professionally with students, parents, colleagues, and administrators. If a parent calls or e-mails to discuss an issue concerning their child, you must get back to the parent the very same day. This may mean calling during your planning period or your lunch. I learned the importance of this lesson early on. One of my tenth graders, "Katie," plagiarized a scene she had written in my Theatre I class. Before I left school that day, I had a message on my desk to call her father. I knew what it was about, and I used the clock to avoid the call. It was late, and I would call him in the morning. Big mistake. The avoidance on my part gave Katie's father time to e-mail my principal expressing his displeasure over his child's being accused of plagiarism as well as my lack of professionalism by not contacting him. By not making immediate contact the day before, the situation had only gotten worse. When I contacted Katie's father, we discussed the situation, and through professional dialogue, he understood why she did not receive credit for the assignment. He apologized for sending an e-mail to my principal, and I reciprocated for not having contacted him the day of the incident. Issues must be addressed immediately. Although you will be tempted not to return a call or respond to a nasty e-mail in order to avoid conflict, you will just end up making things worse for you and your students. Communicate with courage.

Dorothy's journey ultimately took her to visit the wizard. She felt confident that this all-powerful man of Oz would give her companions what they sought: The Scarecrow his brain, the Tinman his heart, and the Lion some courage. She also thought he would be able to send her home to Kansas. When Dorothy and her companions finally arrived in the Emerald City, they were greeted by an enormous head of fire that turned out to be nothing more than an illusion. The wizard was just a simple man behind a curtain. Dorothy was faced with the stark reality that her hopes would not be fulfilled by "the great and powerful Oz," and her journey would never end.

In our own personal teaching journeys, we are often seeking a Wizard—some person who is miraculously going to solve all the things that need fixing in education. This mythical, all-knowing, all-seeing being will somehow magically set everything right. Sometimes we seek this person in our principals, our superintendents, our school boards, and even in our President. The truth of the matter is the wizard we seek does not exist. The true solution in education is you, the classroom teacher. You have the power and the capability to make students exceed far beyond their potential. The effectiveness of the classroom teacher is the single biggest factor in determining the success of students. The power of a teacher is more awesome than any mythical wizard we may seek to right the ills in education.

The moment Dorothy realizes the wizard does not possess the powers to fix or solve her problems, Dorothy is liberated. Like any good teacher, she gets the Scarecrow, the Tinman, and the Lion to realize they have already exceeded their potential by implementing brains, heart, and courage throughout their long journey together on the yellow brick road. Dorothy taught them to appreciate their innate gifts and abilities, and the three worked so hard for her because she had faith in them. Students will work just as hard for you, the teacher, if you believe they can achieve beyond what they thought to be possible.

Although Dorothy had improved the quality of life for her three friends, she still needed to get home. The wizard was exposed as a fraud. He fled the scene in a hot air balloon, leaving Dorothy with her dog, Toto, and her ruby slippers. What Dorothy doesn't realize, until it is made crystal clear to her by Glinda, is that she possessed the magic and the power all along. The key to success was always there—it just took time for Dorothy to realize it. She never needed a wizard to get her home after all. Dorothy has her own revelation, the same type of "aha" moments we wish for our own students. The ruby slippers are our teacher magic—they possess a magical combination of brains, heart, courage, high expectations, passion, dedication, and energy. Effective teachers realize they wear ruby slippers every day of their teaching careers.

In second grade, I knew that *The Wizard of Oz* would always be a part of me. On my ongoing teaching journey to success, I now know that there will be many joys and challenges. Some days, you will run into your own Wicked Witch more than once, but with brains, heart, and courage, you will be able to continue your journey, widen the road, and create multiple golden paths for you and your students. Keep your Glinda close by and whatever you do, never take off your ruby slippers. As you travel the yellow brick road to success, you will discover there's no place like the classroom.

Author's Personal Collection

Stephanie Bishop with her former student, Vanessa Hope.

About the Author:
Stephanie Bishop graduated from Virginia Tech in 1996. During her ten years at Prince George High School, Stephanie taught theatre. Her students were three-time state theatre champions (2002, 2004, and 2006). In 2001, she was honored with the prestigious Milken National Education Award. In addition to teaching theatre, Stephanie also served as lead teacher, fine arts department chairperson, and Summer Fine Arts Academy coordinator at Prince George High School. In 2006, she earned an endorsement in educational leadership from Virginia Commonwealth University. Stephanie now serves as assistant principal of J.E.J. Moore Middle School in Prince George, Virginia.

Chapter Six

Lessons from the Second Year: What I Learned from First Grade

Linda Koutoufas

1999 Virginia Teacher of the Year

It is what teachers think, what teachers do, and what teachers are at the level of the classroom that ultimately shapes the kind of learning that young people get. —Andy Hargreaves and Michael Fullan

My second year of teaching was almost my last. Four days into the opening of school, I was convinced that any success I'd experienced in the first year had been a fluke and that I was a failure. The chaos that was evident in my classroom gave testimony to this fact.

After what had been a relatively easy first year of teaching, I had foolishly begun to think of myself as a seasoned teacher. "Relatively easy" in my case meant that I'd had the luxury of at least one hour of free time each weekend after pouring over a curriculum guide, planning lessons, grading papers, phoning parents, rounding up equipment for science projects, and responding to student journals. My class, a combination of second and third grade students, had been small, fairly homogenous, and well-behaved. Because I had been involved in a year-round school pilot project, much of each subject area's pacing had been mapped out for me. So here I was, no longer new to teaching. I looked forward to the second year as a time when I could expand my instructional repertoire rather than concentrate on mere survival.

These thoughts were soon shattered by the noise and disorder of my classroom. At one point, I stood in the doorway and requested that the teacher next door observe the goings-on in my room. I asked if the activity and disarray that I saw was typical of first graders. As her eyes widened and she carefully backed away to the safety of her own classroom, she shook her head and regarded me with what was either sympathy or alarm. I knew I was in deep trouble.

I might have had a chance if my class had been of somewhat average size. Today, many similar high poverty schools average between 12 and 16 students in their first grade classrooms, but I counted 32 five- and six-year-olds in attendance on day one. We gradually ballooned to 36 by the end of the year. In this heterogeneous mix was "Stanley," a legally blind child who needed all material and text to be reproduced in large font, and "Jim," a veteran of at least five former kindergartens and preschools, the last being a Montessori school, which had expelled him for creatively covering the teacher's desk in blue paint. I didn't think that anyone was ever expelled from a Montessori school. At least six students were reading well above grade level; yet, there were three who had never attended kindergarten; the alphabet was another language to them. In addition, the class makeup was three-fourth boys whose center of gravity had not yet become accustomed to sitting in chairs for any period of time and whose birthday months all ended in –er: September, October, November, December. It was my understanding that the Virginia Board of Education felt that children were better off in school at a younger age than at home, but I wondered why they were all clustered in my classroom.

I was in no way prepared to teach first grade, much less a first grade of 32. First grade is a different animal. Although they are young and adorable, their toothless smiles hold a deep, dark secret: they instinctively sense when a teacher is not prepared for any part of the day. Forget to cut the construction paper into squares for a project? Need to run a few more copies of an assignment? Out of chart paper for recording a story? The typical first grader's intuition goes into high gear on these occasions, and the network alerts every-

In late September of 1987, I prepared to enter the education profession with passion, idealism, and a commitment to make a difference. What I did not realize was that I also needed electricity for the portable in which I would teach, and as a result, I was temporarily without a classroom. I received a phone call from a veteran teacher and my soon-to-be mentor, Linda Koutoufas, who told me that because it might be a while before my portable was certified, I was welcome to spend time in her classroom. This invitation turned into an unbelievable opportunity.

Although I had planned and organized, I had yet to realize the essentials required for my journey as a teacher. Linda possessed the great gifts that outstanding teachers seem to own: deep knowledge of content, the ability to facilitate learning, the need to make magic in the classroom, the ways to inspire students, the compassion required to understand students, and the necessity to make sacrifices in order to give the gift of education. Linda was and still is my mentor and my coach who graciously shares her expertise and her passion for teaching. The lessons I learned from her are embedded in my teaching, and I am proud to call her a colleague and a friend.

—Frances Hatzopoulos, Virginia Beach City Public Schools
2006 Teacher of the Year

one in the room of your failure to be ready to teach. It is as if a signal is sent that tells the group, "Time for us to take over."

During the previous year, I often passed by other teachers' first grade classrooms and stepped back for a second look. What I saw resembled an oasis of calm—little angels clustered at tables, working in groups, always on task cutting, pasting, and coloring while their teacher smiled benignly--an adored ruler surveying her peaceful kingdom. As I listened to the happy murmuring of young voices, I wondered, how hard could it be to teach a first grade class?

The question was answered often during that first week of my second year. I watched in agony as my class walked, or rather lunged toward the cafeteria. While other classes followed the hallowed silver line embedded in terrazzo tile, mine showed no semblance of order. Other classes made bubbles with their mouths or raised fingers to their lips to remind them of the "quiet in the hallway" rule. Mine was busy negotiating with each other for better lunches or practicing for the Olympic high jump using the exit signs on the ceiling as targets.

First grade *was* hard—not for the students, but for their teacher.

I knew I had to gain control, but how? Salvation came in two forms. The first was an invitation to visit the principal, who ushered me into her office after noting the sagging shoulders and dazed expression that had become permanent fixtures of my outward appearance. She drew me in and offered a bit of advice. Get your routines in place, she suggested. Make your students practice, practice, practice until it becomes automatic. Be consistent. Don't be fooled by their outward charm and youthful appearance. If you don't maintain control, they will do it for you—but they won't be happy. Children need structure, and although they may hide that fact, they cannot function well without it. Provide routines, consistency, enforcement, and consequence. Once you do that, they're all yours.

Better advice has never been given. I had been wary of imposing consequences on such young children, some of whom had never attended kindergarten, but I had been mistaken. My students sought the security of structure, and without it they were totally lost. Once I enforced simple class rules and followed through on what I said would happen, calmness and civility reigned.

Although happy with the change that took place in my classroom, I sensed that we were somehow living in a police state, with me as dictator and head bully. I now had the perfect line marching in step to lunch. When I barked an order, it was obeyed. But I sensed wariness on the part of my students; there was an edge in my classroom, and I wasn't comfortable with the atmosphere I had created.

It was at that point that I met the person who would have the most impact on my career as a teacher. Jan was a fellow first grade teacher, and although she taught on my grade level, I had little chance to talk with her due to the differences in our year-round schedules. She was one of the veterans I had observed during the previous year who made first grade look easy. But, as I came to discover, it looked easy because she knew how to work with young children.

What Jan had done was to create a caring and respectful relationship with her students. Classroom rules were created, but most

James Madison University

Linda Koutoufas welcomes Special Education teacher, Helen McClain, into the teaching profession during the pinning ceremony at the Teachers of Promise Institute at James Madison University.

often there was little need for consequence because Jan subtly pointed out how well children were doing and communicated how much she appreciated their behavior. As I marshaled my class to lunch, I passed by her open door and caught the positives that were an automatic part of her speech. "I like the way Toby is keeping his hands to himself." "Markisha, thank you for clearing your space so quickly." "Sharon, aren't you kind to help Tara put her papers away!" Always the positives. And, I noticed, on those rare occasions when someone acted out and was held to a consequence, a choice was always offered. "Darren, you have the choice to come to the rug now or miss the story. It's a wonderful story, and I know you would enjoy it, so I hope you make the right choice." If a child was given a time-out or a cooling-off period, the choice of when to return was left entirely up to him. When he felt he could follow the rules, he was more than welcome to return. No time limit was imposed. The responsibility was placed directly on the child, and it worked. The relationships Jan created were never severed and the fact that she believed in her students' ability to do the right thing was never questioned.

As I got to know Jan better, she generously volunteered to take a group of my students to her classroom for reading instruction. It soon became obvious that she was well ahead of the times, not only in regard to instruction but also in understanding how to reach, motivate, and elicit the best from children. We now know from researchers who study brain function that children, who feel they have no choice or little control over their learning, close down and often learn new information based only on habits and instinct or through rote memorization. Yet, when students feel that they have some control and some choice in their academic environment, much more learning takes place. When a student believes he or she has some say, creativity abounds, and problem-solving along with complex decision-making comes much easier.[31]

Add to this the research of James Comer of Yale University regarding relationships and learning. Comer asserts that "No significant learning can take place without a significant relationship."[32] In Jan's class, children were treated with respect. Yes, these were five- and six-year-olds, but they instinctively knew when someone cared enough about them to be demanding yet supportive and enforced structure, but in a positive way. What we finally know about what works best, Jan knew and was practicing 30 years ago. Hers was a special gift and a rare talent. For some, it is intuitive, but it can also be taught and learned. By watching and listening, I uncovered the secrets of teaching, not just first grade, but any grade. Establish relationships of respect and caring, and kids will respond; demonstrate your faith in them, and they will make the right choice. These relationships are the threads that hold instruction, curriculum, and all the pieces of academics together. If they are cut or if they are never created, the fabric of education unravels.

Jan taught me many lessons during that year and the years that followed, but my students taught me as well. "Tomas" was a very young first grader, a below average student who, I suspected, was

capable of more. His family had emigrated from the Philippines to
New York City and then to Virginia Beach. Both parents worked
long hours at minimum wage jobs, but there was never any question
that Tomas was well-loved, well-cared-for, and that all basic necessities were provided. At the time Tomas enrolled in my first grade
classroom, he did not qualify for free lunch; therefore, one of his
daily necessities was a brown paper bag lunch. Tomas hated that
brown paper bag. At lunchtime he would quickly empty its contents
onto the table, crumple the bag, and hide it. I noticed that he
watched the other children, who either enjoyed a cafeteria-provided
meal or proudly displayed their lunchboxes decorated with the latest
cartoon characters or action figures. Tomas had neither of these, and
his discomfort in the cafeteria was evident.

A few weeks into the school year, a volunteer happened by my
room to offer her third grade son's used lunchbox to any student who
might want it. It seemed that third graders had reached the age when
aluminum containers no longer held any mystique or charm. The
lunchbox she offered was one depicting the Power Rangers, inar-
guably the action figures of choice for my boys. I knew immediately
to whom it would go.

Shortly after I privately offered the lunchbox to Tomas, he and
his mother appeared at my door. Knowing that Tomas' mother
worked two jobs, I was taken aback by her tears. I sensed I had a serious problem. But, no—while Tomas beamed, his mother explained
that she and her husband usually worked a 12- hour day in order to
afford to stay in the Virginia Beach area and allow Tomas a quality
education. Specialized lunchboxes did not fit into their tight budget.
Tomas's pleas to own a lunchbox like his peers had gone unheeded
until that afternoon when I provided the one he'd always wanted.
The family was grateful, but I was embarrassed not to have thought
of this solution sooner. I learned another valuable lesson that day,
and one to which I still adhere. Little things count. To me, a Power
Ranger lunchbox was a trivial thing, a matter of a few extra dollars.
To Tomas and his family, it might very well have been the difference
between paying for heat or electricity. The lunchbox might be a sta-

tus symbol to some, but most importantly in the end, it was a teacher's validation that Tomas was important and valued. From that day on, Tomas flourished because he knew I had his best interests at heart.

Today, I work as a project specialist in a high poverty school. Every day, I work with children who have already faced more challenges in their young lives than I have in more than 50 years. Yet they manage to greet me each day with a ready smile and a willingness to work hard. While walking the hallways, however, I encounter other children who avoid my eyes. Perhaps their life histories have taught them that adults are not to be trusted. They may already have been beaten down by life, by the bus stop bullies, or by unintentional sarcasm from a teacher. These are the children, according to Marian Edelman in her poem, "A Prayer for Children," ". . . whose pictures aren't on anybody's dresser, who don't get dessert, and who are born in places we wouldn't dream of."[33] To these children, I say, "Hello!" "How are you?" Or I acknowledge them in any way I can. This greeting may be the only bright spot in their day, and it may come from a total stranger, but I intend to provide it and prod my fellow educators to do the same. Never pass a child in a hallway without giving some acknowledgement or recognition. It is at least one positive that we can all provide at no cost and with little effort.

In my journey to become a better teacher, another of my instructors was "Neil." Neil was in my third grade class. After several years of teaching first grade, I transferred to a third grade position. Neil was the kind of student that many teachers tend to write off after the second month of school. He made average grades—nothing stellar had been achieved, but there were no failures either. He was quiet, rarely volunteered, and read at an average to slightly below average rate. His academic progress never earned him a second look one way or another. He was definitely, or possibly deliberately, under the radar and as invisible as a ghost on the darkest night.

Under the radar, that is, until I assigned a project on Washington, D.C. That year, our curriculum included a unit on our nation's capital. Students were required to learn about the history and monuments of D.C. In my class, each child chose a monument or memorial, researched it, drew it, wrote about it, and read that description on a tape recorder in order to create a class filmstrip. As the tape rolled, student after student read from his or her carefully prepared script. The Washington Monument, the Jefferson Memorial, and the White House—they all came to life in our classroom. Then we came to Neil, who had requested to report on the Lincoln Memorial. Neil stepped to the microphone empty-handed. No script, no paper. As I reached to hit the pause button and demand an explanation, he began to describe the history of the Memorial, the life of Lincoln, and the Civil War. Finally, Neil recited the entire Gettysburg Address word for word from memory. My hand remained frozen above the tape recorder as the class and I listened spellbound to an individual we had discounted as unmotivated and sub-par. Yet here he was, teaching us, me included—and a history major to boot—all about Lincoln and the Civil War. At the conclusion of Neil's speech there was silence, and then spontaneous applause. Even third graders recognize giftedness when they see it.

Neil's gift was that he was a Civil War aficionado. His love for the history of the Civil War had led him to learn all he could about that time period. For the rest of the year, Neil was our Civil War expert. As his classmates' admiration grew, his self-esteem rose. Reading from books with a Civil War theme enabled him to shine. If any subject could be connected to the Civil War, we made that connection. At the end of the year, Neil received honor roll recognition and a special award as our class historian. I learned yet another valuable teaching lesson—know your students. Had I not stumbled upon this student's remarkable expertise and used it to foster his self-confidence and academic progress, he may never have shared his talent with us. He may never have enjoyed his classmates' respect and might not have grown to his full potential. But I still wondered, "How many other Neils have I missed?"

Getting to know students takes time. In an elementary class of 30, and especially in a middle or high school class period with more than 30, teachers struggle with the daily preparation and paperwork that are a routine part of the job. But getting to know students is an integral part of developing relationships and is an absolutely essential part of the job. By developing relationships, we are teaching students. Without them, we are merely teaching subjects.

During my second year, I began to formulate my essential beliefs about teaching. These are the observations and musings of an elementary school teacher, but they apply to all educators and to anyone who cares about children.

Keep an Open Door and an Open Mind

Teaching cannot occur in closed-door, isolated classrooms. Make your room an inviting place, not only for students, but also for colleagues. Welcome suggestions from others; ask for feedback from those you most admire. Don't try to do it alone. The teacher down the hall may have a great idea for using technology to teach a lesson on Civics, but you'll never know about it unless you ask. It's OK to admit that you didn't think about it first. Seek advice. Ask for help. These days, asking for assistance is seen as a sign of a reflective, proactive teacher. Leave your ego at the door, try the suggestions others offer, and appreciate their efforts.

Know the Experts

Become familiar with those who have done the most research in your field. Buy their books, read their articles. Join a "Teachers as Readers" group. If your school does not have one, seek out others who are new to teaching, include the veterans you admire, and start your own group. Always consider yourself a learner. You not only become a role model for your students, but also you put theory into practice when and where it counts the most.

Listen to Yourself

This may be the hardest piece of advice to follow, but it may be the one with the most impact. Forget the video camera—taping yourself visually can be a scary thing. Try it with audio. Prior to a lesson, turn on a tape recorder and then forget that it's there. Later, in the quiet of your classroom or home, listen. Assess your lesson as you hear it. Check your tone of voice. Pay attention to the types of questions you asked. Were you asking higher-level or lower-level questions? Monitor to whom you asked those questions. Were you directing them to one particular group of students, such as aiming the higher-level math questions at the boys rather than the girls? Listen to the feedback you gave students. What was your wait time? Did you allow time for a higher-level question to be processed, or did you take a response from the first child who raised a hand? Did you allow discussion of a question by small groups before you asked for the answer? Remember that asking the right question is far more important than giving the right answer. This activity may be uncomfortable, but the benefits are enormous.

Let Kids Know That It Is Acceptable to Make Mistakes

Model this truism in two ways: by acknowledging your own mistakes and by admitting that you, the teacher, do not have all the right answers. I once confused two of my students' names on the first day of school. I consistently called Nick "Eric" and Eric "Nick." I told my class that this was unacceptable and that I needed to do something to focus my attention on saying their names correctly. So I placed a glass jar on my desk. Each time I called one of the boys by the wrong name, I placed a penny in the jar. This concrete action made me pay more attention to what I was saying. Within a few hours, Nick was "Nick" and Eric was "Eric," but the activity had far-reaching consequences for all of us. I demonstrated that even teachers make mistakes. I showed that there was no harm in making a mistake as long as I learned from it. Although I never planned on it, my class became the most attentive one I had ever taught. Because I agreed to keep the penny jar going and acknowledge other mistakes with a contribution, my students became the best listeners in the universe. They hung on my every word, hoping to catch me in error.

Exposing your humanity to students can be a frightening experience, but it's worth it. I eventually created a class of risk-takers—students who were not afraid to risk unique and brilliant answers because they knew they would be supported and that, if incorrect, I would take the time to guide them to a correct answer. They also knew that I would acknowledge the fact that I wished I'd thought of their unusual answer and that I envied their thinking process. Needless to say, the penny jar stayed on my desk for many, many years. (All profits went to a charity of each class's choosing.) There were days when no pennies were contributed on my part. But there were also days that I entered the classroom, pulled a dollar from my purse, deposited it in the jar, and demanded of my class, "Don't ask any questions."

Savor the Joys of Teaching

Take the time to appreciate the "light bulb" moments. It's the time when everything clicks, and the kids get it. Enjoy the experience of having a parent tell you what you mean to his or her child; what your expertise has wrought; how your influence has shaped or changed that child's life. Take time to find pleasure in the fact that your animated classroom discussion spilled over to the dinner table of a student you thought was barely attentive; that you made sense of algebra for the student who is normally a poster child for math anxiety; and that the eight-year old boy who spends most of Saturday watching cartoons was found in his room reading a book you recommended. Celebrate what the world considers little things but that you know are milestones. Kids will thank you later. They recognize good teaching even if they can't articulate what it is. They appreciate concern and kindness. They will remember not just what you taught, but how you taught it, and they will love you because you made it real and accessible for them.

Learn from Your Students

Many years ago, I brought my parents to my classroom to partake in a holiday activity. Normally this would have been a simple endeavor because over the years they had come to many school functions and always enjoyed meeting my students, but my mother had recently suffered a series of strokes. She had become mentally and physically impaired. Having become accustomed to considering my class as part of my family and having faith in children, I decided that my students would enjoy meeting them. Several volunteers were on hand to assist with our ornament-making project, so I was comfortable in asking my parents to attend. After my father wheeled my mother into the room, I made the introductions and then became absorbed in assisting several students. I forgot to check on mom until my father discreetly directed my attention to the corner of the room where he had parked her wheelchair. There sat my mother, brain-damaged from strokes, surrounded by children and paying rapt attention to her tutors— three of my most academically challenged children and two students who were headed for the "Disruptive Student Hall of Fame." Patiently but adamantly, they insisted that she could indeed create her own ornament, and as I watched, they guided her through the steps, applauded her efforts, and cheered her on as she glued sequin after sequin to a styrofoam ball. "We knew she could do it, Mrs. Kou," they told me. "She just needed a little direction. And we told her it was OK to make a mistake."

For me that day, the lesson was about compassion and expectation. The future for those students changed because I was humbled by what they had done, and I learned from it. My mother's disability meant little to them. They sensed in her a spirit similar to their own, and they showed their faith in her by doing what good teachers do. They broke down a simple concept into a step-by-step process, demonstrated how it worked, guided her through it, and expected that she would learn it. Their expectations for her had been higher than mine for them. I looked at them differently from that time on and demonstrated my confidence in their abilities by setting the same high standards for them that I did for the rest of my class. I helped them get there, and they succeeded. As is often the case, we see only what we look for. I had not looked hard enough or far

Author's Personal Collection

Linda Koutoufas and Jack Bridgeford conduct a science experiment.

enough. These students may have benefited from my transformation, but I consider myself the real beneficiary of this lesson. I will forever remember them with a sense of deep gratitude.

Which brings me to my final bit of advice: Unless a teacher communicates that he or she has high expectations for all students, two distinct sets of classes are created: The "cans" and the "cannots." These classes are not necessarily created by a family's educational level, their socioeconomic status, or the neighborhood in which they live. The distinction is created through a school culture. As an instructional specialist for my school division, I visited almost every school in my city, but most frequently, I worked in high poverty schools. The greatest difference I observed was in regard to the staffs' mindset about each school's population. In some buildings, the mantra went: "These kids can't ..." Early on, the staff had decided that the majority of children were unable to achieve any sort of success. As I listened, teachers listed a variety of factors: Absentee parents, lack of family involvement, homelessness. This message was clearly communicated to the student body, and as students usually do, they lived up to the teachers' expectations—they failed.

Yet in other high poverty schools with the exact same challenges (including the one in which I now work), such negativity is forbidden. The phrase, "These kids can't...," which I equate with a terminal illness, is simply not allowed. Students with difficult family and environmental issues thrive because their teachers expect them to excel, and these teachers communicate this fact to students through their verbal comments, their body language, and their written notes on tests and projects. They know that in addition to hours of after-school tutoring, mentoring, and one-on-one attention, the best thing they can offer these kids is a strong dose of confidence—teacher confidence that these very special children can achieve as much as or more than anyone in the city. Written comments such as, "I know this was hard, but I'm so glad you stuck with it!" go a lot farther than "Weak! What were you thinking?"

It should come as no surprise that children are influenced by our expectations of them, both stated and unstated. Kids aren't fooled. They can read body language much better than adults, and they recognize when there is a disconnect between the verbal and nonverbal message. The nonverbal is always much more accurate. If our mission is to positively impact the children we teach, we must communicate in every way that we believe in their ability to do well. It ought to be every teacher's dream that the classroom is such an inviting and invigorating place for all students that the kids don't want to leave. What it eventually comes down to is the attitude of the teacher. The idea is not to convince students to give up their dreams, but to foster those dreams through enthusiasm, patience, and genuine interest. Kids learn what they're taught. If they're taught that they are not smart because they are disadvantaged, that they lag so far behind their peers they'll never catch up, or that they do not fit the teacher's image of what a model student should be, then they will become those things. Teachers who personify, embody, and foster these mistaken ideas are not teachers; they are demolition experts, and there is no place for them in education. What is called for in this remarkable profession are builders, artists, and sculptors. We need people who will mold children to be successful, paint their future for them, and build their confidence through insightful teaching and powerful instruction. We need positive people teaching kids and their families. We need people who understand that often, the only barrier between hope and hopelessness is education. My fondest hope is that we in the profession will have our hearts captured by children, that we will learn the lessons they teach us, that we will learn from each other, and that when we leave the profession, we will be proud to have enhanced others' lives.

Official White House Photo

The 1999 Virginia Teacher of the Year, Linda Koutoufas, with President Bill Clinton.

About the Author:
Linda Koutoufas, 1999 Virginia Teacher of the Year, spent 32 years in the Virginia Beach Public School System as an elementary teacher and administrator. She has testified in Congress on teacher quality and was designated as a Woman of the Year by the *Virginian-Pilot* newspaper for her work on gender equity. She currently serves as a project specialist for College Park Elementary in Virginia Beach and is a mentor in the Old Dominion University Career Switcher Program.

Chapter Seven

Great Teachers Teach Differently: Maximize Your Impact in the Classroom

Alexander B. Carter

2003 Milken National Educator

The mediocre teacher tells. The good teacher explains. The superior teacher demonstrates. The great teacher inspires.

—William Arthur Ward

Terror. This describes my general feeling the Friday before I would teach my first day of classes at C.D. Hylton High School as a fully licensed and certificated high school history teacher. Like most new teachers, I spent the week prior to the first week of school going to meetings with my new colleagues in Prince William County and preparing my units to start the year. All week I strutted around the school projecting a sense of calm confidence. "How's it going?" my fellow department members would ask. I'd say, "Great!" Helpful administrators would inquire, "Anything I can do for you?" "Nope," was my reply, "I pretty much have it under control." But the truth was, I was quaking in my boots.

Don't get me wrong. I was reasonably confident that I could be a good teacher. I had completed my student teaching experience the previous semester and discovered that I had a certain talent for standing before a group of students and getting them to learn. I was comfortable planning units and lessons; I could align my content with the curriculum and develop pacing guides; and I felt that I could manage behavior in a class reasonably well. What I didn't know was how to begin. How do you actually get a class going?

Enter my hero, my knight in shining armor, Mr. Walter Bailey. Now understand, I've never needed a knight in shining armor before. I stand 6 feet, 3 inches tall, and I was at least a passable athlete during my day. Mr. Bailey, my Social Studies department chair and mentor, stands 5 feet, 4 inches tall and weighs 120 pounds soaking wet. In my world, however, he stands as a giant. What a character! Every day that I saw him teach, he was nattily dressed, wearing a bow tie with matching suspenders. Always the consummate professional and instructional leader, he had been electrifying classes and infusing a love of history into students for 30 years. I could not fool him; he saw right through the calm façade. Around 1:00 P.M. on the Friday before school started, he asked me what was wrong. I confessed: "Mr. Bailey," I said "I don't know what I am going to do when they walk into my class for the first time!" He replied, "Relax, kid. Just go over the administrative 'first day' packet they've given you during your first period class. Then come to my second period and watch me open the year. You'll see how to start a class."

The weekend passed all too quickly, and the first day of school had arrived. When the bell rang for first period, I followed the guidelines provided to me by the administration. After the "Pledge of Allegiance" and morning announcements, I carefully checked every student's schedule while calling roll—that killed eight minutes. I slowly introduced myself and told them how excited I was to be their teacher that year—six minutes gone. I handed out my course syllabus and class rules, reading every word on both pages—12 minutes more. I recited every excruciating word on pages one through eight in the "Code of Behavior." I had run out of material and noticed that there were a few minutes left in class. I asked if anyone had any questions. They did not, and so there I stood, staring out at a bored throng of 14-year-olds, as the last 90 seconds of my first ever class mercifully expired.

Finally the bell rang, and as my students shuffled out of the

The most notable thing about Mr. Carter is his raw determination to see every student in his class experience success. He doesn't lavish all of his attention on the students in the front row—those students who enthusiastically take notes and nod along with his lectures. It's the students in the back of the class who are less focused on achieving that he forces to sit up and take notice of the material he is teaching. He refuses to let them slide through, regardless of their protests. And those students in the front? He makes them work harder than they ever thought possible, and they love him for it.

—Abbey Scheflen, former student

room, I gathered my things. I hustled across the hall to Mr. Bailey's room to see what he would do with his second period because I was determined to make a far better impression on my next class. I was hoping to learn how to do that from his demonstration. When I arrived, he pointed to his desk, which was situated in the back corner of the room. Without a word, I took up my position to watch a master at work.

Mr. Bailey positioned himself at the door of his room, welcoming his students to his classroom with a firm handshake, a stiff bow at the waist, and a "How do you do?" He would quickly glance at their schedule to ensure that they were assigned to his class. Determining that their names did, indeed, appear on his roster, he then pointed them to the area of the room where they would find a desk with their name already printed on a three-by-five card. I noticed that he was immediately taking control of every aspect of his classroom. You see, Mr. Bailey owned this space, and everyone else was merely a guest in his realm. As the students came in, I noticed that they already had a sense that something different was going to happen.

What I didn't notice is that Mr. Bailey had strategically placed a small metal trashcan away from the wall about five feet behind where he stood when welcoming students to his class. If I had noticed that trashcan, I might also have noticed that it was bent and dented from years of abuse. As the last 30 seconds of the break between classes wound down and all of his students made their way to their assigned seats, I saw Mr. Bailey casually talking to a teacher across the hall. When the bell rang, however, I couldn't believe what I saw next.

No sooner had the electronic tone sounded to begin class when

Mr. Walter Bailey with his famous intensity, enthralls his students with powerful instruction.

Carol Bailey

Mr. Bailey suddenly wheeled on his heel, took two steps and kicked the small metal trashcan, sending it flying through the air and across the room. Before the can struck the opposing wall of the room, Mr. Bailey was already teaching. Not taking roll, mind you, or passing out the course syllabus, the class rules, or any other piece of typical first day administrativia—he was teaching! He didn't even introduce himself! He began class with a two-minute, mind-blowing introduction to human nature and the development of civilizations. The students were enthralled. He brought out a statuette of a fat little naked lady and passed it around the room, asking his students what they thought it was. By the time they figured out it was a totem of the "Earth Mother," a common religious idol worshiped by ancient nomadic cultures, they were his! He had only just met these students a few minutes before and they were already on the edge of their seats, hands in the air, flailing so that they might get his attention and be recognized. I knew right away that it was what great teachers do, or rather what great teachers do differently, that makes all the difference in the classroom.

Lesson Number 1: Great Teachers Don't Take Roll
At Least Not During the First Five Minutes of Class

The most important thing I learned from Mr. Bailey is that you never get a second chance to make a first impression. Students are almost always willing to give the teacher their undivided attention at the beginning of a class. Great teachers know this fact and capitalize on this unique opportunity by ensuring that the first few minutes of class consist of only powerful instruction.

Just a few minutes of really powerful, interest-based instruction hooks the student into your plan for the day and ensures that each is primed for a full day of learning. The most common mistake I see teachers making is the failure to capitalize on this opportunity during the very first minutes of a period. This mistake is a tragic waste of one of the most valuable assets you have as a classroom teacher: the natural curiosity of the student. Students want to learn. They want to be interested. They want to be involved. But during the first few minutes of class, many teachers fail to exploit the students' natural desire to be interested by asking their students to sit idly by as the teacher muddles through the bureaucratic minutia of teaching (checking homework, taking roll, etc.). When teachers make this common mistake, the student's natural curiosity, which should have been focused on the day's instruction, inevitably becomes directed to something else. Time after time, I see educators let students off the learning hook by making a weak first impression.

The First Day of Class: Shock and Awe

I call it the "miracle of the first day." It has happened countless times all across our country as students show up for the first day of school. They are excited, nervous, eager, and curious. As the day begins, their anticipation of what is to come is at an all-time high. Every student is ready to give you every ounce of their attention, but what do most teachers do? We bore them to death! We drone on about our class rules and codes of behavior. We describe the countless hours of hard work expected of them. We make them sign administrative documents and forms *ad infinitum.* The only thing most of us don't do on that first day is actually teach. What a waste. Instead of "turning them on" to the prospect of a great year of learning, we "turn them off" with our administrative minutia.

Now I assure you that most of your students will forgive your first day transgressions and will accept you eagerly when you decide to really start teaching on the second day of school. In fact, your top students will actively look for reasons to adore you and value your class. These eager little beavers will wait patiently for you to plow through the copious (albeit necessary) administrative mumbo-jumbo that every school across the country finds important to safely and efficiently run the school. But there is another group of students in your class who won't be so forgiving.

The Paradox of the Reluctant Learner

It is a little known fact that even your most reluctant learners also come to school on that first day of school full of hope and anticipation. They want to be successful, but for whatever reasons (social, academic, behavioral) they have always struggled in school. "This year will be different," they hope. "This year I am going to get it all together." Then that first class starts, and it's the same old thing; they get bored and they regress into old and familiar patterns. Yet with the national focus on ensuring that each and every student be successful, these students, who are historically the lowest performing group, are precisely the students that we need to get on our side right from the start! I can tell you from experience that all you have to do is give these students one chance to disengage from your instruction, and they will take full advantage of it. They don't just disengage—they reengage too. What they are now engaged in, though, is rarely going to benefit your instructional plan for the day, and is usually disruptive. So what can you do? You never let them off the hook. Seize their attention: You "shock and awe" them during those very first seconds they are in your class, and then you never let go. Never give them the excuse they are looking for to disengage.

So just how do you do that? Well, it's simple: You teach. Don't waste the precious first minutes of the first day with the typical "first-day materials." Begin your first lesson with a demonstration of what is most exciting about your class. Show your students why you fell in love with your subject and why you are a teacher. Demonstrate how incredible your field is! Once you have them hooked, you can get around to the assigned administrative tasks. But never, ever do those tasks until you've accomplished your first and most important goal:

Engage their interest in your class.

I am a history teacher, so I usually start my class with a favorite story or by challenging my students to engage in a discussion on a controversial issue. I have to admit that on the first day of school I always secretly wish I was a chemistry teacher. If I was, I can promise you that within seconds of that first bell ringing something would blow up! That's right— smoke, fire, a loud bang—a real explosion. Those students would be putty in my hands before the first five minutes were up! But it doesn't matter what your subject is—you love it! Let your students see the passion that you have for your field and show them how they might come to love it, too. Passion and excitement in the classroom are contagious. If you can get them to understand how much you love your subject and how excited you are to share that with them, your job will be much more rewarding for the rest of the school year.

> *"Good teaching is one-fourth preparation and three-fourths theater."*
> —Gail Godwin

Now please don't misunderstand me; the duties you are assigned by your administration on the first days of school are truly important and necessary. It is a good idea to review your class rules and your syllabus. It is beneficial to describe your classroom procedures and strategies for success in your classroom. But these things don't need to be reviewed and explained at the beginning of your first class. You must first demonstrate why your class is worth their time and effort. Only after you have demonstrated that point of view, should you cover all of these other items. Without generating student interest in your class it is all moot anyway, isn't it? Remember, you never get a second chance to make a first impression.

Not Only the First Day: Start Every Lesson This Way!

Now once you have accomplished your goals on the first day of school and you have all of your students excited about your class, plan to begin every class period with the same thought and care, each day establishing a level of interest and excitement that will remind the students why they love your class. Too many teachers in our schools start every class by routinely calling roll. Can you think of anything less interesting or more mundane? Why not get the students started on a thought-provoking writing prompt, or a discussion of a piece of music, or warming up with a math problem. Then, once the students are actively engaged in the learning process, you can quietly take attendance. Remember, if you lose your most reluctant learners in those first few minutes of class, you may spend the rest of the day trying to reel them back in.

Lesson Number 2: Great Teachers Make It Personal:
And Take It Personally, Too!

When I saw "Philip" walk into my classroom with a swagger, I knew this kid was going to be different. Freshmen generally don't swagger on the first day of school. As class began I saw that he was on his own agenda. Talking to girls, making wisecracks—he was really enjoying himself. The problem was that he was already causing a major disruption to my glorious first day of class! Trying to bring him around to getting on the same page as me, I began to ask him questions. He wouldn't give me a serious answer, but he always gave a clever one— a clear demonstration of his innate wit and intelligence. I would laugh at his response, but then pose another question, keeping him in the "hot seat." About three minutes into this exercise, he relented, realizing that I wasn't going to stop questioning him until he gave me a straight answer. I won that first battle, but I got the sense that this situation was on the way to being a perpetual year- long struggle. I decided then and there that I wasn't going to engage in this fight. I needed to end it by establishing a relationship, and fast!

At 6:00 P.M. sharp that evening I knocked on the door of Philip's house. When his mother answered the door, I explained that I was her son's second period World History teacher. She was shocked. "He couldn't already be in this much trouble!" "Not at all," I answered, "I just wanted to see where he got that great sense of humor." She invited me in and explained that they were just sitting down to dinner. Before I knew it, I was at the table, tucking into her meatloaf and green beans. Within minutes, I knew the answer to my question about where Philip developed his quick wit. The speed at which one had to interject one's thoughts and opinions was lightning fast. If you wanted to be heard in this family, you better be quick! If you hesitated, you missed your opportunity to be noticed. Everyone at the table was fair game, parents included. They were merciless…loving, but merciless. It was kill or be killed at this table; no one was safe from ridicule.

After dinner I explained what had happened in class that day. I told Philip and his mother that, while I appreciate his quick wit and wry sense of humor, I have an important job to do. I need all students to be focused on the same goals, including him. I told Philip that I knew that only very intelligent people have the ability to formulate jokes as fast as he could, and I was interested in seeing what kind of scholar he could be if he applied that intelligence to my class.

You understand, I was determined to be in charge of that class. I explained to Philip and his mother that there simply was no time to engage in casual, verbal sparring every day. I agreed, however, that there may be occasions where his humor would be appropriate, and when that was the case, he would have some leeway. I needed to know if we could develop an understanding that there were times when he needed to hold back. He said he could live with that. I left satisfied that we had reached an accord.

At the end of the first quarter I could honestly say that Philip was among my favorite students. Although his work wasn't as academically impeccable as some of the others in my class, his insights into history were impressive and his contributions in class had become less for comic relief and much more to the point. He was a pleasure to teach. I asked to see his report card. When he sheepishly handed it to me, I was shocked! The B he received in my class stood alone among a sea of Fs. I asked him how this could have happened.

"I don't like those other teachers," he replied. "I'm not going to give them the satisfaction."

At that time I learned the second lesson that all great teachers know. Your top students will do whatever is necessary to make the grade. Your lowest achieving students, however, will only work for teachers that they truly care about. These students often don't recognize that the only ones they are hurting are themselves! They don't see that it is their futures that are at stake. The only reason they will work hard is if they care if their teacher cares. The only way to make that happen is for the teacher to develop a personal relationship with every student. It's as simple and profound as that.

> *"No significant learning happens without a significant relationship."*
> —Dr. James Comer

Many times in my career I have begun discussions with teachers by asking, "What is most important to you as a teacher?" It is amazing how often this question stumps them. Great teachers know that student learning is the answer. It is important that every educator commit to this goal as the driving force behind his or her instruction. If student learning is your goal, you must be willing to do what is necessary to achieve it and that means developing personal relationships with your students.

To be honest, your top students are already motivated to achieve. They are already interested in their schoolwork and are focused on their own personal goals and agenda. Whether these goals include earning straight As, achieving a high GPA to get them into college, or gaining knowledge and experience to further their career goals, they will learn regardless of who is teaching them. They are focused and determined, and they are the type of students who will learn the material despite their teachers if necessary. In short, these students are exceptional and will succeed.

The rest of your students, however, need a strong personal relationship to motivate them to want to learn. In fact, your most reluc-

Carl Long

Establishing a personal relationship with every student pays huge dividends for Principal Alex Carter.

tant learners will actively resist learning if they feel that the person teaching them doesn't care about them. They will only care to learn if they know the teacher cares that they learn. It is up to teachers to demonstrate daily that it matters to them that every student achieves success in their class. I'm not saying you have to be easy on your students; I'm simply saying that you need to show them you care.

Many young teachers fall into dangerous territory when trying to establish a personal relationship with their students. They become their students' friend, confidant, or enabler. The fact is that students don't need their teachers to assume these roles in their lives and, truthfully, students don't want this from teachers either. What students want and need from their teacher is for them to be their guide, resource, and role model.

Students Want Teachers They Can Trust

Students have to be able to know that what their teachers are asking of them is good and important. Great teachers establish a sense of trust between themselves and their students. This trust convinces the student that every assignment the teacher asks them to do is worthwhile and relevant to their progress. Great teachers invest the time necessary to build this trust early in the year so they can reap its rewards all year long. They demonstrate to their students every day that the hard work and attention spent in class will ultimately contribute to achieving a better life and a happier future.

Students Want Teachers They Can Respect

Too many teachers fail to realize that students are constantly watching them. They notice when you're not feeling well. They notice when you're not prepared. They notice when you're taking a break. Too many teachers expect their students to do "as they say," not "as they do." This is not realistic. When a teacher gives the class a meaningless assignment and then disengages to answer emails on the computer or do paperwork for the next 20 minutes, that teacher is sending a very clear message to his students. Students need to see their teachers giving all of their efforts toward furthering their students' success, and the students will, in turn, reward this by working diligently for their instructors.

Students Want Teachers They Can Accurately Predict

For your most reluctant learner, every day in class is a personal challenge, and sometimes it can be frightening. Students want their teachers to be fair and consistent, and they want to know what to expect from their teachers every day. They need to know that the classroom is a sanctuary where they can take a risk without fear that their mistakes may be ridiculed. Any attempt by these students needs to be rewarded with praise from their teachers. In order to feel safe, students need to know they will be treated with the same respect every day. Predictability from all of their teachers is paramount.

How can you establish that "personal relationship" with your students without crossing that invisible line? Here are some strategies that I've used to great effect:

- Meet and greet your students at the door before every class: This is harder than it sounds. You're going to be tired from the last class and you really will want a break! But the investment you make by interacting with your students prior to class and talking to them as individuals will pay huge dividends when class begins. They need to see you as a person who cares about them individually and is interested in their lives, rather than just as a teacher who cares only if his pupils are doing their class work.

- Call on every student by name every period. This is difficult and a challenge, but it's still very important. The research on this practice is clear: Students who are called on by name are more attentive and retain more knowledge than those who feel anonymous. Don't ever let any of your students feel that they are overlooked or unimportant to you.
- At least once a week provide personal and specific feedback regarding student performance. Students need to know that the work they are doing for you affects you personally and is important to you. This feedback can be positive or constructive criticism. It doesn't really matter. They just need to be reminded that their work is noticed and of value to you, their teacher.
- Go the extra mile for your students. Do things for your students that let them know they are more than just clients in your classroom: Go to their sporting events, attend the school play, celebrate their birthday, or make a home visit. The effect of these "extras" is incalculable. Especially for your most reluctant learners, these extras will make all the difference. These are the things that great teachers do routinely to demonstrate their personal commitment in their students. They are hard to quantify but they mean the world to their students.

There are many other ways to establish that personal relationship with your students, and I encourage you to work at it each day that you are teaching. The payoff is well worth the effort.

Lesson Number 3: Great Teachers Energize Every Class:
Creating the Best Environment for Learning

By my sixth year as a teacher, I started to really feel that I was making an impact on my students. I became more reflective, not just on the big things that make instruction work (planning units and lessons, crafting meaningful assignments and assessments, aligning the curriculum with the state standards, etc.), but I was starting to look at the little things that could transform a good lesson into a great lesson. I came to realize that different lessons required a different feeling, tone or energy from both me as the teacher and the students as learners to have a great impact. I learned that I could manipulate the students to get them to adopt an energy level appropriate to the day's lesson, which made all the difference in making every lesson exciting.

It is always obvious to me when I am in a great teacher's classroom. There is an energy that you can feel instantly upon entering their space. Great teachers learn to set this energy level and seem to know just how to make it work for the lesson they have planned for that day's instruction. This energy level is quickly grasped by the students, and they innately attune themselves and their behavior to suit the day's work, thus saving valuable time for instruction. I know this sounds strange, but it's true, and it really works.

In my classroom, I identify three different types of energy levels, or "intensities," that I actively attempt to create for the lessons that I have prepared. I call these energy levels "High Intensity," "Medium Intensity," and "Low Intensity." These intensity levels are particularly suited to the type of instruction that will be taking place in the classroom for that day. Each energy level helps my students to adopt the attitude that will be appropriate to their roles in that day's lesson. The intensity level is reflective of the tone the teacher projects during the lesson.

High Intensity Energy
High Intensity=Students Quiet and Passive (taking notes, listening, etc.)

This energy level is best when the teacher is the center of attention. On "high intensity" days, the teacher is leading the class in discussion or delivering a lecture. "High intensity" days are perfect for beginning a new unit, where the students need a clear understanding and introduction to new material or for when students are presenting projects to the class. On days of "high intensity," the teacher immediately takes charge. Even before the bell sounds to signal the beginning of class, students can sense that today is a day for them to be attentive and focus their attention on the teacher. The teacher directs the students to take their seats, asks questions like, "Are you ready to learn today?" or makes declarations like, "I hope you ate your Wheaties this morning!" These comments create an atmosphere of excitement and expectation without really eliciting any response. Students generally just smile and take their seats. That is exactly what you want. Without having to say, "Students, today the expectation for you is to sit quietly and be attentive," your students will already be sitting quietly and you will have their attention. This really does work.

Medium Intensity Energy
Medium Intensity Energy=Students Talking and Productive

This energy level is perfect for days when the students are the center of attention (Hopefully, this will be the default energy level for your classroom). I set the energy level at medium on days when the students will be doing cooperative learning, discussions, group work, or any other type of creative assignment. Some teachers have a tendency to shy away from this type of instruction because the first time they try it, they realize that success is completely dependent upon the cooperation of their students. If the students aren't willing to participate, the day's lesson will fall flat on its face. What teachers sometimes fail to realize, however, is that with just a little advance preparation, the students can be "primed" to share.

On medium days, great teachers intentionally create an atmosphere of sharing. Students recognize that their teacher is open to their input, and they follow his lead. Really great teachers will have created conversation areas by pushing the student's desks together into groups. By asking questions as the students enter the classroom, great teachers get the students talking with one another even before class begins. These questions don't necessarily even have to be related to the subject matter (i.e., "Did you see that game last night?"). The teacher simply wants the students to begin discussing things so that once the students get into this proper state of mind, it's easy to transition the focus of conversation to subject-related matters once class has officially begun. Setting the energy level before the class even begins makes this type of lesson more enjoyable, less stressful, and more effective for both the teacher and the students.

Low Intensity Energy
Low Intensity Energy=Students Quiet and Productive

Great teachers want to establish low intensity energy on days of assessment, intensive study, extended writing, or any time individual quiet contemplation will be required. On "low intensity days," you want your students to be quietly focused on the task you have assigned them.

On these days, I never allow my students to begin talking. I do this by creating a "library-like" atmosphere in my room from the very beginning of class. You can do this, too. As students arrive at your room, stand at the door, almost acting as a physical barrier against the noise and chaotic activity in the hallway and the quiet sanctuary of your classroom. Greet your students with a low whisper, welcoming them to class and asking them to go silently to their desks and get out their materials for the day. On test or quiz days, you might suggest that they review their notes as last-minute preparation for the assessment, promising that if everyone is on task, you will extend this study and review period beyond the first few minutes of class.

I still find it amazing, but students almost always follow these directions perfectly. By the time the bell rings, the class will be sitting quietly in their seats with their materials out and ready to begin the day's lesson. Not only will you be able to avoid having spending the first precious minutes of class time quieting them down, but the level of intensity and concentration that is achieved will be superior and enhance student performance.

All teachers must remember that they have the most important job in the world. The students who are now in their classes are the future of our nation. It is incumbent upon us to do everything we can, whatever is necessary, to ensure that they will be prepared to meet the growing challenges of an ever-changing world. It is a monumental task but one that is immensely rewarding. I wish you all the best of luck as you undertake this exciting challenge and hope that each of you will teach differently and dare to become great!

Tyler Mallory

Alex Carter at C.D. Hylton High School.

About the Author:
Alexander Carter graduated from James Madison University and began teaching history in 1995. During his 9 years in the classroom, Alex coached football, sponsored the Student Council Association, and was active in the organization of student cultural exchanges to France and England. Some of the honors Alex received in recognition for his contributions were the "Outstanding Performance Award" in 2000, he was named a finalist for his division's "Teacher of the Year" in 2002, and most notably, Alex was among the 100 outstanding educators in the nation to be honored with the 2003 National Milken Educator Award. After receiving his M. Ed. from the University of Virginia, Alex transitioned from the classroom and into school administration and now serves as the principal of Brentsville District High School in Northern Virginia.

Chapter Eight

No Excuses, Only Success: The Pine Spring Way

Deborah Tyler

2004 Milken National Educator

They who educate children well are more to be honored than they who produce them; for these only gave them life, those the art of living well.
—Aristotle

It is always an amazing scene to see 450 elementary school students gathered together in an auditorium. There is an incredible energy level, and the crescendo of noise fills the room while their teachers skillfully manage and maneuver the children into their proper seating locations. The purpose of this particular assembly, however, was shrouded in mystery. The principal, Deborah Tyler, had been told only that she should expect numerous dignitaries from Richmond, including the Superintendent of Public Instruction. Moreover, the Fairfax County superintendent and several members of the school board were expected along with a large contingent of the press. Several parents had also spontaneously appeared, tipped off to the assembly by the fact that their children had been told to dress in white and black, a positive indication that the entire school would be singing that day, and they surely did not want to miss the perform-ance. It was obvious that something big was going to happen, and it was an honor that Pine Spring had been selected as the venue for this important event. It was a happy school. It was immediately obvious that the students loved their teachers and that the respect was mutu-al. Debi Tyler was like a celebrity—she could hardly walk a step with-out a child running up to hug her. This was a very special place, indeed.

Pine Spring Elementary School is located in Falls Church,

Virginia, just a few miles west of the nation's capital. The region has become a crossroads to the world, and the school's demographics reflect this diversity. The students come from 25 countries and speak 14 different languages. It is also designated as a Title I school since many of the children come from poor families—48% qualify for free or reduced lunch programs. These socioeconomic factors certainly pose many obstacles and challenges for educators. Elsewhere, these factors have become a perennial excuse for poor test scores and a justification for sub par academic performance. That is not the "Pine Spring Way," however. Debi Tyler does not tolerate excuses and rightfully demands success for these children. To achieve that success, she assembled a talented group of educators who are similarly committed to this vision.

After all of the children had quieted down, the purpose of the assembly was finally revealed: To recognize Principal Deborah Tyler for outstanding work and professional excellence. Lowell Milken, the chairman of the Milken Family Foundation, was personally on hand to present the award along with a check for $25,000.

We asked Debi Tyler to share with us her important work at Pine Spring Elementary. P.B.-S.B.

The day I received the Milken award, on October 13, 2004 was in recognition of over 20 years of service to public education. When I embarked upon this journey in 1982, no one could have ever told me that I would someday become a principal or receive a national award. I always loved being a teacher and found joy each day in working with students. There is nothing more exhilarating than seizing on those "teachable moments" and feeling the energy that accompanies students as they make connections and realize their potential. I often compare it to an athlete who trains year after year and, after many false starts and defeats, finally makes it first across the finish line. Teaching gives me the same adrenaline rush that is described by many athletes, although I must admit I've experienced my fair share of failure and setbacks. Yet, many of my friends in the business world complain about their jobs and don't like to go to work in the morning. I have always been blessed by loving what I do,

Deborah Tyler has always put her heart and soul into education from her days as an elementary school student to the present. Her experiences as a graduate student, a special education teacher, and an assistant principal helped her build knowledge and skills. She has grown from a quiet, studious elementary school student to a dynamic, vocal leader and advocate for students.

Ms. Tyler ably oversaw student education at Pine Spring Elementary School in Falls Church, Virginia, where she worked as a teacher, assistant principal, and principal over a period of 18 years. The staff, students, and community at the school appreciate the rich student diversity comprised of students from 25 countries speaking 14 different languages. The school includes 20 general education classrooms, four classes for learning-disabled students, and a school-based program for visually impaired students.

To meet the needs of this diverse student body, Deborah Tyler provided carefully planned staff development for her faculty. These activities enhanced student achievement and supported her commitment to lifelong learning. Teachers planned together, grappled with new ideas, and discussed and conducted research. In addition, Ms. Tyler conducted frequent walkthroughs in her classrooms and used the information gathered to focus conversations about teaching and learning in the school with both individuals and groups.

In conjunction with her staff, Ms. Tyler established a program targeting at-risk students. The needs of each student are reviewed by a committee who periodically discuss the student's progress and makes plans to help the student. These plans may involve having the student work with the school's math specialist, be assigned a mentor, meet weekly with the counselor, or participate in an after-school remediation program.

In 1999, due to low scores on the Virginia Standards of Learning tests, Pine Spring received funds to boost student achievement. Additional resource teachers were hired. Ms. Tyler used these teachers to reduce the pupil/teacher ratio during language arts instruction, provide small group math remediation, and offer enrichment in science, social studies, and mathematics. The success of these programs is evidenced by the fact that Pine Spring was designated a 2006 Title I Distinguished School for reducing the achievement gap while raising the achievement of all students.

Deborah Tyler's dedication to the school reached beyond the staff and students to the community. She and her staff paid particular attention to parent participation with the total school program. The monthly newsletter is published in both Spanish and English and offers a wide variety of opportunities for parent involvement and education.

The dedication and expertise of Ms. Tyler have been recognized both within Fairfax County Public Schools and in the broader education community. Her walkthrough process is the focus of an ASCD video on classroom walkthroughs. In 2004, she received the Milken Award for outstanding leadership. Fairfax County administration selected Ms. Tyler to open a new elementary school in the fall of 2006 where she will continue to build a school dedicated to providing the best possible education for every child.

> —Mary Helman, Fairfax County Public Schools Elementary Curriculum and
> Instruction Coordinator (Deborah Tyler's 5th grade teacher)

and I still feel invigorated around children. For me, though, the New Year never starts in January but rather begins in September.

I am now approaching my 25th year as an educator. I still marvel at how far I've come and the personal growth I've experienced. Over the years, I have been fortunate to work with some of the most outstanding educators in the field, and they have helped shape my career and philosophy of education. I will always be grateful for their positive influences on my life.

When I was a young teacher, I was at the same crossroads that many of you are now facing. I had just gotten my first job, and I was positive that I could change the world. My career began in rural West Virginia where I was hired as the school's special education teacher. Armed with all of my up-to-date and new- found knowledge, I was determined to level the playing field for all of our special education students. I arrived at my new school with great hope and enthusiasm. The school had approximately 300 students but only one special education teacher—me. I was expected to meet the diverse and unique needs of students at every level from kindergarten through sixth grade. My meager classroom was, in actuality, a "temporary" trailer located behind the main school building. This was during the era of the self-contained classroom; Public Law 94-142 (Education of All Handicapped Children Act)[34] had just been enacted. Special education students were expected to be given greater access to public education, but in fact, there was little mainstreaming, and these students were separated from their peers. The concept of inclusion was still years away.

The general education teachers were happy to have a place to send the special education students. My students' disabilities ranged from mildly mentally challenged to learning disabled and physically handicapped. I had some students with cerebral palsy and others with muscular dystrophy. In addition, we were now facing children with the newly diagnosed attention deficit disorder (ADD). This disorder was still in the infantile stages of medical treatment. Caffeine, a stimulant, was prescribed to actually slow these children down. So one of my students had the distinction of enjoying his very own, personal coffee break every morning. The rest of the class had little problem with this practice. In fact, we were all quite grateful when it was time for his coffee break.

Another underlying factor that I had to face was poverty. It was a huge obstacle for these students to overcome since many were living in homes with fixed or subsidized incomes. Maybe it was my beginning teacher naiveté, but I refused to let any of this get in my way. I truly believed, and still do, that education is the great emancipator and that all students deserve a fair chance.

Fortunately, the school where I worked was small and warm. Most of my colleagues were very helpful and cared deeply for our students. The principal was also supportive and took me under her proverbial wing. One of the things that worried her most was the potential negative influence that a few of my colleagues could exert upon me. She warned me that the teacher's lounge was a lethal place for a new teacher. Forewarned, I founded a close camaraderie from the other teachers which helped me flourish.

As a novice teacher, I experienced the usual ups and downs. I would plan these grand lessons that somehow faltered in their implementation. So there I would be, late at night, alone in my trailer, changing my plans and searching for something different and looking for better resources. It is inevitably true that your first year of teaching is an exhausting one and that you will learn much from the process of trial and error. Everything you have gleaned from your college courses and even from student teaching cannot adequately prepare you for the reality of your own classroom. If you can make it through that first year, though, the confidence you gain will prepare you for future success. I have come to believe that new teachers really hit their stride as skilled educators during their third year, and only if they have been fortunate enough to have had an effective mentoring program and strong administrative support.

After years at my school, I felt ready to leave the security and comfort of my hometown to pursue my career as part of one of the nation's top school systems, Fairfax County. The most significant contributing factor in my willingness to make this dramatic change had been my students. The lessons I had learned from them were invaluable, and they had given me confidence. These precious students had placed their trust in me even when I was an inexperienced, anxious teacher. Most importantly, they never gave up on me no matter how I struggled or how many mistakes I made. They were my inspiration. When I announced that I was moving away, it was very difficult. We were all sad. Still, my students gave me a going-away party and presented me with a wooden plaque on which they had all carefully carved their names. Now, many years later, I still have that plaque and I cherish it. Whenever I gaze upon their individual names, I hope that each of them is living a fulfilled life. I treasure that simple piece of wood every bit as much as my Milken award.

Fairfax County has always prided itself as an innovative school system on the cutting edge of education with high expectations for its teachers. These expectations filter down to the students as well with most destined for higher education and prestigious, high-paying jobs. The Fairfax County Public School (FCPS) system is the twelfth largest in the nation and has a well-deserved reputation for academic excellence. It touts one of the country's highest per capita incomes with the majority of its citizens holding advanced degrees. Still, despite all of this obvious, suburban affluence, there are pockets of poverty and, like many other jurisdictions, rapidly changing demographics. There is a substantial African-American base as well as a growing immigrant population comprised of second-language families.

My new school, Pine Spring Elementary, was located in Falls Church, Virginia, about ten miles west of the nation's capital. In the late 1980s, the school found itself reflecting the region's growing diversity. Located in a long-established housing development, many of the neighborhood families had opted for private schools as the school's population shifted from a white majority to one with a growing Latino, Middle Eastern, and African-American student body. The school also had a large number of learning disabled students and, at the time, housed the only program for the visually impaired in the county. It was also one of the most remarkable schools I could ever imagine. Pine Spring was a place that empow-

Philip Bigler

Deborah Tyler joins student Matthew Hoang in Ms. Heather Young's music class at Eagle View Elementary School.

ered teachers and put students first. Teachers actually had input in both governance and policies; the faculty was determined to focus on kids and work together to achieve their goals. Given the many opportunities for real teacher leadership, I witnessed firsthand the impact that stellar teachers could have with the support of a committed principal. I yearned to learn more. These early experiences led me back to graduate school to earn an administrative endorsement in hopes of someday becoming a principal.

When I shared my intent with my teacher colleagues, though, it was met with some initial trepidation. They feared that I would become part of an "administrative establishment," one that was isolated from the realities of the classroom and callous to the genuine needs of teachers. In order to help allay their fears and improve my leadership skills, I got them to agree to let me practice what I was learning with them. The feedback they provided was invaluable and, again, I learned that the most practical lessons did not come from the college classroom but through our day-to-day collaboration as educators committed to a common goal. I learned what teachers truly expect and need from their administrators. A level of trust and mutual respect is critical to effective leadership. I initially thought I would take my new-found knowledge and be assigned to work as an assistant principal at another school. Little did I know that fate would allow me to hone my skills as assistant principal at Pine Spring.

Public education was again changing in the 1990s. There was an outcry of dissatisfaction with America's schools. Citizens were right-ly asking: What is being taught? Were the students actually learning? Are the public schools doing their job? Demands for an increased accountability led to an era of curriculum-based standards and state-mandated testing programs. Standardized testing of students was hardly a new phenomenon in our schools. Indeed, we had been administering tests for decades, but the results were used primarily to qualify students for enrichment (gifted) or special education programs. Little was being done to help those students who scored in the middle. The annual cycle continued, but the test reports were merely stockpiled and stored in some isolated central file room.

During the decade, state legislatures, school boards, and even the federal government embarked upon an ambitious program of implementing standards-based testing as an effort to ensure public accountability. The hope was to enhance the credibility of the public schools. The Commonwealth of Virginia was among the first states to actually implement a comprehensive testing program. Students in grades three and five in the elementary level were required to participate in the pilot testing of this new program. The children would be tested in English, math, social studies, science, and technology. We all faced this challenge with some trepidation and with limited insight. Little could we know how this would initially challenge us and forever change our views on instruction.

The Virginia Standards of Learning (SOLs) tests arrived in the spring of 1998 at Pine Spring Elementary. Now that I was an assistant principal, I also had assumed the role of test coordinator. On this maiden voyage into the uncharted seas of high-stakes testing, we were required, without exception, to test every child in the third and fifth grades. This testing even included all of our second language and special education students. No accommodations were allowed regardless of how long a student may have been in the United States or whether he or she had an Individual Education Plan (IEP) to address some learning disability. Accommodations and exemptions would not come until later. The tests were unsealed and distributed, including Braille editions for our visually impaired students. The hallways were as quiet as a monastery. The only sound that could be heard was the scratching of hundreds of number 2 pencils on scantrons as the students diligently worked through the questions. We had begun our descent into the mysterious world of standards-based testing.

A few weeks later, the initial test results were reported. Schools throughout the state had done poorly. Pine Spring was among them and we were devastated, especially when an article appeared on the front page of the *Washington Post* indicting our efforts as teachers. The gist of the article was that, despite the Fairfax County Public School system's stellar academic reputation, several of its elementary schools had recorded a "sub par" performance on the first round of SOL testing. The fact that the majority of these schools were grappling with increased diversity and poverty was of little consequence. Needless to say, our staff morale plummeted.

Fortunately, our school superintendent, Dr. Daniel Domenech, was himself a Cuban émigré and a product of a second language environment. He instituted a creative, bold approach to address the poor test scores. The 20 lowest performing schools were designated as Project Excel schools. Dr. Domenech concentrated monetary and instructional resources to help support these schools. Each school was given one year to implement an instructional model. Full-day kindergarten and uniform school days were included in the plan (previously, all elementary schools in FCPS closed two hours early on Monday for teacher planning, but now many of these schools gave up that option to increase instructional time). I applauded the efforts of our superintendent and his commitment to reallocate resources to the system's most needy. In a school system known for its affluence, it was the only right and moral thing to do.

My immediate boss, Principal Andrea Warner, wanted to take full advantage of Dr. Domenech's initiative. We were both committed to bringing Pine Spring into full accreditation to avoid sanctions. The school had already created a strong "Teacher as Researchers" group, and we had long-established committees for all of our core curriculum areas. From this solid base, we as a faculty analyzed every piece of test data we had on our students. It was then charted, graphed and examined. We consulted with the county's Instructional

Services Department to determine "best practice" teaching methods and to obtain the latest materials on brain research.

In an effort to retain quality teachers at the challenged schools, the superintendent had proposed a seven-percent pay increase coupled with additional contract time. We discussed this collectively as a staff and decided to take the money. One of the teachers, though, went home, did some calculations, and returned the next day with some startling statistics that she shared with the faculty. Once the seven-percent salary increase was factored into the additional contract time and taxes were taken out, it didn't amount to that much money. The staff already came to work early and stayed late because it was necessary to get the job done. So we assembled again as a full staff to discuss this dramatic revelation and, in the end, we voted to forsake the money in return for an additional allocation of resources to help our students. Many outside the world of education would find this preposterous, but it showed the dedication and commitment of our teachers.

Our intensive studies of our school data made it very apparent what we needed to do. All of the current research on effective schools showed that it is not programs but people who successfully turn schools around. We had just the right people in place to do this at Pine Spring. We already had a reading teacher and a Title I targeted assistance Reading Recovery/ Step Up Language Arts teacher. So, if we added a good Language Arts specialist, this individual could give our students and teachers additional literacy support. We also hired an additional Reading Recovery teacher who served a dual purpose. She would work on improving reading skills, and then in the afternoon, she would be our school's primary math specialist. Another math specialist, social studies/science specialist, and technology teacher were likewise added. The schedule was also modified to increase time for more art, physical education, and music. The additional resources that came from the surplus funds would also help us implement a reduced student-teacher ratio classroom model.

One of the things that we were determined to retain was a strong Fine Arts program. During our year of reflection prior to the implementation of our change, we had discovered the connection between music and increased reading and math performance in our brain research studies. Using this knowledge, we decided to add to our music program. Our students would have the opportunity to begin studying strings in fourth grade and band in grades five and six. Chorus was a mandatory subject for all of our fifth and sixth graders despite some dramatic variations in the quality of voices. We also purchased 25 portable keyboards and added a piano class for our later grades.

We presented our proposal to the Superintendent of Instruction, Nancy Sprague, and to the director of Elementary Instruction, Gloria McDonnell. These women were true instructional leaders in the Fairfax County Public School system and committed educators. I was nervous sitting with these remarkable ladies as Andrea Warner began her presentation, but she talked and they quietly listened. They had a few questions and added some recommendations, but most importantly they embraced our ambitious agenda. With their approval, we began to investigate how we could fold these additional resources into a viable master schedule that would increase the amount of collaborative time for teachers and their teams. Several existing schedule models were given to us for additional research and study. Finally, the Pine Spring plan was brought to the superintendent and given his official sanction. Our model was totally unique from those of the other 19 Project Excel schools.

One of the most important aspects of our school's program was our faculty's annual retreat, which took place every spring and involved the entire staff. The purpose of this event was to reflect and plan for the upcoming school year. Our first retreat after the SOL results now took on a whole new significance. We eagerly shared the student data we had accumulated and discussed our new instructional model. We then wrote the job descriptions for recruiting the new specialists.

The master schedule we finally devised gave teachers up to 90 minutes for grade-level collaborative planning time every day. The math, technology, and social studies/science specialists were combined into the master schedule along with art, physical education, and music to give classroom teachers additional planning time. This additional time allowed us to fine-tune our assessments and further analyze student data while providing embedded staff development. The Special Education teachers, English Speakers of Other Languages (ESOL) teachers, and other specialists were likewise expected to participate in joint grade-level planning. It was paramount that everyone at the school had the same level of competency and commitment when it came to raising expectations for every student.

In order to gauge and assess the progress of Project Excel schools, Dr. Domenech implemented an accountability formula. This formula was based on the scores from the Stanford 9 standardized tests, which were administered in fourth and sixth grades, coupled with those of the SOL tests in grades three and five. He wanted each school to demonstrate a statistical five-point gain based on this formula. Schools and teachers would receive a bonus based on their students' improvement. The highest standard, gold, would result in a monetary pay raise for the entire staff as well as additional funding for the school.

The next spring, the SOL tests predictably arrived on schedule. By now, the state school board had approved some limited accommodations and exemptions for special education and second language students. Still, we all said silent prayers as the students delved into the tests. They fully realized the importance of their performance both to themselves and the school. When we finally packaged up the tests, we sent them to Richmond with a great anticipation of the forthcoming results.

Every August, Fairfax County hosts a leadership conference prior to convening classes. All of the members of the superintendent's leadership team, the school board, the board of supervisors, department heads, and principals and assistant principals attend this massive conference. The conference is held at Fairfax High School because of its centralized location, but parking is always at a premium. After circling the parking lot several times, I finally found a coveted parking space, but by the time I entered the school's auditorium, the lights had already been dimmed and there was no place to sit. So I stood in the back as the superintendent at the podium announced the preliminary results from the most recent SOL tests. He stated that overall he was very pleased with the scores and that the Project Excel schools in particular had shown great progress. There was one school, he continued, that had far exceeded the others. Based on his new accountability formula, this particular school had achieved not only the required five-point gain, but also had, in fact, achieved a stunning 15-point improvement. He paused for dramatic effect and then asked the principal of Pine Spring Elementary, Andrea Warner, to stand and be acknowledged. The auditorium spontaneously erupted with thunderous applause and cheers. Standing alone in the back of the room, my knees suddenly felt weak and my eyes filled with tears. Our dedicated teachers and wonderful students proved it could be done—that nothing was impossible. Poor children and second language students can achieve and do so at high levels when they are given the appropriate resources and have committed, dedicated teachers.

The next article in the *Washington Post* was lauding our initial successes, but we all realized that there was still a lot of work to be done. Pine Spring was still not fully accredited, and we still had to make additional progress. Our initial success, though, helped build our confidence and validated the choices and decisions we had made for our school. It was with renewed vigor that we once again looked at our students and mapped out our additional plan of action.

In the winter of 2001, Andrea announced her retirement and asked me to consider applying for her position. I knew that there was much at stake, but I also believed that the school system would want to maintain and build on her successes. Obviously, there would be strong competition for this principalship. Although I had the support from the staff and community, it would be difficult to replace such a great leader. So, with only a slight hesitation, I took a deep breath and applied for the job.

I was named the principal of Pine Spring on July 1, 2001. My first thoughts were of my predecessor. She had accomplished so much, but I knew my main goal would be to bring the school into full accreditation. Based on our continual assessment and evaluation of instruction, the staff and I decided to add even more specialists. Because we realized that the role of the social studies/science specialist was far too much responsibility for one person, we added an additional person to share this task. At the same time, our rising poverty rate elevated us to school-wide Title I status, and we were authorized to add a Step Up Math position to support a full-time and part-time primary math specialist.

Our plan called for continual assessment of our students so that we could use these data to tailor and focus instruction. Our staff development was embedded and research-driven, meaning that the teachers not only embraced student learning but their own learning as well. Their extended planning time provided them with the opportunity for grade-level collaboration on a daily basis, which was complete with release time for quarterly vertical team meetings. It required some creative scheduling but it was possible. For example, teachers and specialists in kindergarten through grade 3 would be released in the morning for their staff development, planning and vertical articulation. In the afternoon, teachers and specialists in grade 4 through grade 6 would meet. We also used in-house educational consultants to work with the staff on a regular basis.

At Pine Spring we were committed to all our children. It was critical to us that no child became anonymous or felt abandoned. We had established an Identified Student Committee several years prior to the advent of the Standards of Learning Tests. This committee included the principal, the assistant principal, lead special education teacher, lead ESOL teacher, a reading teacher, and school counselor. The committee met three times a year. Its purpose was to identify and help students who were having difficulty in reading, writing, and math. Other specialists, who worked with particular classes or students, would also be expected to attend. Each case was documented on a matrix with detailed recommendations for additional student support. This committee also served as our forum for making special

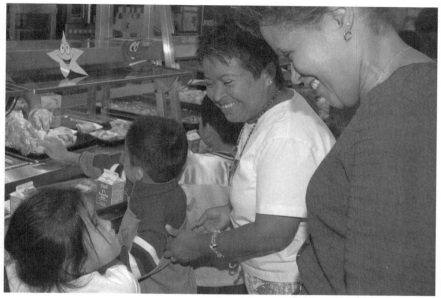

Philip Bigler

Hallie Tran stands patiently in the cafeteria line for lunch with her kindergarten instructional assistant, Ms. Barbara Palencia, and Principal Deborah Tyler.

education decisions, deciding on retention, and summer school recommendations. It was imperative to identify problems early and resolve them before they became a permanent obstacle to a child's educational future.

With everything finally in place, we faced the spring 2002 Standards of Learning tests with a renewed sense of optimism. Our faith in our students and ourselves was justified because this time we made it to full accreditation. Our success made us a model and demonstration site for the entire school system. Teams of principals and teachers were frequently visiting our school to see the "Pine Spring Way." I would tease my teachers and tell them they were coming to watch them wave their magic wands and miraculously solve all problems. One of my teachers actually gave me a magic wand as a gift, and I displayed it proudly in my office. In truth, we know deep down that our success was predicated on the tremendous willingness of our staff and community to accept our students where they are and from there to continually adjust and challenge them to excel. As importantly, we set our expectations high and did not compromise our standards.

Nothing has ever been static in my career. In 2005 I was given the opportunity to plan for the opening of a new elementary school. I was deeply honored since it showed the faith that the school system has in me. Still, it was very difficult to leave Pine Spring, the place that gave me such personal and professional fulfillment. The school is in good hands, though, and it is my sincerest hope that I will be able to translate some of the great lessons I learned there to my new school, Eagle View Elementary. Once again, I know the importance of a quality faculty, and we have assembled a talented group of educators who will truly make a difference.

Today, our schools are portrayed in contradicting ways by our national and local media. Depending upon the fickle mood of a reporter, it can be the best of times or the worst of times to be a public school teacher. I choose to believe that, despite the many challenges faced in education, it is still an exciting time to be an educator. This era of increased educational accountability has created a new breed of educators. These teachers are fully cognizant of the profound impact they can make on the success of their students. They know that a one-size-fits-all approach will not succeed and that we all must work diligently and honestly to reach across cultural, economic, and ethnic lines to uplift our students. The best teachers in our schools today keep current and embrace change. In doing so, these educators bring a respect and honor to their profession through their willingness to work very hard to achieve their goals.

Philip Bigler

Deborah Tyler, Principal of Eagle View Elementary School, 2004 Milken National Educator.

About the Author:
Deborah Tyler earned her bachelor's degree from West Virginia State College and a master's degree from Marshall University Graduate College. She received the elementary-middle school principal endorsement from George Mason University. Ms. Tyler became principal at Pine Spring Elementary in 2001. Under her leadership, students made significant increases on the grade 3 and grade 5 SOL tests. Pine Spring, which is a school-wide Title I school, is fully accredited and is meeting the achievement objectives of the federal No Child Left Behind Act. In 2004, Ms. Tyler was selected to receive the Milken National Educator's Award. Criteria for selection include exceptional educational talent via instructional practices in the classroom, school and profession; outstanding accomplishments and long-range potential for professional and policy leadership; and an inspiring presence that motivates students, colleagues and the community.

Pine Spring Elementary received the Distinguished Title I School award in 2006. Shortly after receiving this award, Ms. Tyler was appointed principal of the under-construction Eagle View Elementary. Ms. Tyler oversaw the construction, facilities, staffing and instructional programs for the county's newest elementary school.

Chapter Nine

All Together Now! What's Special About Special Education

Sheri Maeda

Disney American Teacher Honoree in Team Teaching, NBCT

The highest result of education is tolerance.
—Helen Keller "Optimism," 1903

Even after 30 years of teaching, the first two weeks of school for me are a blurry parade of unfamiliar faces, names, voices, and, now, of special needs. A teacher's basic responsibilities include the academic progress, social development, and emotional well-being of students. We must also become familiar with a range of physical, emotional, and learning needs; collaborate with parents, psychologists, guidance counselors, learning resource teachers, physical,- occupational,- and speech therapists; and figure out what instructional and interactive strategies best support the learning and achievement of students with special needs. It's easy to be overwhelmed. Hard to believe, but there was a time within the span of my teaching career when special needs were not identified, when teachers were on their own in teaching students who learned differently. But now, that is not the case as the teacher log below shows.

Teacher Log, Second Week of School
Monday: Planning Period. Meeting to review IEP for a student with severe macular degeneration.
Tuesday: Before School. Conference with parents concerned about support for a student who suffered a sudden and

devastating personal loss during the summer.

Wednesday: Lunch. Meeting with the school nurse for all teachers of students with diabetes; administration of insulin injections to be demonstrated and practiced.

Thursday: After School. Meeting to review a 504 Plan for a student with Attention Deficit Hyperactivity Disorder (ADHD).

Friday: Planning Period. Meeting with learning resource teacher for all teachers of students with autism.

So what can you do? How can you best interact with so many other professionals, some of whom might have very different perspectives? How can you make your way through the briar patch of information you are expected to know about your responsibilities under the laws and regulations governing special education? And perhaps most importantly, how can you best serve your students with special needs?

Ask for as Much Information and Background on your Students with Special Needs as You Can

The information or accommodations written in the Individualized Education Program (IEP) or 504 Plan are there to ensure access to education; they do not tell you about the student's home life, successful past learning experiences, or how best to teach the content of your curriculum. Moreover, many of these details are not written anywhere. You have to know to seek them out. The first time I encountered a student with Asperger's Syndrome, a high-functioning form of autism, I found that "Kyle" had particular difficulty with writing assignments demanding revision. If he wrote anything at all, he would make no changes to it. He was mostly noncommunicative, although he had a group of peers in the class who were friendly and engaged him as much as he chose to be.

The learning resource teacher provided me with general information about Asperger's that helped to place Kyle's learning within a

I've known Sheri Maeda for almost all of her thirty-one-year teaching career. She has stimulated my thinking about teaching and learning, shown me new ways to approach literature, and inspired me to be more creative with my classes. Sheri is always probing, thinking, trying to figure out why students do what they do, wondering how to make something work just a little better. She thinks broadly about lesson design, but she also thinks carefully about individual students. Sheri has always invited other teachers to think with her about teaching and learning. She writes about teaching, and she teaches other teachers, participating in and leading summer institutes for teachers. An English teacher, Sheri has worked closely with many biology, technology, and especially social studies teaching teammates over the years. As a department chair, she designed staff development opportunities that fostered sharing, collaboration, and discussion. Through her years of thinking and talking about teaching, Sheri has developed a classroom that is active and student-centered. She understands how to help students learn the same material in different ways, and she is always generous in sharing her ideas with other teachers.

—Roger Green, National Board Certified English Teacher, Thomas Jefferson High School for Science and Technology, and Fellow, National Writing Project

wider framework, but it was the specific background that she gave me in response to my informal inquiries that was most informative. What was it like, to work one-on-one with him? What classes did he enjoy? In which subjects did he do well? How involved were his parents/guardians in his school progress? What approaches had worked well, and what had failed? Thanks to the details I gathered from a series of informal conversations, I learned when to gently but firmly insist that certain assignments be handed in and when to fall back, letting him make his own decisions. I also made sure to structure assignments with elements in which he could successfully participate, if not excel, such as information-gathering and retrieval and web site design. I was surprised and gratified when Kyle returned before he graduated to say goodbye and say that he had enjoyed the class.

The following year another student with Asperger's was assigned to me. The descriptive material I received on "Aaron" was nearly identical to the packet I'd received on Kyle, but like any two individuals, they were very different. The strategies that had worked with one did not necessarily work with the other. Again, the background story and impressions shared by the resource teacher were most valuable in determining how to work best with Aaron. Where Kyle rarely communicated directly with me, Aaron could be his own best advocate.

Early in the year, he told me that he had to see instructions and assignment descriptions written down. "I can't remember them if you just tell them to me." I agreed that, in addition to writing everything on the board, I would be sure to post my assignments, instructions, and grading rubrics online. As it turned out, Aaron's self-advocacy helped many other students who were more visually oriented; they all benefited from having the class materials available to them online.

Learning resource teachers, therapists, and other specialists work intensively with students identified with special needs. Some are itinerants and must travel among a number of schools to meet with the students assigned to them. Those who remain at a single school may not have specific planning periods assigned to them. Whenever I had a question or concern, I would begin with e-mail or written notes, scheduling face-to-face meetings when necessary. I found that each specialist willingly provided me with useful feedback, information, or suggestions whenever I requested it, and they did whatever was possible to support the student's achievement in my class.

Listen Carefully to Everyone Who Has Something to Say about the Student

Having just one student with special needs in a class introduces regular, intensive interactions with many more adults: parent(s) or guardian(s), guidance counselor, administrator, resource teacher and/or specialist. Since each of these individuals brings his or her perceptions, expectations, and background of experiences to any meeting or communication, each provides a puzzle piece that can contribute to a better understanding of the student.

After a sudden, startling outburst, a student with an emotional disability couldn't articulate what had set her off. After speaking with her guidance counselor, my teaching partner and I learned that none of us had much knowledge of this student's history, since she was new to the school. Together, we sought her resource teacher, who described circumstances in which she had observed "Susie's" outbursts of angry frustration. Speaking with her parents provided us with a sense of her emotional life at home. Teachers who had taught her previously gave us impressions of her behavior in certain classroom situations. The information we collected helped her counselor, my teaching partner, and me to determine how best to structure and define Susie's assignments and activities in our class.

When Asked to Share Your Thoughts about a Student, Speak and Write from Observation

This cardinal rule of teaching and writing applies a hundred-fold in special education. Specifically describe only what you have observed because descriptions of concrete behavior give you common ground for basing your discussions about a student. I've often received e-mails or phone messages from parents who are distraught at their students' low grades. I recall one in particular. A parent expressed shock and some anger at my teaching partner and myself, since "Jessie" had always been a good writer and passionately interested in humanities." Our response was concerned, measured, and exclusively factual: Jessie's work was consistently late; her quiz scores were low; she shrugged off our offers of assistance; she tended to be absent on test or presentation days; she fell soundly asleep in the middle of class, even when engaged in an interactive activity with other students. We asked if they could help us to understand how we could help Jessie to succeed.

Their next message was very different from their original one, and it provided us with helpful insight about Jessie's moods and behavior. The family had experienced the loss of Jessie's only sibling less than a year before, and Jessie was deeply grieving that loss. Jessie was not sleeping at night, and she tended to stay up late because she had difficulty concentrating on her homework. She insisted that her parents not notify the school about her situation, and regretfully they had complied. The behaviors we had observed at school were being acted out at home. As sad as we were to learn of this family's situation, knowing this background gave us the means to work better with Jessie and address her behaviors as a product of her grief. Slowly, hesitantly, Jessie recovered her energy and enjoyment of life, participating more actively in the class. Her story illustrates how often we do not know what we're seeing. Jessie's situation also shows that sometimes a student doesn't have to be identified with special needs to need special attention, at least for a little while. The key is to observe. As we say in writing instruction, "Show, don't tell."

Take Nothing Personally, or It's All About the Student

Often, other teachers try to be helpful by telling "war stories" about confrontational parents or ineffectual counselors and administrators. These tales of horror can only increase your level of stress and mistrust. In the face of such negative myth-building, remember that, like you, everyone is trying to do his or her best. It's just that sometimes we bump each other along the way.

"As a teacher, I try to remember the frustration I had as a parent of a kid with special needs," says Jamie-Ellen Spessard, elementary teacher in Goochland County, Virginia. At best, parenting a child with special needs means reams of paperwork, multiple visits to specialists, and hours of communication with school system offices. "A lot of the time, I'd come in to a parent-teacher conference seemingly angry with the teacher. But I wasn't angry with her, I was actually frustrated with a school system I couldn't figure out."

Each member of a student's special education team has a common goal: to provide the student with the appropriate access and skills to learn. Try to establish rapport because you're part of that team of people who want to ensure the student's success. Sarie Feld, a retired pediatric physical therapist, describes the teacher-therapist relationship most supportive for the student as one where a teacher

Philip Bigler

Sheri Maeda evaluates student projects during a simulation on immigration at Thomas Jefferson High School for Science and Technology.

"sees how we can work together or is interested in learning how we can work together to facilitate a student's progress." Indeed, collaborating with other adults with the success of a student as a common goal has provided me with challenging, ongoing professional development.

Be Flexible and Use All the Resources Available

The teacher-centered model doesn't work in our diverse classrooms today, and it does us a disservice by ignoring the skills our students will need in a future of rapid change, technological development, and economic uncertainty. To successfully work in the twenty-first century, our students will have to solve problems independently, communicate clearly with a variety of others, and collaborate productively with small and large teams of people. Such skills must be taught and practiced in school if our young people are to be fully prepared to meet the challenges of this new century. The increasing numbers of students identified with special needs in our classrooms gives us another reason to reevaluate and revise our teaching practices. If we are to reach and engage all of our students, flexibility and differentiation hold the keys.

One word best describes a student-centered and differentiated classroom: Busy. Individuals know what they are responsible for doing, whether they're by themselves or in a group. Students confer with each other or seek information from print, electronic, or human resources. From day to day, the room is configured differently to match and support the activities taking place: Theater seating for guest speakers or presentations, large circle for class meetings or seminar discussions, small clusters for peer writing revision or focused discussion groups.

Within such a classroom, it's difficult to immediately identify those students with special needs since each student works to complete a part of a complex task that will ultimately contribute to the learning of the whole group. Jan Vallone, an Advanced Placement (A.P.) U.S. history teacher and my American humanities partner, and I developed an ongoing project for our students that required small groups to work together to produce online chapter summaries of the history text. The chapter reviews were due for uploading when we studied the material in class, and they were available to our students before unit tests and the A.P. U.S. history examination in early May. The project demanded that group members read and synthesize the content of their chapter, develop a way to visually present the most important concepts and facts, and transfer their product to an online format. Jan and I noticed that the project design allowed our students with special needs to contribute fully. One student with an emotional disability, who had difficulty with personal interactions, could work on his own and e-mail his section to the other members. Another student with Asperger's syndrome contributed his factual mastery and computer skills. Along the way, these students' peers learned to work productively with them and appreciate their talents as well.

An unexpected benefit of designing a differentiated classroom was that Jan and I had the chance to observe more authentic student behaviors. Instead of reporting exclusively on a student's ability to sit through a lecture or presentation, student-centered activities enabled us to witness and describe complex patterns of interactive and independent behaviors. Student-centered activities also supported the development of a variety of skills, such as visual design, planning, and organization; task delegation; and synthesis of information. As a result, we, in turn, learned more about all of our students, both as individual learners and as teammates.

Having a student with special needs assigned to your classroom gives you the opportunity to become a learner. When encountering situations that are unfamiliar, don't be afraid to say you don't know, ask for some time to determine an informed course of action, or brainstorm best approaches with any or all of the special education specialists who serve your school and students. "Mark," a student who was eventually identified as having a severe case of dysgraphia, grew increasingly frustrated in my English class whenever I asked students to write spontaneously. When he refused to write at all, I first thought that he was experiencing writer's block. I wondered if Mark just didn't want to write. He complained persistently about his frustrations, but without a clear idea of what was wrong, I felt helpless and admitted as much to him. I asked the school's learning specialist to intervene. With her assistance and that of his parents, Mark's learning needs were identified, and I could take concrete steps to assist him.

While he had great difficulty with the coding process of putting pen to paper, he had no difficulty using a keyboard, but I taught Mark before computers were widely available in classrooms. For a lengthy writing like an essay test, I would schedule the entire class into a computer lab so that everyone could word-process their work. When I couldn't schedule the class, I would arrange for Mark to meet the learning specialist in the lab or even in the office of a generous school administrator. For short, spontaneous pieces, I arranged with the guidance department to send a student assistant who would transcribe Mark's thoughts as he verbalized them; often, I would transcribe. Classmates took turns taking class notes on carbonless copy paper. While all of these solutions were the best we could offer at the time, they were cumbersome and singled Mark out as different and dependent. In the years after he left my 9th grade classroom, his parents gave him one of the earliest versions of a laptop computer, which he took everywhere. Mark proudly showed it to me and declared, "Look! I can write on my own!"

Especially in the areas of assessment and assignment development for students with special needs, I learned to take into account everything I'd learned from others and from my observations of and feedback from, the students and their classmates. Working with teaching partners gave the bonus of additional perspectives on what was observed and how to adjust our practices to meet the different needs of our students. Whether I worked with teaching partners or not, I found that all my assignments could be structured to both stretch students and encourage them to exercise their strengths. Similarly, when determining standards for assessment, I could adjust for reasonable, attainable, yet challenging benchmarks for students with special needs.

Some of the most successful adjustments to my assignments have been suggested and implemented by students. A student diagnosed with Frederick's ataxia, a rare, degenerative neurological condition, and another with macular degeneration, the deterioration of the retina that is rare in young people, were able to participate fully in every aspect of the class as a result of revisions made by the students themselves along with their classmates. In dramatic performances, for example, all of the students in their play groups together worked out the staging so that one played Benvolio in *Romeo and Juliet* and the other played Creon in *Antigone* because each, according to their group members, was the "best one for the part."

The impetus for rethinking my evaluation practices with students with special needs often has come from students. In the process of completing an intensive and long-term group project, the students working with "Henry," a student identified with an emotional disability, approached Jan, my teaching partner and me. Their list of grievances revolved around Henry's inability to communicate with them. The more they pushed him for his part of the work, the more he retreated into himself. Two days before a deadline, two group members hastily completed Henry's part; another stayed up all night integrating the last-minute material into the project. They were angry and frustrated. Our meeting with Henry was just as difficult. He, too, was angry and frustrated, but he was unable to help us understand how his group could better communicate with him or what could be done to ensure that he handed in his part of the work. Jan and I agonized over a course of action.

We consulted Henry's learning resource teacher, who advised us that he had had similar difficulties in other classes. She also emphasized that if we could alert her to the topics for which Henry would be responsible, she could try to assist him by helping him to schedule and write up his independent research. We wanted to be fair to all of the students involved, and we wanted to be sure that our accommodations appropriately challenged all of them. Jan and I decided that, given the nature of the project, we would assess Henry's work separately from that of the group. We hoped that the change in assessment policy would help Henry to practice responsibility for himself and that it would remove the pressure and resentment felt by the other group members when he didn't follow through. Henry continued to participate in the group's meetings, and volunteered to do his share of the research each quarter. We made clear to the other group members that, when we graded their project work, any omissions of the material Henry had agreed to complete would not be counted against them.

While Henry was not able to contribute any written research to the project, he did make significant progress in the oral presentation component of the assignment. He became increasingly comfortable speaking in front of the class on his topics. At the group's final presentation of the year, Henry dressed in a suit and took the podium to discuss the causes of the Great Depression in America. His team mates applauded and encouraged him that day. It was one of the few times we saw him smile.

Consider the Alternative

Thirty-four years ago as a second-year teacher, I taught a student who profoundly expanded my perspective on all of my students since that time. At first I thought "Jason" simply did not like senior English. He bombed the reading quizzes I gave to check student reading. He rarely handed in a writing assignment and, politely but doggedly, refused to participate in class discussions. I inquired of teachers who had taught him previously. They told me little more than that he was, to put it politely, "an underachiever."

One late winter morning, the class read aloud Robert Frost's "Nothing Gold Can Stay." For the first time all year, Jason raised his hand and spoke hesitantly but eloquently about the impossible coexistence of perfection and time. I was ecstatic and perplexed. After class I asked him how someone who could so incisively interpret a poem would not hand in his work or complete his reading for class.

"I have dyslexia," he replied. Over the next weeks, he had to educate me about what was then a mysterious condition that caused him to see letters backwards or upside-down. Jason's revelation began a period of trial-and-error on my part to bring him more fully into the class. His girlfriend agreed to read short stories or essays to him. I sought assistance from the school librarian to obtain audio versions of full-length works, and he used a tape recorder to compose written pieces. All of these strategies worked to varying degrees, and during the second semester of his senior year, Jason made remarkable progress.

Yet the process was isolating, in that no colleague could provide any more information or feedback than I got from him. His guidance counselor was aware that Jason's parents had taken him to be tested, but had no understanding of dyslexia or how to work with it. There were no resources readily available for an inexperienced teacher trying to manage the learning of 149 other students as well. That year I had a tiny glimpse into what life at school must have been for this intelligent student who didn't decode written symbols in the same way as the rest of us. To this day I regret the years he must have lost as a result of unwitting, but systemwide, marginalization and ignorance.

Too late for Jason, but not for the countless students since identified with special needs, the Rehabilitation Act of 1973, the Individuals with Disabilities Educational Improvement Act (IDEA) of 1975, and the Americans with Disabilities Act (ADA) of 1990 have completely changed our educational landscape. Identification of students with special needs has improved. As public facilities, schools have had to ensure reasonable access to those with disabilities. IEPs and 504 Plans ensure that students with special needs receive necessary educational services to support their learning. Professionals like occupational or physical therapists, speech or hearing specialists, and learning resource teachers work directly with students while acting as resources to classroom teachers.

More recently, I've taught students identified with a variety of learning disabilities including ADD, ADHD, dyslexia, dysgraphia, and Asperger's syndrome; as well as those with medical diagnoses such as lymphoma, diabetes, and Frederick's ataxia. While my calendar of meetings and e-mail exchanges with parents, resource teachers, and therapists has expanded, I've not missed the gnawing anxiety in isolation that accompanies either not knowing what's causing a student to flounder or not knowing how to help a student succeed.

Not long ago, I watched as my former student with Frederick's ataxia graduated from the high school where I'd taught him. As his class and the faculty spontaneously rose to give him a standing ovation, I felt the satisfaction of having been part of a large network of people who had supported his high school journey. Yet, isn't this true of all the students we teach?

Upon reflection, I see that I've been the beneficiary of some profound lessons arising out of the increasing integration of special education in the general classroom. To begin with, I've been inspired and challenged by the courage of each student with special needs whom I have taught.

Teaching students with special needs has given me the opportunity to sharpen my professional skills and develop new ones. I've had to problem-solve the most effective instructional and interactive teaching strategies just as I expect my students to ask and answer their own questions as they learn.

Finally, by collaborating with other professionals in assisting students in the face of daunting challenges, I've had the privilege to be part of a community of people dedicated to learning. What a powerful educational model, where all participants learn together and teach each other from their expertise and strengths.

Marilyn Schoon

Humanities teacher, Sheri Maeda, is recognized as a 2000 Disney Teacher Award Honoree.

About the Author:

Sheri Maeda, with Philip Bigler, was a 2000 Disney American Teacher Honoree for Team Teaching. National Board Certified in Language Arts, she taught English and humanities for 30 years in Fairfax County, Virginia, 21 of which were spent at Thomas Jefferson H.S. for Science and Technology. She is a Fellow of the National Writing Project and has worked closely with the John F. Kennedy Center for the Performing Arts, the Corcoran Gallery of Art, the National Museum of American Art, and the Folger Shakespeare Library on programs integrating fine and performing arts in the classroom.

Chapter Ten

How Do You Spell Success— "S-U-C-C-E-S-S"

Charla Faulkner Crews

2000 Milken National Educator

There is a place in America to take a stand: it is public education. It is the underpinning of our cultural and political system. It is the great common ground. Public education after all is the engine that moves us as a society toward a common destiny . . . It is in public education that the American dream begins to take shape. —Tom Brokaw

One of my best friends in school was a cheerleader, which meant I also knew all of the cheers. Even now, when one of my current students asks me how to spell success, an instinctive response is triggered that even the renowned Russian psychologist, Ivan Pavlov, would take notice. What is the response?

> "S-U-C-C-E-S-S
> That's the way you spell success
> S-U-C-C-E-S-S
> That's the way you spell success!"

The phrase must be repeated, and I have to fight an irresistible urge to display the accompanying hand movements.

When you finally earn a degree in education and become a licensed teacher, you automatically gain the ability to create a mysterious, special language filled with acronyms. In your career as an educator, S-U-C-C-E-S-S. as an acronym will work for you.

Give Me an S! (S for Students)

As a senior majoring in education at Norfolk State University in 1982, I was required to write my own personal philosophy of education. Several years later, I understood the importance of this requirement, given that it forced me to determine the foundation for my beliefs as a classroom teacher. The task was challenging because amidst all the educational jargon I encountered, I discovered that what really was important was the students. Now, after many years in education, many reflective moments, and many experiences, the fundamental foundation of my beliefs continues to be where it should, and that is with the children.

What an awesome opportunity we have as educators to impact the future. It is awe-inspiring to realize that the very children you teach today may grow up to be the nation's bankers and businessmen, nurses and doctors, and politicians and civic leaders. It is incumbent upon us to enter our classrooms each day believing every child who has been placed in our trust by their parents has the potential to become someone great. There will be times when it is hard to believe in some children, but those are the times when we must believe even more.

Several years ago, "Joe" was in my third grade class. He was a struggling student and often had days when his behavior got the best of him. Although I had many conferences with his parents, we didn't always agree on how best to meet Joe's needs. His parents were caught in a continuous cycle of blaming Joe's teachers for all of his problems, rather than actually exploring ways to advance his emotional and academic growth. Joe and I slowly began developing a positive rapport, and we both understood that I had to contact his parents whenever he misbehaved in class or didn't do his schoolwork. Sometimes it seemed as if we were at a standoff. Joe wouldn't do his part so I would contact his parents. Different discipline strategies would work for two or three weeks, and Joe's grades and behavior would temporarily improve. He would work diligently until something or someone would set him off again, and the cycle of conse-

I have known Charla Crews for many years but learned first-hand about her dedication to education when my son, Ethan, was in her fourth grade class at Meadville Elementary School. Ms. Crews nurtured my son's naturally inquisitive nature that his teachers in the past dismissed as 'lack of focus.' She told me that Ethan was very smart with a great gift that would serve him well in life. What we needed to do was help control his natural curiosity, not destroy it.

Ms. Crews had an idea for Ethan. She initiated a 'parking lot' for his observations during class. The parking lot consisted of a sticky pad and a board. Ethan would jot down his questions or comments and post them on the board as they occurred to him, and when the lesson was complete, she would go over the questions with him.

Throughout Ethan's fourth grade year, he was able to keep his focus on the main objectives by 'parking' his observations for a short while. It was great for his self-esteem to know that someone was interested in his ideas. A simple idea from a great teacher made a significant impact on Ethan. For my child, Charla Crews made an impression that will stay with him for years to come.

—Mary Jane Collie

quences would begin anew.

This particular year, we had a holiday party just before winter break. No matter how much you tell a child and parent that teachers don't expect gifts, some students will still bring tokens of appreciation during the holidays. Others desperately desire to give their teacher a gift but can't afford it. When some students would confide in me that they wanted to give me a present but weren't able to, I would smile and always reassure them by saying, "You can give a gift that doesn't cost one penny. Give me your good manners and good behavior."

At the class party, one of the many exotic delicacies was individually wrapped marshmallow rice treats. Joe became so excited because this was his all-time favorite snack, and he couldn't wait to get one. He was in the middle of one of his rougher weeks, but he told me he wanted to give me a gift. I gave him my usual "no gift" reply and he smiled and said, "Okay." Finally, when the marshmallow treats were distributed, all of the children were eating and enjoying a good time. As the students were lining up to leave for their much anticipated two-week vacation, Joe asked if he could speak to me privately outside. He looked up at me and handed me a very special gift—his own marshmallow rice treat. He very quietly said, "Thank you," and gave me a quick hug before running outside to his school bus.

Joe's cycles continued after this but I continued working on strategies with his parents and him to improve his behavior. Toward the end of that year, his positive cycles were lasting longer and his parents consented to a special education evaluation. Today, Joe is having success in high school and receiving important special education services, and I often see him and his parents in our community. Personally, I will always cherish the memory of that individually wrapped marshmallow rice treat and from him I learned that every student has potential. It is our task as teachers to provide occasions for that potential to be revealed and we must remember that our work is all about the students.

Give Me a U! (U for Utilize Resources)

As educators, we are privy to many opportunities and resources. Scores of teachers fail to understand that they don't have to reinvent the wheel every year, but rather just use it to its full potential. Acquiring appropriate classroom materials can be expensive and the reality is that annual school budgets do not cover everything for effective instruction. In truth, most teachers will spend their own hard-earned money to ensure that they are able to provide a quality education for their students. Donna Winchester, staff writer for the *St. Petersburg Times* Online, cites the following statistics based on a poll of teachers in two Florida counties in a recent article entitled, "Many Teachers Buy Supplies for Students."[35]

- Forty-five percent spend $100 to $500 a year on items for which they are not reimbursed.
- An additional 28 percent say they spend $500 to $1,000.
- One out of every five teachers reports spending $1,000 or more.
- Newer teachers, the ones who make the least—often spend the most.

These statistics are not the exception but the norm in our schools. Therefore, it behooves every teacher to maximize existing resources and to take advantage of other opportunities to improve instruction. There are several ways that may assist in locating and making the most of available resources.

- Ask the Parents: When developing classroom projects and activities it is important to keep the parent informed. Generally, parents are more than happy to send additional materials to school for special projects, especially if they already have such supplies at home or they can purchase these items conveniently when buying groceries during their routine shopping excursions.
- Search the Web: There are numerous resources for teachers available on the Internet. Every teacher should set aside a few minutes of every week to search for new, free or inexpensive online materials. Moreover, there are many grant opportunities that reward teachers for their innovative thinking and their willingness to try researched-based strategies.
- Utilize federal, state, and local education agencies: The U.S. Department of Education (www.ed.gov) has an entire section on its website devoted to classroom teachers. There is a wealth of information available including teaching materials, staff development opportunities, and other resources. Your state department of education and your local school district will, likewise, have outstanding materials available.
- Your Community as a Resource: Most people are excited to provide classroom materials, if they are convinced that they are directly benefiting children. Others may know how to obtain additional support from the community, but it is always important to check with your building administrator about your school system's individual guidelines for procuring donations in advance.

Over the years I have had the opportunity to work with many teachers whose projects were successful because of the collaboration among parents, students, and fellow faculty members. It is through creatively utilizing all available resources that you will ultimately be able to provide engaging and creative educational experiences for your students.

Give Me a C! (C for Colleagues and Commitment)

During the last decade, there was an increased demand for accountability and accreditation of the nation's public schools. This created a new awareness and a sense of urgency in many schools and divisions throughout Virginia. Teachers were no longer passive entities who had policies and mandates thrust upon them, but were now included in the decision-making process, and often expected to lead the way towards improving our schools.

Teachers underwent professional development and had to learn a new vocabulary including such words as goals, expectations, standards, stakeholders, continuous improvement, and quality assurance. Our fellow teachers were no longer isolated, but rather became true collaborative colleagues. One positive result of the makeover was that many teachers, who once thought of themselves as "only teachers," learned to see themselves as members of a true profession. They began to conduct themselves accordingly and began to see their fellow "colleagues" to include all of those who worked in the school for the benefit of children. We would not be able to teach, and the students would not be able to learn, without those other crucial partners including the bus drivers, custodians, cafeteria workers, and office personnel.

A true sense of professional bonding can only occur when we work together as a team to provide quality educational experiences for all of our students. We, likewise, share a resolve to work through those inevitable situations that threaten our ability to provide a quality education. This takes time, commitment, and change in order to create a strong tie between diverse people. Bonding is a continual process and requires dedication from veteran teachers, administrators, and novice educators, alike. Paramount to this process is an understanding that each must be committed to doing what is best for students.

Hard work and effort are needed to grow strong, positive working relationships with colleagues. As singer and songwriter, John Mayer, said, "Life is like a box of crayons. Most people are the 8-color boxes, but what you're really looking for are the 64-color boxes with the sharpeners on the back." I have been fortunate because most of the professional educators I have had the pleasure to learn from and work with have all been those "64-boxes with the sharpeners on the back." I have encountered some educators, though, who have failed in their careers. Still, I want for every child in our schools, a teacher that is committed and dedicated. The best advice I can give to new teachers is to seek out the best in your field and learn from them.

Our commitment manifests itself by constantly reminding us that children are at the center of everything we do. A teacher is forced to make decisions everyday that will have a profound influence on the lives of his or her students for years to come. The old adage, "to teach is to touch lives forever," is a breathtaking responsibility. It is incumbent upon us to center everything we do on the children.

Self-discipline is a vital component of the commitment equation. A little known secret is that self-discipline is just as important in being a successful educator as it is in being a successful student. A teacher must practice self-discipline in order to meet all of the deadlines assigned by administrators and expected by parents and students. One of the worst feelings is to have a child look at you and ask, "Have you graded my test yet?" The guilt is worse when a student asks that question several days after the exam and their work still hasn't been graded. Students need immediate feedback while a task is still important to them to learn and grow and it is the teacher's responsibility to provide that in a timely manner.

In order to be the best teacher possible, it is essential that we first take care of ourselves in order to take proper care of our students. Commitment to self-discipline is required in our personal lives. Countless teachers stay up late at night grading papers and creating lesson plans which only makes them tired and irritable the next day. A lack of proper rest will eventually take its toll, as will lack of exercise and poor nutrition.

Self-discipline also requires restraint. Good teachers only conduct professional and constructive conversations within the confines of the teacher's lounge. As a professional, it is vital to know how, when, and where to comment and it sometimes takes a great deal of self-discipline to stay silent when you merely want to vent your frustrations.

On Wednesday, October 4, 2000 the Milken Family Foundation Award was presented to me at Meadville Elementary School. After the surprise announcement, I received countless well wishes from colleagues, friends, and relatives. One of the most memorable ones came from my mentor, Mrs. Irene Peters.

I had been teaching for several years prior to moving to Meadville where I received my award. Mrs. Peters was a well-respected, veteran teacher who taught next door to me. As we worked together for the next few years, she became my own personal mentor. She was never paid for helping me or given any prestigious teaching award. In fact, her contribution to education was never properly or sufficiently recognized. She had retired and was in the hospital on the day I received the Milken award, but I went to see her shortly after the official announcement. I wanted to talk about other things, but she wanted to make sure that I knew how proud she was of me and my accomplishments. Each and every day that I teach, I still use a bit of what I learned from her. She helped me with the usual types of things that most mentors do, but I am blessed that she helped me to realize some more important things as well. She taught me the value and honor of being a teacher. She also said that I should cherish every opportunity I am given to be a part of my students' lives.

Our colleagues influence our professional lives in countless ways, and I am forever thankful that I was able to share my special moment with Mrs. Peters shortly before she passed away. I am eternally thankful that I was her friend and colleague. She helped define my teaching style and mold my professional reputation. Indeed, she was one of those 64-color box people that you should seek out.

Charla Crews working with division staff in the computer lab on technology integration.

Give Me Another C! (C for Collaborate)

For many years, education was a lonely, isolated profession. Teachers were with their students all day. Planning time was as equally isolated because of scheduling and other assigned duties. There were times when teachers only saw each other in the parking lot or the lounge and had little opportunity for adult one-on-one conversation or collaboration. Thankfully, times have changed and educators have discovered how vital it is to collaborate during an age of increased accountability. Schools now expect teachers to work together to maximize time and resources as well as to benefit from the wisdom of others.

Collaboration is actually just an adult form of a routine teaching strategy we use all the time with our students—cooperative learning. Today, there are many opportunities for teachers to collaborate in small teams. Just like in the classroom, our schools have educators who bring varying talents and skills to the table. Each member of a cooperative learning group has a responsibility. The goal is for each member of a collaborative team to fulfill a specific responsibility and maximize the benefits from this professional collaboration. It is important for teachers to remember:

- We too have a lot to learn from one another.
- We all have a stake in the quality of education in our schools.
- We are all working to attain the same common goal, the best education for our children.

Teacher collaboration is a win-win situation because it enables us to work better and smarter while eliminating the self-imposed isolation of the past.

I love my current position as one of four instructional technology specialists in the Halifax County Public Schools. Part of my job is creating innovative resources for teachers to use based on areas of specific need as determined by state and local test data. Last year, we were privileged to work with teachers from all over the division in various capacities as they related to instructional technology.

Our office has collaboratively worked with various schools and the students to document their work. In each situation the students and teachers were able to celebrate a project that was completed through true collaboration. While it is true that one educator can provide a good education for a few students, true collaboration allows for a great education to be provided for many more students.

Give Me an E! (E for Education)

As committed educators, we must continue to learn throughout our lives. Our contemporary students have grown up wholly in a digital world. They are accustomed to being entertained, receiving instant gratification, and knowing things about computers that many of their current teachers could never have comprehended. The students' wealth of knowledge and involvement in the information age must be respected and teachers must give their students opportunities to express themselves using the modern tools with which they are familiar.

In order to meet our students' diverse needs, we must be knowledgeable of the current trends and technology. It is imperative to stay
informed and to upgrade our skills and knowledge, even with the
very real constraints placed on an educator's time.

Gaining such knowledge does not have to be in a traditional college classroom setting. Now, online classes are routinely available and
professional organizations provide numerous online resources.
Educational websites provide for learning about new strategies and
techniques while web pages and "blogs" allow us to exchange freely
ideas and information with educators from all over the world.

Likewise, there are numerous professional development opportunities which allow us to improve our teaching methods.
Traditionally, the overall goal of education was to help prepare students for either college or the work force. This goal remains the same
today, but different factors have been added to the formula for how
best to succeed. Students of the past generally competed for jobs and
employment opportunities with others from nearby areas, while our
contemporary students are actually competing on a global basis. In
his remarkable book, *The World is Flat,* author Thomas Friedman
argues that to be successful in this global culture, "it...take[s] the
right imagination and the right motivation... [that this is a] generation of strategic optimists, the generation with more dreams than
memories, the generation that wakes up each morning and not only
imagines that things can be better but also acts on that imagination
every day."[37] Indeed, they must be able to communicate and collaborate with people of varying cultures, and it is our job to prepare
them for this reality. We can only do this if we, as educators, operate
on a more global level so that our children will be successful in this
exciting new future.

I started my teaching career years ago as a long-term substitute
on Chincoteague Island, Virginia. Because of where we lived on the
Atlantic Ocean, the first grade students were knowledgeable about
ducks, and our region had become somewhat famous because of the
hand carved wooden decoys made by many of their families. They
also knew about the famous wild ponies of Assateague. Each year

there was a "Pony Swim," made famous in the novel *Misty of Chincoteague* by Marguerite Henry.[38] My own hometown, South Boston, Virginia, was much different. It was in the heart of tobacco country. Fields upon fields of tobacco could be seen when riding down major highways, and the smell of cured tobacco could be smelled all over town in the late summer months. My first grade students and I talked about the places we loved so dearly, our hometowns. They learned about my culture and ancestral roots, and I eagerly learned about theirs. Was this global education? Well, not quite, but it was an important learning experience that helped me to understand and embrace the need for students to be knowledgeable and appreciative of different cultures. To be an effective educator, you must be a lifelong, global learner.

Give Me a Double S! (SS for Safety & Structure)

Psychologist Abraham Maslow has described safety as one of the most important human needs. All children need structure; some, more than others. Structure helps provide both security and safety; and students learn what to expect. Teachers need structure, too, because it provides similar benefits.

As a classroom teacher, it is crucial to provide a safe and welcoming environment for our students. Classrooms should be arranged in a way as to create a natural flow so that students can move about freely without tripping over each other and they need to keep their bulging bookbags safely out of the aisles to prevent injury. We can also implement several simple practices to ensure physical safety in the classroom. However, there are other considerations in creating a safe environment.

In our schools, you will have students from a variety of circumstances. Some will come from rural homes, others from the city; you will have children from traditional two-parent households and those raised by relatives; you will teach students who aspire to go to college while some will graduate from high school and go to work. Despite such diversity, they all come to us wanting and needing organization and security. They all have the same need for this structure. Children need to know that, regardless of what goes on in their own personal world, their classroom will be a stable, caring, and safe place day after day. It becomes their comfort zone and sanctuary. Our students will soon know that through our positive classroom management that they are, at least for awhile, safe from emotional stress.

Good teachers are aware of the other needs that their students may have. Many children come to school without having anything to eat in the morning. Contrary to popular belief, these students don't come only from low-income homes. There is a staggering number of children who rely on their school lunch for their one complete meal of the day.

My mother-in-law was the cafeteria manager for over twenty years at Meadville Elementary School where I taught. During her career, she fed many generations of students. She had an uncanny ability to remember what most of the children liked and didn't like. She made school meals an adventure and exciting activity. When we celebrated Dr. Seuss's birthday, she put green food coloring in the eggs to the delight of the kids. During the time of critical state testing, she would make sure that everyone had a nutritious breakfast, but most importantly, the students knew she cared for them.

One morning however, my students came to class from breakfast quite upset. They were whispering to each other and wouldn't quiet down, so I finally asked what had happened that seemed to have traumatized them. They knew the cafeteria manager was my mother-in-law, so there was some initial hesitation. Finally, one of the children confided: "Mrs. Crews, you have to check on what your mother-in-law is doing in the cafeteria." "What's wrong?" I inquired. "I don't know, but you need to see what is wrong with her." Alarmed, I hurried to the door and desperately looked for someone to cover my class. I again asked the children to tell me why they thought something was so wrong. "She gave us stale doughnuts," one of them volunteered. "She didn't even put the glaze on them. She gave us the glaze in a little cup." I quickly looked at the breakfast menu for the day, and it was all I could do to keep from laughing. The children's routine and stability had been suddenly interrupted by the fact that my mother-in-law had served them bagels with cream cheese. From this incident, I became even more convinced that our students need structure and safety and teachers need it too.

Put it together, and what does it spell? It spells Success!

As a veteran educator, I applaud your commitment to teach. I hope that you will use some of this advice during your own personal journey in education. You, too, can be creating your own cheers and definitions for success. Feel free to shout it out and share it with your colleagues.

Author's Personal Collection

Milken Educator, Charla Crews, working with students in Halifax County, Virginia.

About the Author:
Charla Crews, a product of the Virginia Public School System, has served as a classroom teacher, instructional and technology lead teacher, and program coordinator. She is currently the Language Arts Instructional Technology Specialist for Halifax County Schools in Halifax County, Virginia. Charla earned her Bachelor of Science degree in Early Childhood Education from Norfolk State University. She earned her Master's degree in Curriculum and Instruction/LD, and licensure in Administration and Supervision from Longwood College. She is a 2000 recipient of the Milken Educator Award, a 2001 recipient of the Virginia Lottery Excellence in Teaching Award, and has twice been included in *Who's Who Among American Teachers.*

Chapter Eleven

Life Lesson: A Thirty-Something-Year-Old Needs the Experience of Student Teaching

Gus Teller

2005 Virginia Teacher of Promise

That which does not kill me makes me stronger. —Frederick Nietzsche

The summer of 2005 was finally coming to an end. I, Gus Teller, would finally get my very own classroom at Hidden Valley High School in Roanoke, Virginia. However, like many other first year teachers, this was not actually the case. Instead, I was destined to be a "floater." My classroom was actually a cart that I would push from room to room. Still, I couldn't believe it—no more practice, no more nagging from my advisor. I was no longer a student teacher, but rather a real teacher. As everyone who has ever been a teacher knows, the first year is tough; in fact, it proved to be the hardest endeavor I have ever undertaken.

I approached it thinking I was in fairly good circumstances. I knew in advance the two subjects I would be teaching and I'd started working on my syllabus and lessons months prior to the first day of school. I had my textbook along with the Virginia Standards of Learning (SOLs), so I had a fairly clear idea about how to move forward. I'd be lying, though, if I claimed that my lesson plans were complete as the first week of school approached. I felt I had a good start, however.

I had met with one of my colleagues a couple of times during the summer, and his help and insight had been critical in my preparation. I was also relieved to know that we still had one glorious week of planning at the beginning of the official school year, giving me ample time to seek any additional guidance and help. My first fantasy about teaching, however, was about to be shattered: The myth of uninterrupted working time to prepare lessons and get ready for class during so-called teacher workdays.

I was fortunate to actually have two days to work on my lessons, but as the week progressed, it was soon loaded up with other outside duties and endless meetings. In fact, this first week before the start of school should really be dubbed, "Welcome to administrative paradise." First came the procedures for students with IEPs and 504 plans that had been created to address their special needs. I had to create a special category in my file cabinet for an entire series of IEP and 504 plans and locate its long-lost keys since these files were strictly confidential. The keys finally turned up after a relentless 48-hour search. I then learned that I had been assigned a homeroom with 26 freshmen. They would rely on my "extensive" knowledge about coursework required for graduation to help them formulate their future plans for their next academic year and to chart the rest of their high school careers. Over the course of the year, their parents would rely on me to help their children sort through these academic challenges. Being brand new to the school and a self-proclaimed expert in German history left me ill-prepared to address the realities of high school freshmen. I began to perspire when I contemplated the difficulties I would face in dealing with all of the administrative tasks and paperwork required of a homeroom teacher since I was a "classroom-less" floater.

I rationalized that there was no need to panic. Any stressful administrative work and deadlines would be more than offset by the fact that I would be primarily teaching dual enrollment U.S. History. These students would receive college credit for the quality time they were spending with me. Moreover, I surmised that they should be easier to teach since they were either driven intrinsically by a desire to learn or extrinsically by parents who were pushing them to get a

I admit I would not be called a "reader." And read about boring history? All the complicated names and terms would drag me down until I quickly lost interest. I cursed school for requiring history, and I cursed myself for ratcheting up to the college-level option. Never did I expect to walk into a class with so much energy and excitement.

Mr. Teller used three tools to transform his classroom: humor, variety, and student involvement. A master at lightening the mood, he often told jokes when we were taking notes, breaking from the usual rote presentation. A weekly session allowed for class discussion on the notes and reading material we had just covered. PowerPoints were sleek and easy to understand while class note outlines were posted on the Internet so absent students could easily access them. Working in groups was a comfortable routine. Many of the projects were hands-on, such as creating PowerPoints, making a newspaper, constructing a website, acting in skits, and presenting poster board projects. Mr. Teller purposely designed group projects that required everyone to participate and share their perspectives in order to complete the task. His laid-back class didn't put a lot of pressure on us, yet he pushed us to work to our highest ability.

Mr. Teller doesn't teach history; he celebrates it. Even I, a reluctant reader, want to read more history now. It was Mr. Teller who taught me not only about history, but also how to love it.

—Meghan Neel, Hidden Valley High School, Class of 2007

head start on college. I quietly comforted myself with this knowledge until a colleague shattered my delusions by informing me of all of the additional administrative duties required of dual enrollment teachers. She asked me how I planned to keep student copies of all their assignments as well as the term paper requirements that were specifically designed for such students. I was proud that I had already crafted many of my long-term assignments, but after hearing about these specific writing requirements for the course, I quickly realized that all of that work needed to be revised. My vision for the course included short, concise writing assignments following each unit. However, this plan apparently was not compatible with the four- to six-page research papers that the students would be expected to write every quarter to receive college credit. I couldn't remember ever being contacted by anyone regarding these specific policies for dual enrollment students, nor was I ever informed that I needed to follow a specific assignment blueprint. The bad news continued as my colleague gently told me about the dues that had to be collected for the community college where the students would receive college credit. As she continued, I quickly began to realize that the joys of teaching highly motivated students would involve even more administrative hurdles. "Was I hired to teach or administrate?" I didn't even have a classroom, and I looked at my floater cart with even more trepidation.

The administrative duties kept piling up, complicating the other challenges associated with that first year of teaching. As the school year progressed, however, I somehow was able to fulfill these many administrative challenges in addition to performing what I naively thought would be my sole duty, teaching. My ability to deal with the many challenges of teaching came from something I would never have initially predicted—student teaching.

Many pre-service teachers question the importance and validity of student teaching within their college teacher preparation programs, seeing it as artificial or irrelevant. I was among them. Look, I'm a 37-year-old, first year teacher with two children, a lovely wife, and a dog. I did everything in my power to avoid student teaching because I, too, was skeptical of its value. I was going on job interviews before the start of my student teaching internship believing that I had all the ability and life experience to begin teaching and did not need to waste my time student teaching.

As I now look back on my first year, I can clearly see what really caused me to look so dubiously on the value of student teaching. I had a lot of real life experiences that got in my way of grasping the importance of, and need for, student teaching. I didn't go into teaching until I was 36 years old and only after going through quite a few twists and turns. First came getting an A.B. degree in European history in 1992 followed by a brief flirtation with becoming the world's finest hotel front desk clerk. I then decided that getting a Ph.D. degree was the direction I wanted to go in my life but after dabbling about in the doctoral world, I discovered that a life filled with esoteric research wasn't really what I wanted. My Ph.D. degree morphed into an M.A. degree experience from 1994-1997, which was then followed by another deviation, this time into the world of commercial aviation before I finally realized that becoming a public school teacher was my true calling. Still, I had many misconceptions about the value of student teaching that were clouded by my previous experiences. I now know why I developed these false impressions and have come to realize that things aren't always what they seem.

Misconception Number 1: Based on the Teacher Preparation Course-work, Student Teaching Will Be a Waste of Time

So why aren't things always what they seem in relation to student teaching? I went to school at Virginia Polytechnic and State Institute (Virginia Tech) part-time for four years while my wife earned tenure at the same school. This arrangement allowed me to take a rich variety of courses before performing my actual student teaching internship. The majority of these courses gave me important knowledge that I would use later in my student teaching. While taking the required teacher preparation courses, I often told my wife how challenging it was for me to manage and balance my time now that we had two young children and that wonderful dog. After successfully completing courses in my teacher preparation program, I foolishly believed that student teaching would be a breeze. Why couldn't I just skip all this nonsense and just start working with kids?

As I look back on the courses I took before beginning my student teaching, I realize I was developing an effective routine. During the period between earning my master's degree in history and enrolling at Virginia Tech, five years had elapsed. We had two children, and my wife and I continued to grow in terms of our life experiences. I had to learn how to work more effectively and better manage my time because of the demands created by my responsibilities as a new father and as a student.

The classes that I took during my teacher preparation program seemed manageable, but it was what I learned in these courses that proved invaluable to both my student teaching experience and my first teaching position. During my internship, I was teaching several students with special needs who challenged my abilities. My course-work pertaining to such students did much in preparing me for the challenge of teaching these kids. I gained exposure to the variety of strategies needed to teach them. For instance, my coursework on educational psychology emphasized the concept of prior knowledge and gave me insight into how people learn and how they best remember what they have been taught. When I was earning my master's degree, I learned a lot about history, but I never studied how human beings actually learn or about concepts such as prior knowledge. Learning these concepts during my teacher preparation program improved the way I taught because it forced me to keep in mind how I could make course content more appropriate for my students. Likewise, the content reading course I was required to take introduced numerous strategies for making the subject matter more relevant to kids. This particular subject taught me how to craft better lessons that would be more interesting to students. Yes, the courses I took during my teacher preparation program were different in their overall intensity, but they still proved invaluable, especially when I needed to apply what I had learned to my student teaching.

Misconception Number 2: I've Got Enough Content Knowledge and Don't Need Student Teaching!

As a history major at the undergraduate and graduate levels, I developed the false belief that my content knowledge would be enough to make me a great teacher. I often complained to my wife that student teaching would not help me improve content knowledge. I rhetorically asked: "How many people can discuss in detail the failures of German diplomacy in the 1930s?" I surmised that an accomplished understanding of subject matter was more important than anything student teaching would offer. Kids only needed to be exposed to someone with a good grasp of the "facts," one with an amusing delivery, and they would become eager learners.

Content knowledge is, indeed, critical in teaching social studies at the secondary level. Having such knowledge allows a teacher to answer student questions easily and with confidence, but I soon learned that content knowledge alone was not enough. Teachers need to develop the ability to take their understanding of past events and somehow make them relevant to the very different lives of the contemporary students they teach. Much of the details of history and social studies, which may be extremely interesting to the teacher, often seem old and boring to students who are used to instant gratification and getting cutting edge information quickly and electronically. My students use Ipods and cell phones more regularly than they breathe. No matter how fascinating Josef Stalin's purges may be to me, those purges are ancient and distant events for the students.

During my student teaching experience, I taught sophomore World History II and was confident that, when lecturing about German Unification and Otto von Bismarck, the students would appreciate the interesting circumstances that led to these historical developments and the nature of this remarkable man. After all, I rationalized, I had a good sense of humor and could make almost anything amusing to the students, thereby keeping them engaged. Much to my chagrin, the students wondered how this old man who governed Germany over 100 years ago had any relevance to their lives in Roanoke, Virginia. Besides, there really isn't a whole lot of amusing data about Otto von Bismarck.

My failure was to recognize the reality that just having a personal grasp of content did not translate into student motivation. It was only through my student teaching experience that I learned this important lesson about motivation. My teacher preparation program had actually equipped me with valuable tools for teaching, and I now had the forum to put them into actual practice. I learned a key strategy that would greatly improve my lectures through the use of technology, and I experimented with implementing it during my student teaching experience. Instead of dry, boring lectures, I began to create multi-media PowerPoint presentations on a regular basis. I made sure these presentations were filled with high interest visuals including pictures, video clips, and historical quotes. I also punctuated the content with any amusing and wacky information I could find.

PowerPoint made my classes more interesting and was far better than just overheads and straight lecture. Many of my students thanked me for using this technology.

Still, no matter how glitzy or interesting, there will always be students who don't like any type of lecture. I realized that I had to mix my teaching style with frequent cooperative learning activities, strategies I learned during my teacher preparation program. During the midpoint of my student teaching, I momentarily paused to ask for student feedback on how they learned best. After weeding through some of the desperate pleas for "all video, all the time," I found their comments helpful, allowing me to modify further my presentation of content. Had I circumvented the student teaching process, I would never have had the opportunity to experiment and make mistakes with my teaching. While I might have ultimately arrived at the same strategies on my own, it would have been a struggle and taken longer. My first year of teaching was stressful enough without having to develop and experiment with new teaching styles.

Misconception Number 3: I've Taught at the Grad School Level! Why Do I Need to Student Teach?

When I was earning my master's degree, I taught undergraduates in various discussion sections of their larger history classes. This kind of teaching was my favorite experience during my graduate work, especially when teaching a class on the history of Nazi Germany. We discussed class readings during the discussion sections and I, along with the professor, created a number of activities to encourage students to contemplate how they might have reacted had they lived during the nightmare years of the Nazi ascendancy.

What was so rewarding about the course was the high level of discussion generated with the students during these sections. The topic was both familiar and repelling, thanks to the proliferation of film and books on the subject. The students readily embraced the topic and were eager to join the discussions. Our conversations and activities were stimulating; we pondered some serious questions and found some answers. I loved the content and went on to write my Master's thesis on the relationships between Nazi and American businesses. My success with this course helped form my perceptions of myself as a teacher. I thought of myself as a natural teacher, and I resented the idea of having to go through an internship since I believed I already had mastered the art of teaching.

I didn't realize how different public school teaching was from that at the university level. From the first day of my student teaching, I quickly came to realize that there was quite a range in student abilities. Sure, I had read about how students varied, but it took the actual classroom experience to make me fully aware of all of the implications. Some students loved taking notes and listening to me; others preferred active learning in the form of presentations or group work; and another group of students would rather do anything than be sentenced to the same classroom with me. In itself, the last group was much different from the university where students work hard to get admitted and pay exorbitant tuitions. Furthermore, university students have considerable freedom to select specific courses that interest them, while all high school students are forced to take the same history courses. University professors have the flexibility to develop their courses in a way that reflects the instructor's expertise, while public school teachers must follow a prescribed curriculum. It was through my student teaching experience that my eyes were opened to the fact that students needed the proper tools (e.g. scaffolding, study guides, concept maps) to understand what I was trying to teach them, one that would require me to experiment with a wide variety of methods.

Misconception Number 4: What Is the Value in Observations?

It was my understanding that once I was finally assigned to a school district, my administrators would spend some time observing me, but I was under the impression that these occasions would be rare. As my student teaching approached, I was anxious and felt dubious about the value of my advisor's observing my teaching. I based this skepticism on four factors. First, I had already been observed by my college professors while handling undergraduate sections in graduate school and these observations were complimentary. They gave me confidence that my teaching methods were quite good. The student feedback from these sections had also been largely positive.

Second, I believed that classroom observations were extremely subjective, much like having someone else review your writing. In other words, everyone has different writing methods and criticism is expected when one's writing is read by another. A reviewer might make stylistic suggestions that may be contrary to the writer's preferred style. Similarly, criticisms of my teaching from an observer might be useful to the person making the critique but might not be compatible with my teaching approach.

Third, I thought constant observation would be an intrusion that would affect my teaching. I surmised that such scrutiny might change my teaching or take away my freedom to do things the way I wanted.

Fourth, I was 36 years old and not 23! Why did I need to be observed when I had had so much professional and life experience? Subsequently, I began to dread these upcoming evaluations.

Instead of approaching student teaching with such a negative attitude, I should have thought about my experiences at summer tennis camp that I regularly attend. I love tennis. The one thing that has greatly improved my game has been participation in these summer camps where I am observed by professionals who regularly offer constructive criticism and recommendations on how to improve my game. Anyone who has ever seen me play will understand that criticism usually comes from all directions, but I always took their observations and constructive suggestions to make me a better player. I can take such advice and use it effectively to improve my game.

I finally came to embrace the frequent observation of my teaching. One of the best pieces of advice I received from my advisor was in regard to my lack of eye contact with my students while I was teaching. Certainly, no student would have had the nerve to tell me this, and I doubt that I would have ever identified this problem myself. By not establishing eye contact, I was violating one of the core beliefs about teaching, which is to establish empathy with your students in the classroom.

My advisor's observations led to an overall improvement in my teaching strategies. Through the feedback I received from an observer who paid careful attention to classroom dynamics and student behavior, I got a better feel for what I needed to modify. Like all teachers, I had moments where I was afraid to change strategies because I was comfortable, even though I knew that it was important for me to vary teaching styles. An objective observer can report if a particular teaching strategy is ineffective or if it is, in fact, working. For example, I had a difficult time understanding that lots of noise during cooperative learning assignments could be a positive sign of student interest and involvement. Without an observer, I would have concluded that a cooperative learning assignment involving the creation of a poster detailing the motives for European Imperialism in 19th century China had been unsuccessful because of the high noise level in my classroom. Surprisingly, both my cooperating teacher and advisor told me that the loud group discussions were indicative of students staying on task. Because I was all over the room and had to spend extra time with certain groups, it made it difficult for me to grasp the overall effectiveness of the lesson. That day, though, I had a second and third pair of eyes in the room that provided me with insight into things I couldn't see. As a result, I became a better teacher.

Misconception Number 5: What Can Student Teaching Teach Me? I've Managed the Cargo Conversion of Commercial Aircraft

After completing my Master's degree, I didn't immediately go into public education. In truth, my experience in graduate school left me a bit confused about where I wanted to go next. I was frustrated that I could not focus on what I loved about my graduate school experience. It was teaching, but rather than make the connection that being a public school teacher would provide me with the things I sought, I changed careers instead.

After going through a long and ultimately unsuccessful application process to become an intelligence analyst for the CIA, I shifted my sights to the world of commercial aviation. I've always loved airplanes. As a kid, I could identify every type of commercial aircraft in service by both make and airline livery (insignia). This uncanny ability earned either admiration or the designation "plane geek" from friends, relatives, and even my spouse. Fortunately, a startup commercial airline was in need of an administrative assistant. My father-in-law had been with the company, and through his connections, I landed an interview. I was offered the job and in less than a year, I was working in the material department, ordering aircraft parts and sending aircraft components out for repair. By my first year anniversary at the company, I was placed in charge of managing the material side of cargo conversions for the airline. The airline purchased old passenger jets and converted them into cargo freighters. During the six-month conversion process, I had to ensure the aircraft parts were fixed and made it back to the plane on time.

This particular job involved no technical knowledge on my part. What it did require, though, was an ability to manage people effectively who were out in the field removing and installing the parts that I was tasked with sending out for repair and/or replacement. The position also required a strict adherence to timelines and organizational skills. If an aircraft was late by even a few days, it generated huge financial losses for the airline. I was constantly stressed out and fatigued, yet I had an immense feeling of pride in being part of a team responsible for getting an aircraft back into service on time.

Given the demanding nature of my work with the airline, I was confident I could easily make the transition to the classroom. The year before I began my student teaching, I interviewed for a position with Roanoke County Schools, hoping to prove that my content knowledge and life experiences were adequate preparation for a career in teaching. I clearly remember lauding my experience in commercial aviation as though it was the perfect substitute for student teaching. I could not conceive that student teaching could serve up any challenge I couldn't handle. Needless to say, I was stunned when

New teacher, Gus Teller, in his classroom teaching World History.

Piper Durrell

I was not offered the job. Later, to my astonishment, I discovered that the primary reason I had failed to get the position was because of my lack of student teaching experience.

No doubt, my commercial aviation experience was a challenging and important experience in my life, and it has helped me during some of my tough times as a teacher. I always have clear goals and timelines permanently lodged in my head that are essential to pacing my classes in preparation for the annual SOL exams. Given what I now know about student teaching and classroom teaching, I understand why Roanoke County required that additional level of experience. While things did not always go as anticipated with the airline, my aviation job involved working with paid professionals who were motivated to keep planes safe, stay on schedule, and earn their pay. Teachers, as professionals, also have clear goals and objectives. However, students don't always come to class with the same academic goals. Some students are motivated intrinsically or extrinsically, but others are not motivated at all. Teachers must challenge and engage these reluctant learners in their course content. The challenge of reaching unmotivated students was something that my aviation background could not teach me. It was only through my involvement in an excellent teacher education program, one that required a student teaching internship, that I was allowed to practice and experience the difficult task of crafting lesson plans intended to motivate students of varied needs.

A good example of this was my effort to teach the beginning of World War I. Fully comprehending how the war came about was a struggle even for me. Getting students to understand it was even tougher. The first thing I had to learn was how to make the opening of the conflict relevant and explain it to my students in a different way. I began my lesson with an introductory activity or anticipatory set designed to get the students immediately interested in the topic at hand. I read a story about a bench clearing brawl involving two major league baseball teams. The description of this major league baseball fight emphasized the uncontrollable nature of the event. Once the first baseball player threw a punch, his team ran out of the dugout and was met at mid-field by the opposing club. As the fight continued, it was difficult to restore order and break up the combatants. I then began my lesson on the outbreak of World War I, emphasizing the same uncontrollable nature of events, and I continued to compare it to a baseball fight. Through this baseball example, the students were better able to grasp the spontaneous origins of World War I. Students who don't receive fat airline paychecks need some other incentives to develop an interest in learning. It was through student teaching that I learned to develop motivational lessons that helped spark student interest. I could have delivered dozens of aircraft on time, but without the experience of student teaching, I would have had a much rougher time helping students achieve success in the classroom.

Misconception Number 6: This Additional Work While Student Teaching is Worthless!

I did a lot of complaining during student teaching. It was extremely challenging creating lesson plans daily and implementing them. On some days, I admit, the day's lesson plan wouldn't be completed and fine-tuned until minutes before class was to begin. It would then continue to be tweaked and modified all day long during my different preparations. Yet, the work was not confined to just creating lessons and teaching them. My student teaching internship was made all the more challenging by various associated requirements.

I was tasked with some more difficult things: Writing an educational biography; crafting a report detailing student comprehension;

reviewing various articles on issues in education; creating an online activity with a Virginia Tech history professor; and building my online student portfolio. These tasks were in addition to my classroom responsibilities. The student portfolio was by far the most difficult project I have ever worked on. It required pulling together all of my experiences and work from student teaching as well as the entire college teacher education program and preparing a comprehensive yet understandable website. This assignment forever banished from my mind the idea that my teacher preparation program wasn't rigorous.

The last few months of my student teaching experience were replete with stress from the portfolio project as well as from other projects. I kept questioning why I needed to do additional assignments when I should be focusing on my teaching. Was my advisor trying to kill me? Did my constant teasing about his British heritage cause him to delight in the misery he seemed to direct my way? My fellow colleagues and I often complained that all these tasks were taking away from our ability to be the most effective teachers we could be in addition to ruining any opportunities for a substantive social life.

Once I had finished my teacher preparation program and had another beautiful Master's degree diploma framed and ready to hang, I thought how wonderful it would finally be to just teach in the fall. No more teaching portfolios or article reviews would interfere. I could focus on putting together great lessons and not have to worry about all these other things. How wrong I was.

The first thing I discovered when I actually became a practicing teacher is that I couldn't just teach. Fortunately, during my student teaching experience, I had been prepared to multi-task. All of those additional assignments hadn't been given to us by an evil, arbitrary advisor, but instead they were carefully designed to prepare us for the million different directions we would be pulled while teaching. Additionally, by completing my student portfolio, article reviews, and the other aforementioned assignments, I had been forced to reflect and rethink my approach to teaching, which is important for all teachers to do on a regular basis.

Are the administrative duties still overwhelming? Yes, the

administrative stuff can be a killer. However, I had a cooperating teacher during my student teacher experience who had largely shielded me from these mundane, routine matters (probably fearing the administrative duties would forever alienate me from education). I greatly benefited by having an internship that forced me to work at more than just teaching, and it taught me how to handle a slew of additional tasks.

Misconception Number 7: Who Needs Detailed Lesson Plans Like This?

During the early stages of my student teaching, I was paired up with a partner to work jointly on lesson plans. As any experienced teacher knows, lesson plans are indispensable because they provide a clear compass and direction for the class and the course content. A plan also lets others quickly understand a particular lesson's objectives and goals. I had seen the lesson plans my cooperating teacher used, and they were clear and concise. If I had been a substitute teacher, I could easily have followed them and understood what I was required to do. This clarity is an essential component of all good lesson planning.

The lesson plans I was required to write to fulfill my college requirements contained additional elements as well. These consisted of such things as a discussion of the National Council for the Social Studies (NCSS) standards and background information that related the lesson plan to previous classes and how the content was to be taught. The NCSS standards were developed in 1994. They focus on ten thematic strands within the social studies, including culture, global connections, and power authority and governance. Every lesson plan we developed had to relate to at least one of these strands in some way.

Focusing on the Virginia SOLs at least made sense to me given how much emphasis was placed on these standardized tests. Tweaking a lesson to encompass the NCSS standards was incredibly time-consuming, especially when coupled with writing detailed background data for my lesson plan. Once again, I cursed my fate every night as I typed up these formulaic lesson plans. Once again, though, I did not fully appreciate the benefits these plans would have for the future.

During my first year of teaching, I was fortunate to work with several alumni of Virginia Tech's teacher preparation program. These colleagues told me that my lesson plans would be much simpler now that I was through with my student teaching. One colleague confided that my experiences during my first year of teaching would actually be easier than the entire student teaching process.

Indeed, I found that my lesson plans needed only to address the SOLs and required only a fraction of the detail that was expected of me while I was at Virginia Tech. I was so relieved and happy not to have to pour so much energy into addressing the things my professors required. As the year moved forward, and much to my amazement, I came to miss those detailed lesson plans. What the heck was wrong with me?

Teachers need clear direction and succinct goals. I'm not sure I would have had time during my first year to focus on the details I was forced to address as a student teacher. I found that my lesson plans were not as polished as they had been while student teaching. Subsequently, they were not as effective. Neither was my rationale for conducting a particular lesson as clear as it had been. By applying the NCSS standards and background information, I had been forced to think more carefully about the SOL objectives and how I might make them more relevant and exciting rather than simply plugging in SOL-generated historical bullet points. Being forced to write detailed lesson plans prepared me to become an effective teacher.

In sum, the writing of my lesson plans during student teaching was admittedly extremely tedious, but it forced me to focus and think about the entire educational process. I actually plan to increase the detail of my lesson plans in my second year because I know it will lead to more thoughtful and better teaching.

Putting the Misconceptions to Rest

I have survived my first year of teaching, and I am a better educator now. I brought many life experiences and prior lessons to my job, but it was only when these things were combined with the experience and opportunities of student teaching that I became a truly effective educator. I have no doubt that the process enhanced my abilities to deal with the numerous teaching and the administrative challenges faced by new teachers. Had I skipped student teaching and miraculously landed a teaching position, I would never have realized how much I missed, and I would have had to struggle to become a better teacher.

Piper Durrell

TOP Teacher, Gus Teller.

About the Author:
Gus Teller earned his M.A.Ed. from the Virginia Polytechnic Institute and State University in 2005. Prior to graduating, he was selected as a 2005 Virginia Teacher of Promise and attended the 2005 Teachers of Promise Institute, an event cosponsored by the Virginia Department of Education and the Virginia Milken Educator Network. This institute is a professional development program that focuses on advancing teacher quality and encouraging new teachers to remain in Virginia. Additionally, Gus was a 2005 Mid-Atlantic Regional Teachers Project Meritorious New Teacher Candidate. Currently he lives in Blacksburg, Virginia, with his wife Shannon, his two children, Molly and Sam, and his golden retriever, Zuzu. He spent his first year teaching primarily Dual Enrollment U.S. History to eleventh graders at Hidden Valley High School in Roanoke, Virginia. After spending most of his salary on fuel costs driving between Roanoke and Blacksburg, he has made it back to his community and will be at Blacksburg Middle School teaching eighth grade civics in 2006-2007.

Chapter Twelve

Lessons from Lindsay: A Teacher's Epiphany

Jennifer K. Presson

2001 Milken National Educator, NBCT

Education is not the filling of a pail, but the lighting of a fire.
—William Butler Yeats

A colleague stopped me as I sped down the hall on the way to check my mailbox and return a couple of phone calls. She had been approached to provide homebound services for an elementary-age student. Unable to assume this commitment at the time, she wanted to know if I was interested. Interested? Yes! Did I have the time to commit? Honestly, no! I was already working with a group that provided after-school services to youth. I co-taught the kindergarten through fifth grade classes, and I found that the younger students were both a balance and challenge to my middle school lifestyle.

I hesitantly took the contact information without making a firm commitment. I was considering it, although I was unsure if I could find adequate time. Balancing this argument in my mind was the pull to work one-on-one with a student in need. I had previously worked with two homebound students and had enjoyed the experiences.

I pondered over the opportunity that evening. My husband and I hashed it out during dinner, but I went to sleep without an answer. The next day I followed up with the student's mother, not really knowing whether I would accept or decline. The specific details would help me reach a final decision, I rationalized.

When I first spoke with Wendy, she explained that her daughter, Lindsay, was extremely shy and often withdrawn. Her daughter was part of the preschool program in our school system. She was being treated for an aggressive tumor on her brain stem and would be missing school for her medical treatments. Wendy was very forward and informed me that, if Lindsay did not connect with me, she would need to request another teacher. Not knowing what the future held for her daughter, she was clear in her expectations for homebound services. Wendy's urgency for Lindsay's education could not withstand the delay of working with someone who did not connect with her daughter. While this initially made me nervous, I respected her for placing education as a top priority.

Intrigued with the idea and ready for a challenge, I accepted before I hung up the phone. I sat down and figured out how to rearrange my after school commitments to schedule the hours necessary for Lindsay. Some weekend hours would be required since her rigorous treatments would necessitate ample time for her to recuperate. To prepare for my initial meeting with Lindsay, I read up on the preschool curriculum and characteristics of preschool students.

On a gray, February afternoon at the arranged time, I found myself nervous about meeting this four-year-old. I felt like I was on my way to an audition. Armed with a few lesson ideas and materials, I arrived trying to hide my uneasiness. We all sat together at the kitchen table in order to get acquainted. Wendy showed me the schoolwork that Lindsay's teacher had sent home. We talked briefly about her learning goals while Lindsay sat with one arm flopped across her face. Wendy talked with me about my teaching experience and ways we could try to mesh our busy schedules. She reiterated her need to be an advocate for whatever was best for her daughter. Knowing that Lindsay was often particular about those she warmed up to, Wendy would give our arrangement some time to see how well Lindsay and I would work together. Working with doctors and therapists to balance Lindsay's schedule, she could not afford to shortchange her education. I caught a glimpse of Lindsay's big blue eyes peeking at me. After a few minutes, her mother excused herself so the lesson could start.

I knew I would need to tread lightly and persuade my little student into trusting a new teacher. I asked her a few questions. At first,

As a career high school educator, I knew being promoted to middle school principal would be my greatest test. Little did I know going boldly, yet blindly into this challenge, I would find my guardian angel in one of my own teachers, a five foot three bundle of ideas and energy named Jennifer Presson. Jennifer is an education gold mine and an administrator's dream. Many times as her principal, roles were reversed. The leader became the follower as Jennifer provided uncanny insight to the needs of middle school students and shared her vision for proactive instructional strategies for our school. Her guidance helped me light a fire under our teachers that resulted in huge gains in student achievement and made our school a competitor in the SOL/NCLB arena.

Jennifer was an invaluable resource for me in those days as a middle school administrator, and I still depend on her education know-how and advice. She granted me a true gift by forcing me to examine myself as an educator and raised the bar on my expectations for students, teachers, and myself. Without question, Jennifer Presson has touched my life, and I am a better person professionally and personally.

—Kevin L. Alston, Assistant Superintendent, Suffolk Public Schools

Lindsay barely responded, and then only with a few very lightly mumbled answers. I persisted. I proceeded to take the materials sent from her teacher out of the plastic bin. I talked out loud about each work sample and assignment that I retrieved while butterflies fluttered full force in my nervous stomach.

When I introduced the letter of the week, "V" is for Valentine, a spark flickered in Lindsay's eyes. She left the table and soon returned with her own Valentine's Day cards. She had memorized each of the characters and knew who had sent them. I described the pictures, colors, and shapes on each card and read the name of the sender and spelled it aloud. Lindsay's ears perked up, her arm fell to the side, and she tentatively made full eye contact with me. We spread out her cards in front of us so that we could see all of them at one time. We sorted them by color and later by cartoon character. I assessed her letter identification through the senders' names on the cards. Those cards were Lindsay's only real connection to the normalcy of preschool, which now had been denied to her because of her illness. A simple childhood holiday tradition, one that I had all but ignored with my own sixth grade students, brought a sparkle to

Wendy Debman

Lindsay's sweet disposition shines through in her preschool photograph.

her eyes that I will never forget. That first impromptu lesson was our initial connection.

That February afternoon was the beginning of a powerful journey for us. It established our relationship as teacher and student. Lindsay and I would work together through that semester until she was well enough to return to her preschool class. I kept in touch with her family through the summer, even making trips with them to nearby amusement parks. During her kindergarten year, she was in remission, but then she needed to have an operation on her hips. These surgeries left her in a half-body cast and once again in need of homebound services. When her tumor returned later, she needed additional homebound services while undergoing more treatments—treatments that the doctors were not sure would bring a cure but perhaps provide her more time. Each scan, each appointment brought on the emotional roller coaster of knowing and not knowing. We spent many hours together over the course of the next two years sitting at that kitchen table—teacher and student. She practiced writing, molded clay into shapes, finished patterns, and dabbled with art projects. She learned to write her name, read sight words, add and subtract. I watched her grow and learn; I watched her flourish and struggle.

At that table I learned as well. Not overtly, not in the same measurable way as Lindsay but in a deeper knowledge that came over time. For me this certain insight needed time to grow, develop, and surface. When I peeled away the many layers of teaching—the lessons, the grading, the preparing, the planning, the adjusting—I found that ultimately there was the relationship between student and teacher. It is these relationships that guide you on your journey, and on this special journey, I learned what was important to me as a teacher.

Teachers are fortunate to work with a clientele who are naturally curious and search for knowledge. This natural curiosity may be hidden beneath layers of self-doubt and blanketed with apathy. Like many preschool students, Lindsay was inquisitive. She anxiously waited to see how a story unfolded and found delight in sculpting the letters of the alphabet with various materials. There is magic in watching a four-year-old manipulate clay into a circle and flatten out the sides in order to make a rectangle. Lindsay needed repetition, and she needed variety. Lindsay's teacher provided a vast array of materials as well as numerous resources. I was continually looking for ways to provide variety and experience. I didn't want the confines of our home classroom, the kitchen table, to restrict her learning.

Many students somehow lose their zest for learning by the time they leave elementary school. As I thought about my own sixth grade students, I felt that all too often their learning was restricted to traditional methods and the confines of their classroom. I knew that I needed to be more diligent in expanding their learning experiences so that these adolescents could recapture the magic of learning that I saw so clearly through my experiences with Lindsay. I set out to find ways that would channel my students' curiosity and allow them to reclaim the wonder and excitement of the learning process.

Good teaching shares some of the characteristics of good salesmanship. You should never discount the power of framing a lesson just as a salesman makes his product relevant to a customer's needs and wants. Yes, the Progressive Movement may be enthralling to the history teacher, but I can guarantee you that most students will have to be "sold" on the idea that this era is relevant to their modern lives. To say, "Let's read a chapter about the Progressives and answer a few questions after we are finished," appeals only to a few task-driven students who strive for completion instead of an in-depth understanding of assignments.

About this time in my career, I was fortunate to have the opportunity to co-teach an inclusion class where students with learning disabilities receive instruction in a general education classroom. Instead of being pulled out for special services and accommodations, the two teachers work together to meet the academic needs of all of their students in the same classroom. Luckily, my co-teacher, Kirsten, made students reclaiming the wonder of learning her personal priority as well. Our collaboration helped fuel this belief and better instruct our students. I learned to frame their learning more skillfully by piquing their interests through making connections to something relevant in their lives. For instance, during the unit on the Progressives, our students would actually experience some of the aspects of this era. We would read excerpts from *The Jungle* by Upton Sinclair, simulate working on an assembly line, and role-play the contentious negotiations between management and labor unions. In English class, we attempted to resurrect the literature by constructing models of settings, dramatizing scenes from novels and poems, and inspire writing through props such as clouds or an indoor rain forest.

Kirsten and I instinctively knew we were being successful in rekindling their natural curiosity when the students were eager to arrive at our room each day. Their excitement likewise ignited our own creativity. Their learning fueled our commitment to exploring alternate ways to teach and assess our students. I learned that these student-centered activities had a profound, positive impact on our social studies classes. Students who started out expecting to read and answer questions, learned to debate topics and critically question the established viewpoints provided in the curriculum. We allowed them the freedom to experience what we could. They mined for gold like the "49ers" in California, picking out chocolate chips from cookies with a toothpick; they tried to preserve "the land" that had been despoiled by the intrusion of the settlers. We even cooked "johnny cakes" and churned butter to give them a taste of life on the trail westward. During the study of the world wars, we included assignments that were interactive by allowing students to stage the alliances and sequence of events. A former student, who is now in high school, shared with me that she will always remember the roles and interaction of nations during World War II by how the desks were arranged, each labeled by country and sorted by alliance. We rehearsed the dramatic events of the war and how each nation became involved in the conflict down to the final climatic battles.

Obviously, none of this happened overnight or even within one school year. Kirsten and I were fortunate to work together for three wonderful years. We built a relationship based upon trust, our shared beliefs, and our common work ethic. By exploring the curriculum, we were able to make it real and relevant for our students. We found a new joy in teaching while our students discovered their own love for learning. While the four walls of the classroom were a physical limitation, the class became a new and exciting frontier, and learning became an ongoing journey rather than a final destination.

Another important lesson I learned from Lindsay on our own special journey was to keep a sparkle in your eye and laughter in your heart. Our sessions became a comfort for both of us. I felt a true connection with her, one that I often did not have time to cultivate with each of my 50 plus sixth graders. Some days when her body was fighting against her beautiful spirit, she would need a little extra encouragement and support. One day when she was slow to get started, I mused that she must have eaten a pickle pizza for lunch. She grinned and squealed at such an outrageous thought. Her quirky sense of humor and her smile were never lost despite the ravaging effects of her treatments. One day after our session, we used leftover supplies to make a paper bag hand puppet that had mismatched wiggle eyes. We later named him George, and he became our constant companion at the kitchen table. He often brought that hidden smile to Lindsay's face on a challenging day.

In my teaching, I learned to put on a smile even on mornings when I was overtired or frustrated by circumstances out of my control. By wearing a smile, I could see it reflected back to me on the faces of my students. A simple investment yielded high rewards. I learned to laugh at myself and the mistakes I made. I learned that there is healing in humor.

In the first few weeks of middle school, a sixth grader can be nearly pushed to the edge of insanity by something as simple as a combination lock that will not open. It would be easy to ignore the situation and watch the student struggle by continuing to enter the combination incorrectly. His frustration would boil up and affect the rest of his school day. A few colleagues felt such a hands-off approach taught the students to be tough and self-reliant, but because of Lindsay, I began to see things quite differently. I came to believe that students would perceive teachers as insensitive and unsupportive.

Using humor to diffuse the situation, I often approached with the firm command to stand back. I swished my imaginary magic wand at the lock and then proceeded to request the combination from the mystified student. Entering the combination, I would talk to the student about the process and the lock would miraculously open. He would be quite relieved, but then I would close the lock to his despair. I would coach him through each of the sequential numbers until he was finally able to open it successfully. I knew that I didn't want my sixth graders to be cynical, but I certainly did want them to be self-reliant. I have found that there is always a way to diffuse a tense situation with a little humor while still dealing with whatever issue is at hand.

The few minutes spent with a child struggling with his combination lock paid off in the weeks to follow since it established an important personal connection. Relationships with students are often defined by such moments throughout the course of the school year. A teacher holds the power of choosing how to respond to students: A sarcastic reply or a gentle reminder, a curt retort or a heartfelt explanation, a cheerful greeting or a distant stare. These seemingly fleeting moments ultimately define your relationships with your students.

As relationships develop, a teacher must find that sparkle in each individual student. While I was elbow-to-elbow with Lindsay for several private sessions a week, her special talents and unique traits were easy for me to see. Yet, I had to find the time to discover that same sparkle in each of my many sixth grade students. For some students, it was readily apparent. For others, it remained guarded or lay hidden beneath the surface. There was "Shaun" who openly described himself as a social misfit. He was repeating the sixth grade and constantly slept whenever seated at his desk. I saw early in the year that his fellow classmates were beginning to shun him. He became a burden to keep awake even during small group activities. Yet Shaun enjoyed the challenge of walking backwards down the hallway to see how fast he could get to the cafeteria. It didn't concern him that he often ran into smaller classmates whom he brushed past without even the slightest acknowledgement. My attempts to get to know Shaun were greeted with suspicion. He somehow felt unworthy of my attention. Eventually, I learned what allowed him to sparkle. It was Japanese animation. He was a gifted artist but he kept his drawing out of sight. He used this medium as an escape from engaging with his peers. His artwork, though, provided Shaun with an avenue to teach me about a topic that I knew little about. He was the expert in both content and technique. His artwork, his personal expression, provided an opportunity to let others in, but the trick was to help Shaun shine and help him understand that he had a place in our class with something valuable to offer. While he continued to struggle throughout the school year, he became more trusting of his peers and began to engage in group activities. His classmates soon changed their preconceived opinions of him and sought his expertise when needed.

Students often need assistance in finding their personal strengths and defining what makes them special and unique. When they can see it in themselves, they can then find it in others. A teacher must be their guide on this incredible journey of self-discovery. Without a relationship built up on a foundation of trust and solid rapport, a teacher will never be able to join this expedition with her students.

Through her intense treatments, Lindsay looked forward to our scheduled sessions even when she was exhausted or nauseated. She wanted to learn even when her small, fragile body felt defeated. In kindergarten, during a remission, she had to undergo surgery on her hips. Even while in her confining half-body cast, she wanted to learn, she needed to learn, and we continued to learn together. Lindsay and I worked together on the skills that brought a familiar normality to her childhood and a comforting routine to her days. Her mother, ever an advocate, carefully monitored her progress and brought together many other professionals to guide Lindsay's growth. I had already begun to reap the rewards of working collaboratively with a coteacher at school, but now I was gaining the experience of working with a variety of adults who all had Lindsay's best interest in mind. Each sought to do what was best for her from our own perspective, but we all held only one piece of the puzzle. By collaborating and welcoming new strategies, we collectively mapped out the best possible plan for Lindsay. Just as Lindsay and I worked and learned together, I learned from my colleagues that we must learn and grow together. Learning at its best is continuous and collaborative.

Unfortunately, collaboration doesn't come naturally and teaching can be a very isolated profession. I often found myself starved for adult conversation, but it wasn't until I realized I needed to reach beyond the walls of my classroom, that I was able to enrich my teaching and my career. To develop true collaboration, I needed to take the initiative and reach out to seize the opportunities.

Two colleagues and I took a class together on "word study" in order to better understand the spelling and word attack deficiencies of our students with learning disabilities. We learned to apply this theory to our practice and see the benefits in our students. It provided us a common language to discuss our students' struggles and successes. We each assisted one another to more skillfully help our students address their areas of weakness.

One of the best examples of collaboration that I experienced is when a simple idea develops and improves far beyond what you would ever imagine. Kirsten and I came across an idea in a resource book about setting up a simulation on Ellis Island. We wanted our students to experience what it was like to travel across the ocean while confined to cramped quarters. Then, what it was like to be confronted by intimidating immigration officials while still retaining their hopes of finding the American dream. We set up this small-scale simulation within our classroom. We had to alternate the roles of the ship captain, inspector, and doctor. When Kirsten relocated, I was unsure how I would be able to replicate the simulation, so I enlisted the help of my partner who taught math and science. After we discussed it, we then took the idea to the entire grade level to see if we could expand it into a school-wide event. That is exactly what happened.

Once the concept was shared with the other teachers, everyone began exchanging ideas. We selected roles for our students, and the teachers volunteered to bring in props. Enlisting the assistance of the physical education and exploratory teachers helped to make this activity truly a school-wide experience. The ship, ocean, and Ellis Island were located in the school's gym. Each student assumed their role and learned about their mythical family and their individual talents. They also had to decide what to pack for their voyage to America. Our simulation was complete with costumes and a multimedia presentation that included primary source photos of actual immigrants arriving in the country. Some students successfully were admitted while others were turned back. I watched in awe as the science and health teachers took on the roles of demanding medical inspectors while our art teacher perfected her own interrogation methods. One of the physical education teachers played the role of the ship's captain. He efficiently checked the appropriate documents and papers while sorting a few lucky passengers into the first class section. The others were stuffed into the steerage section of his ship. The students completed a reflection of their voyage that was later used as a springboard for a narrative writing assignment.

Once the students left for the day, I realized the most valuable lesson learned was that by working together as colleagues, we could collectively create something for our students that was exhilarating and better than what we could create independently. The sense of accomplishment was motivating. We had learned to trust each other and see through the details to make a large-scale project work. We found that there was strength in numbers and, although the teachers had sacrificed their precious planning time, there was satisfaction in what this experience had created. It inspired us to reach out toward one another and conquer other tasks together. Indeed, a long arduous journey is best traveled in good company.

After Lindsay recovered from her hip surgery, she was once again able to return to school and resume the normal patterns of a kindergarten student. Within a year, though, her tumor had returned. The doctors were unsure of treatment since her fragile body had already been through so much. Additional radiation and surgery were options, but they could cause more harm than good. As her family anxiously waited for answers, they took joy in every special moment they had with Lindsay.

One gloomy, late winter day, Lindsay asked me to go on a picnic. It was too cold and wet outside for us to venture to a nearby park so instead we feasted right in her living room with all the trimmings of a fine picnic. Apple juice, graham crackers, little sandwiches, and a few books helped us pass the time. To find the joy in simple activities, like a picnic, is a gift that is often overlooked in the fast pace of a school year. Teaching is consuming, tiring, yet rewarding work. Lindsay showed me that it is wise to stop and enjoy a picnic once in a while.

Lindsay's health issues sometimes caused her to slip. I questioned if this was truly a regression or just a temporary defeat. The sight words she had previously mastered had somehow disappeared from her memory. She could remember a few of the words but often, she was simply just guessing. Was her small body yielding to a stronger power? Would her inquisitive mind be able to overcome these seemingly insurmountable obstacles? I decided that these setbacks made her learning and growth even more special. It gave us more reason to celebrate the small successes. Eventually she mastered the sight words again and I learned that occasionally you have to step back to step forward.

In teaching, one can blindly plow through the curriculum as dictated by the school calendar in order to just get the job finished.

However, it will not be a job well done. Good teaching combines the science of content knowledge with the art of adapting, monitoring, and re-teaching. To be successful, a teacher must learn to be reflective in her practice. Only then will a teacher's skills develop and improve. Without such reflection, teaching becomes detached and canned.

It was hard, but I learned that some strategies I worked to implement would work with my classes while others would not. In truth, there can be more learning from failed lessons than from getting it right the first time. Indeed, I have learned far more from my failures and shortcomings than from any of my successes.   It is far too easy to blame others when a project or assignment doesn't work out or yield the expected results. For example, if students fail a test, teachers often blame the poor study habits of their students. However, if those students really understood and knew the concepts taught, then studying would help reinforce what they were supposed to learn. A good teacher must be willing to look deeper into her methods, practice and routines as well as be willing to adapt and change after such self-analysis.

I once formulated a group research project on the artists and musicians of the "Roaring Twenties." I was excited by the prospect of the final student presentations. I had provided my expectations for the assignment and had carefully constructed a grading rubric for students. I divided them into groups and monitored their progress as they completed their class research. I decided not to give them a "sample" presentation since I felt most of the products would then be too similar to what I had shown them. Little did I know then that many of my students were on a path to academic self-destruction. I did not see the signs or the clues that would alert me to the fact that some of the groups were preparing to crash and burn.

When the day arrived for the presentations, I provided ample time for students to rehearse. That is when everything began to unravel. While two groups were ready, the remaining four groups were in various states of upheaval. One group was arguing over their speaking roles, which they had not yet assigned, while another group feuded over forgotten props. The worst nightmare involved a group of four boys. Plaguing this group throughout the assignment was a typical middle school power struggle and an incurable case of the giggles. Now they were in a complete state of dysfunction. One group member had taken home the scrapbook that they had jointly created to reformat all of the sections in the same type font. His group members had reluctantly approved of this plan the previous day, but the boy independently decided that many of the items in the scrapbook weren't good enough. He replaced much of the group's work with printouts downloaded from the Internet. His teammates' work, no matter the quality, had been callously consigned to the shredder. The group members were fuming with anger at his audacity and he was likewise upset that they did not appreciate his gallant, late-night editing.

What I quickly discovered was that many of my students had completely missed the learning goals that I had intended for this project. I could have easily chalked it up to their immaturity or their lack of commitment, but I knew that I needed to really analyze the problem. Yes, some of the students did forget props and others tried to negotiate and manipulate until they got their way, but there was much more to this collective breakdown. I did honestly believe that the learning goals were worthy and appropriate, so I needed to find a way to salvage my project. I had to find the flaws in my preparation and discover suitable ways to counter them. First, I had failed to assign specific roles within the groups which would help establish a delicate balance of power. This was vital so that the roles could be fulfilled with a shared accountability. Second, I learned not just to hover about and try to facilitate group work but to require each group to provide me with a daily summary of their progress and problems. This would serve to give each member an equal voice and would allow students to work out the inevitable frictions rather than allowing them to fester and evolve. Finally, I revisited appropriate use of the Internet and the importance of respecting the work of others. Never again would I assign a project without showing a sample that provided the students with a clear, concrete example of my expecta-

Wendy Debman

Lindsay and Jennifer take a break after climbing to the top of the jungle gym at an amusement park.

tions. I learned to encourage the students to excel and challenged them to become active learners. In the end, my students may not have learned what I intended about the artists and musicians of the "Roaring Twenties," but we all became wiser and better as a result of this experience.

As Lindsay entered first grade, her health had improved but only temporarily. She was becoming quite a reader and mathematician but when she fell ill once again, her current classroom teacher assumed the role of providing homebound services. When I now think back on my experiences with Lindsay and her family, I realize how blessed I was to have had the opportunity to work with them. During her many medical hardships, she had learned her numbers from one to one hundred. She mastered sight words, word families, shapes, basic addition and subtraction, and so much more. Lindsay tragically lost her heroic struggle during the fifth grade, but my experiences with her had an impact on me that would last forever. The cherished lessons about life, love, and teaching that I learned from Lindsay continue to guide me on my journey as an educator. My shifting role from teacher to student allowed me to gain a deeper insight into what is truly important and remarkable about this amazing profession. In Lindsay, I saw her strength and thirst for knowledge; I found daily delight in her curiosity and her courage. I now know the power of building relationships with each student, and I discovered that teaching and learning are very much an uncharted journey. It is imperative to find pleasure in those regular surprise twists that occur every day and discover meaning in those occasional hardships and to always remember a little girl named Lindsay.

James Madison University

Jennifer Presson sharing tricks of the trade at the Teachers of Promise Institute.

About the Author:
Jennifer Presson earned National Board Certification in 2000. In 2001, she was selected to represent the city of Suffolk as Teacher of the Year. The same year she was honored with a Milken Educator award by the Milken Family Foundation. Jennifer Presson taught sixth grade for nine years and now serves as the Middle School Lead Teacher for English and Social Studies for Suffolk Public Schools. She is currently pursuing an Ed.S. degree in Educational Leadership.

Appendix A

Top 10 Lists

Suggestions for a Successful Opening of High School
Letha King Brooks
Heritage High School

It is critical for teachers to be well-prepared and organized for their first sessions with students as a new year begins. That first impression will set the tone for the rest of the year. The following are ideas to help establish a smooth opening of the school year.

1. Be prepared. Have your room arranged and know what you intend to do every step of the way during the first week. Know your subject matter and have contingency plans on hand.
2. Have a class syllabus or class letter, materials list, and other handouts available for parents.
3. Initiate parent contact list by gathering parents' work numbers, mobile numbers, and e-mail addresses.
4. Listen to your colleagues, ask many, many questions, and learn from their experiences. (Do not attempt this alone!)
5. Obtain a class list or yearbook and learn information about your students.
6. Use Open House as an information-sharing forum and steer conversation away from individual student issues.
7. Have a clear-cut objective and mission for your classes and be able to communicate them to your parents and students.
8. Practice how you plan to address your classes for the first time.
9. Establish clear-cut expectations of behavior and classroom procedures on day one (these should be covered in your class letter) and do not deviate from them.
10. Be knowledgeable of school- and district-level guidelines and standards that apply directly to your subject (i.e., Standards of Learning, Advanced Placement standards).

I once read that teaching is the first line of defense for protecting our future. I feel that I am an integral part of a new process each day as I participate in the education of today's young, beautiful minds. My goal is to impact the world of mathematics, one student at a time.

Ten Things Parents Expect From Teachers
Patty Agolini
Woodstock Elementary

Parents want their children to have a "good teacher." We probably agree that this kind of teacher is fair, makes learning fun, and is an educational professional. Often, this teacher is the one who students love; parents are happy because their child is happy. Fortunately, like students, teachers have different personalities, styles, and strengths. We want our children to have a teacher that will help them to learn, grow, and enjoy school.

1. Communicate behavior or performance problems ASAP.
2. Show joy in kids, learning, and life! Let students know that teachers are human, too.
3. Offer tutoring times for students who need it.
4. Make lessons relevant when possible. Supply the answer to the question we hear at home: "When will I ever use or need to know this?"
5. Give students the responsibility to learn and apply lessons. Let students catch the teacher's intentional errors.
6. Have firm but friendly class control.
7. Recognize the unique personalities, abilities, and learning styles of all students.
8. Treat all children with fairness and consistency. Follow the golden rule when tempted to use sarcasm, ridicule, or ostracism.
9. Use varying and appropriate teaching strategies. Don't always lecture or always use transparencies or PowerPoint presentations, or always show a movie. Motivate, motivate, motivate! No matter what they say, it won't be "boring." (And they will still say it!)
10. Have too much fun sometimes!

Never forget the power that you have as a teacher. Even though we may rarely see our child's teacher, he or she is a presence in our home for the school year. On a school day, our child spends more time with his teachers than with us, the parents. The homework that is assigned sets the agenda for the evening. How the teacher and other students treated our child during the day sets the emotional tone of the evening, and it influences our child's self-image for a long time. The teacher's style and personality often determine how well our child learns given objectives and whether frustration or success reigns.

Ten Tips For Elementary Classroom Management
Pam Livingston
Woodstock Elementary

Classroom management will be an important key to your success in the classroom. It isn't just a list of rules with consequences on the wall. It is letting your children know that you care about them, want what is best for them, and lets them know you love to teach. It also involves how you have the classroom arranged and how well prepared you are for the day. These tips have helped me to successfully manage my classroom.

1. Class rules: On the very first day of class, while using a social studies lesson on rules or reading a book on the importance of classroom rules, you help to develop a set of classroom rules with the students. Your school librarian can help you choose an appropriate book in this area. It is important to limit these rules to four or five. Try to phrase them in a positive way. For example: instead of saying don't run, you can say please walk. Share the consequences if these rules are broken. Be very consistent in applying the rules. Be sure to incorporate the students' views by voting on the rules and establishing routines.

2. Behavior plan: Have some sort of visual way to show students if they have a warning or flipped a card. This can be a tree with apples, library card pockets with colored cards they flip, or any other colorful chart that matches your classroom theme.

3. Classroom arrangement: Your classroom should be arranged in such a way that wherever you are sitting you can see your students. If you are working with a group of students at the back table, make sure you are facing the rest of the class so you can still monitor them. Your desks need to be arranged in such a way that they can all see the blackboard, television, and you when you are teaching. The most effective way to group the desks is in groups of four so they can work in groups or alone without a lot of movement.

4. Consistency, consistency, consistency: Students expect you will have rules and consequences, and despite what they may say, they need them. This will be the most important thing you can do for yourself and your students.

5. Be prepared: Teaching begins as soon as your students walk through the door. It is very important to have well-written lesson plans, gathered all of the necessary materials for the day, run off all worksheets, and completed anything else you will need for the day in advance. You might think you

can get some of it done during planning sessions. What if something unexpected happens that prevents you from getting it done? You need to plan and prepare as if you are going to be observed every day.

6. Time: It is very important to use every possible moment of the day with your students. If you are well-prepared, you will be able to use every moment possible. Parent volunteers can help prepare materials, or even work with students in small groups or one-on-one. Get to work a few minutes early so you can ensure everything is in order. It is not a good idea to come in with the students. You will need a few minutes to do a few last things and so you will be ready to teach as soon as they arrive.

7. Disruptive students: No matter how consistent you are, you will still have students who disrupt the class. If they become so disruptive that you can't teach or the other students can't work, it is time to remove the child. You may use timeout in the back of the room facing away from the class. Give them a card that asks, "What were you doing when I asked you to go to timeout?" This gives them something to think about while in timeout for a minute or so. You may need to need to arrange to have another classroom into which they can go to complete some work. Allow students to determine as much as possible when they are ready to return to the class or to their seat.

8. Practice routines: During the first weeks of class make sure you take the time to practice classroom routines. When students are aware of expectations and have practiced them everyday tasks become automatic and there is less disruption during transition time.

9. Transitions: This is the crucial time to ensure that routines are followed. Teachers should incorporate some sort of fun learning activity into transition times, such as a song to reflect what was learned or a chant about a topic, so that there is little or no down time.

10. Be positive: Consistently point out what students are doing well. Use the good behavior of peers to demonstrate how students should act. Congratulate the students on his or her accomplishment or specific behavior—remark on the act, not the child. Use phrases like, "I'll bet you're proud that . . ." Be aware that some students are embarrassed to receive compliments in front of their peers. In these cases, compliment the child in private.

Ten Suggestions for Working with Challenging Students
Julie A. Ruszala
Great Neck Middle School

Children are our future. We should strive to do the best that we can for them. We must be our children's best advocates. We must have faith in all children. When our children see that we believe in them, the sky is the limit. Teachers and parents make it possible for children to dream and set goals for themselves. There is no career, in my opinion, as noble as the teaching profession. We shape the minds of our children for tomorrow. As stated by Aristotle, "Those that know, do. Those that understand, teach." [384-322 BC].

1. Vision: How important it is to have vision for your students! We all know that no one rises to low expectations; therefore, you must set your expectations high for all of your students. I always try to encourage all of my students by letting them know that I believe in them. Sure they may need some help along the way. Sure they may stumble and fall; but offer them a helping hand, allowing them to see opportunities they can achieve. "Vision is the art of seeing what is invisible to others." —Jonathan Swift

2. Goals: One of the first things I do at the beginning of each semester is to have the students write a five paragraph essay stating their goals for the year. When students put their goals in writing, they have a higher probability of achieving them. The students' essays remain hanging in the room as a reminder throughout the semester. "A man without a goal is like a ship without a rudder." —Thomas Carlyle

3. Character: I have made a poster that is displayed in the classroom with those character traits that we as teachers are responsible for in teaching our students. I have each trait defined. The poster is the focal point of the room. When students break rules, I shift classroom discussion to the character traits. We discuss which trait could have prevented the broken rules. We discuss how character evolves through life's experiences. "Character is a long-standing habit." —Plutarch

4. Active learners: I am an advocate of Edgar Dale's Cone of Learning (1969), which emphasizes engaging students in the learning process as opposed to being a passive learner. This practice enables children to interact socially and gives them the opportunity to solve problems and work cooperatively. Since the school's responsibility is to prepare children with the skills necessary for living and becoming productive

members of society, it is essential that children be involved physically with hands-on activities. Children learn best by being actively involved in the learning process. "Our life is composed greatly from dreams, from the unconscious, and they must be brought into connection with action. They must be woven together." —Anais Nin

5. Kindness: When I asked students at the beginning of the school year to share with me the one trait that they admired most in teachers, kindness was the overwhelming response. "Too often we underestimate the power of a touch, a smile, a kind word, a listening ear, an honest compliment, or the smallest act of caring, all of which have the potential to turn a life around." Leo F. Buscaglia "Kindness is a language, which the deaf can hear, and the blind can read" —Mark Twain

6. Understanding: By meeting and greeting students at the door as they arrive to class, I am able to gain an acute understanding of the students' moods through facial expressions as well as their body language. This is an opportunity to diffuse situations before they erupt like a tinderbox. "Understanding human needs is half the job of meeting them." —Adlai E. Stevenson

7. Respect: I find that when I treat my students in a respectful manner, they are willing to do what I ask of them. Respect does not just happen with challenging students. Respect must first be earned. When they see their teacher acting in a respectful manner, they give it back in return. "The secret of education lies in respecting the pupil." —Ralph Waldo Emerson

8. Caring: Getting to know challenging students on a personal level is essential for building a positive rapport with them. When students see you making an effort to learn about them, they know that you care. When they know that you care, often they will give you some insight to where they are coming from. "To lead yourself, use your head; to lead others, use your heart." —John Maxwell

9. Model: It is essential to be a role model for your students. Even the most challenging students will try their hardest when they see you leading others by setting examples through your actions. "Setting an example is not the main means of influencing another, it is the only means." —Albert Einstein

10. Cooperative learning groups: I find that there is one tip that helps me achieve all of the other tips mentioned above: that is setting up cooperative learning groups in your classroom. I spend a lot of time at the

beginning of the school year establishing cooperative learning groups. The students learn what each is responsible for, and they help one another very nicely. Most importantly they interact with students they might not work with. They also learn how to work together as a team. "All growth depends upon activity. There is no development physically or intellectually without effort, and effort means work."
—Calvin Coolidge

As a struggling student, please consider the following:

C all on me when you know I know the answer.
H ave a big heart.
A lways encourage me.
L eave me alone when I am not pleasant.
L et me know that you care.
E ngage my mind with positive role models.
N ever give up on me.
G ive yourself a break.
I nsults are never welcome.
N ewscast my success.
G ive me your best.

As a struggling student, know that I am:

S pecial
T ender at heart
U npredictable
D own hearted
E asily discouraged
N oncompliant, nonchalant at times.
T emperamental
S ensitive in ways you often may not see.

Challenging students need to have teachers with never-ending faith in truly believing that each student can be successful. Inspiring these students can be the most fulfilling aspect of teaching that you may ever need to balance the ebb and flow of your career.

Ten Tips for Preparing for an Open House
Helen McGrath
Woodstock Elementary

Preparation is necessary for a smooth Open House Night for Parents. This is a chance to outline your goals for the year, acquaint parents with the rules you and your students have developed, and set forth your expectations. The following tips will be helpful:

1. Prepare all of your materials for distribution, straighten your room, and prepare your notes several days in advance. (Something always comes up at the last minute.)
2. Welcome everyone, thank them for coming, and share a little about yourself. (college, family, teaching experience, interests)
3. Remember to stay positive and use humor. (I won't believe everything your child says about you if you don't believe everything they say about me.)
4. Explain your typical day giving times and days for extra activities such as art, music, lunch etc.
5. Discuss your homework policy including amount, frequency, and resources (hot-lines, buddy systems etc.)
6. Explain your grading system. (How much do you count tests, quizzes, projects etc.?)
7. Review your discipline procedures both positive and negative.
8. Provide a conference schedule for parents and guardians to sign indicating a convenient time for them to attend.
9. Review any difficult to understand procedures and/or assignments using the overhead. Such things as reading logs, projects and homework procedures are sometimes easier to explain in person. (This is your best time to reach the most people.)
10. Thank everyone for coming and encourage frequent communication. Don't let one person monopolize your time or back you into a corner. Tell that person that you'd like to speak with him/her another time and suggest a conference time.

Why am I teaching after almost 22 years in the classroom? Knowing I make a huge difference in some of my students' lives is all I need to know-- that this is what I'm supposed to be doing with my life.

Tips for an Effective Parent-Teacher Conference
David Connery
Woodstock Elementary

The parent-teacher conference will always be one of the most meaningful encounters of every teacher's start to a successful year. In order to enable teachers to experience a positive outcome, here is a list of the top ten suggestions. Always keep in mind not all of these may suit your particular style; however these ideas will keep you on the task at hand.

1. Send out a pre-conference agenda—list two or three items you have in mind and provide the opportunity for parents to list their issues.
2. Engage in casual conversation to get a feeling of where a parent is coming from—be an active listener.
3. Always be prepared, have samples of the student's work ready, and focus on specific objectives.
4. Set two or three short term goals that will be easily attainable.
5. Emphasize positive attributes and compliment parents on the job they're doing.
6. Encourage parents to focus on rewards first, and then meaningful consequences for their children.
7. Never contradict or undermine a parent's position; however, be ready to offer suggestions, for example, such as ideas to make homework more manageable.
8. Avoid any judgmental statements. If you stay with your plan, this will be avoided.
9. Recap at the end of the conference to go over important topics covered.
10. Follow up with a short note highlighting positive aspects of conference.

Remember that the conference provides an opportunity to develop a rapport between parent and teacher that will work for the good of the student. It is essential that parents are not only kept informed of their child's progress, but also that the teacher communicates his or her commitment to doing whatever is necessary for that child to succeed. Teaching offers the opportunity change lives, not only students' lives, but parents' as well.

Ten Tips for Effective Communication with Parents
Stephen M. Paddison
Woodstock Elementary

As a classroom educator for almost ten years, I have rarely had a problem deal-ing with parents. These are some of the tips I have used (and use) to keep things running smoothly when dealing with parents.

1. Establish a rapport with each parent or guardian that shows you care about their child's education from day one. Get to know the parents; talk with them at school functions, and use their correct last name. Little things make a big difference.

2. Make yourself available to the parents. Whether or not you choose to give out your home number is a personal choice, but just knowing that a parent could call you creates good will.

3. Keep precise anecdotal records so that when discussing behavior or issues regarding a child, you are able to give specific examples for spe-cific days.

4. Send home graded papers weekly in a marked folder and hold each child accountable for returning the folder promptly.

5. When having a conference, involve all pertinent teachers and hold the conference in a comfortable area. Make sure the parents have a chance to speak; do not monopolize the conversation.

6. Use an "Info Line" or create a web page, which gives information on current class events, personal information, and curriculum being stud-ied in the classroom.

7. On the first day of school, send home a welcome letter that clearly states rules, procedures, and expectations.

8. Always attempt to make positive contact sometime before a negative call must be made. In addition, always try to find something positive to say about the student, even when calling about the most egregious situation.

9. Try to send a weekly newsletter updating the parents of events taking place in the class.

10. Finally, remember the slogan, "Parents on your Side!" Our job is about educating their children, and no other job is more important. Some parents are intimidated in a school setting, so you must do whatever it takes to make them feel at ease. Never antagonize or argue with a par-ent. If you feel like a situation is beyond your scope, or has become too much for you to handle, ask your administrator to become involved.

Be yourself, enjoy the kids; show them you care, and everything else will come naturally. In ten years of teaching I have never had a serious situation with a parent, and I know if you follow these guidelines you won't either. Good luck with your chosen profession!

Ten Things That a Principal Looks for During Classroom Observations
Perry Williams
Woodstock Elementary

Whether it's a first grade classroom or one in which an advanced course is taking place, there are certain elements that all principals expect to find in their observations of teachers. These elements reflect that learning is occurring provided by an instructionally strong teacher. Principals ask themselves these questions as they observe, and they expect that the answers are always positive.

1. Is the classroom atmosphere warm, caring, and nurturing with high expectations, students' work displayed, and students actively engaged in the lesson?
2. Does the teacher clearly communicate the objectives, tasks to be performed, how students will accomplish them, and does she make a connection to prior learning?
3. Are students organized in a variety of grouping structures (whole, small, cooperative, partners) to meet high, middle, and low achievers' needs?
4. Is instructional time maximized so that the class starts promptly, pacing is on target, transitions are smooth, and behavioral expectations are positively reinforced?
5. Is the teacher using appropriate assessment data to plan and adjust instruction and to monitor student progress?
6. Are lesson plans aligned with the Standards of Learning; do they maintain students' interests, and are they connected to the real world?
7. Does the teacher provide for higher level questioning, sufficient wait time for student responses, and provide positive feedback to student responses?
8. Are visuals, differentiation activities, cooperative learning strategies, graphic organizers, hands-on activities, and technology used on a regular basis?
9. Does the teacher provide sufficient modeling, guided practice, reinforcement, and application time to ensure that students understand and master skills, strategies, and concepts?

10. Does the teacher provide summary or closure at the end of the lesson to review the objective and reinforce what was taught and learned?

Perhaps the most important item, although intangible, that a principal searches to find is that the teacher has established a strong, positive student-teacher relationship built on trust, respect, and communication. Relationships with students make the difference. Build those, and you will become immortal in the eyes of your students.

Ten Ways to Become a Teacher Professional
Linda Reese
Woodstock Elementary

Teaching is a profession that requires us to interact with may different types of people with varying backgrounds and education. It is important to understand how to interact and develop the skills needed to develop a working relationship with them. This is true for everyone who walks into your building, from the custodians, cafeteria workers, bus drivers, teachers to the parents. Developing these relationships will be to key to accomplishing any endeavor you may seek to do as a teacher.

1. Be friendly and get to know everyone: It is important for you to let those you interact with know that you genuinely want to know him or her, that you appreciate them, and that you will help in any way you can. Take a moment or two to smile and say good morning or ask how they are. If someone wants to share with you, listen. This helps build those relationships you will need later while working on a project or a committee. If others find you approachable, pleasant, and willing to help out, they will in turn be willing to do the same.

2. Take professional development classes: Whenever possible, take professional development classes that will help make you a better teacher. Go back to your building and try out the new strategy. Then share what you are doing with a colleague, your grade level, or the whole faculty. Talk to your principal and share what you are doing and how you would like to share it with the rest of the faculty.

3. Read professional materials: Always try to stay current on best practices. There are many professional magazines and teacher publications that are available. Your school librarian should be able to help you find periodicals. Many teacher stores and catalogs have an assortment of publications on current best practices. The school system's curriculum spe-

cialists can also recommend books, classes, workshops, or periodicals.

4. Websites: The Internet is another wonderful resource for finding strategies for best practices. Visit professional organization sites such as the Association for Supervision and Curriculum Development (ASCD) at www.ascd.org.

5. Have an open and an inviting classroom: Teachers will ask from time to time to visit your classroom if you are doing something they really want to try. Set up a time convenient to both of you and allow him or her to observe. Then, schedule a planning time or meet after school and discuss the observation. They may also share ideas with you to make the strategy better. You may want to observe them when they are using your strategy so you can offer feedback. Parents should always be invited in your classroom, also, as long as it is prearranged.

6. Be willing to share: Whenever you find a teaching strategy that really works, you should be willing to share it with anyone who is willing to listen. Your enthusiasm will be contagious. When others see how well it works, they, too, will try it. Don't forget to include the staff of the school division's curriculum department. Invite the instructional specialists into your classroom to observe a lesson, or offer your classroom as a laboratory for development of best practices by specialists. Take constructive criticism to heart and always thank those willing to take the time to observe your lessons.

7. Apply for citywide and state committees: There are many opportunities outside the classroom to volunteer for curriculum, textbook adoption, content review, or other committees. Apply for committees for which you feel you have expertise to offer. If you are not chosen the first time, reapply when the opportunity presents itself again. Your principal will usually receive news of opportunities to serve; therefore, let him or her know you are interested.

8. Apply to teach staff development classes: Teaching professional development classes is another way to share best teaching practices with other teachers. You must apply for this as well. Often, it helps to make contact with the school division's curriculum department. You may be asked to teach a class that includes a fully planned session, or you may be asked to develop a class based on your expertise and instructional strategies.

9. Grants: Apply for grants to fund projects at your school that will make learning fun and more meaningful for students. There are many organizations that offer money for school projects. Your school system may

also have a liaison who has information on grants and how to apply for them. He or she may also help you write them.

10. Volunteers: When working on a project at school, you may need to elicit the assistance of others. The local community is a rich resource for finding volunteers. Your school may already have a list of local businesses willing to help out. Let them know specifically what you need and when you need it. Follow up with another contact in a few days. Retirement centers or senior living complexes usually have a contact person who can arrange for volunteers. Don't forget parent volunteers and your own school staff.

To grow as a teacher leader, take advantage of all the opportunities presented by your school division, by local institutions of higher learning, and by the state's Department of Education. In this way, you increase your own expertise and offer opportunities for others to learn. In the end, you provide an additional benefit to students who will be taught by a qualified, dedicated individual whose talents extend beyond the classroom.

Ten Ways to Prevent First-Year Burnout
Tara Hollomon
Cedar Road Elementary

Here are my top ten ways to prevent first year teacher burnout. All of these ways have made my first year a success so far. I am not perfect, but I am learning each day and loving every minute of it!

1. Simplify your life! You will need lots of extra time outside of school.
2. Continue your hobbies or interests outside of school for leisure time.
3. Stay positive and stay around positive people. Negative feeds negative.
4. Pay attention to time management. Always use your time wisely. It is amazing what you can accomplish in a 30 minute break!
5. Set priorities. Concentrate on what needs to be done for the day. Work on what comes next later. Don't try to do everything at once and don't expect to be perfect just yet.
6. Self-evaluate! Reflect! Do not be overwhelmed by "bad days." Reward yourself for the "good" things you did each day and learn by the "mistakes."
7. Organize! Have a specific place for everything!
8. Ask lots of questions! You never know until you ask!
9. Reach out for support both in and out of school!

10. Get plenty of rest, exercise, and eat healthy. Your students need you each and every day!

Teaching has been the most rewarding thing in my life! Knowing that I am impacting someone else's life makes all of the time and money I spend well worth it!

Twenty-Five Inspirational Quotations about Teachers and Teaching

Learning is not attained by chance; it must be sought for with ardor and attended to with diligence. —Abigail Adams

Youth is the best season wherein to acquire knowledge. 'Tis a season when we are freest from care, the mind is then unencumbered and more capable of receiving impressions than in an advanced age - in youth the mind is like a tender twig, which you may bend as you please, but in age like a sturdy oak and hard to move. —Abigail Adams

A teacher affects eternity; he can never tell where his influence stops. —Henry Adams

Laws for the liberal education of youth, especially for the lower classes of people, are so extremely wise and useful that to a humane and generous mind, no expense for this purpose would be thought extravagant. —John Adams

Teachers, who educate children, deserve more honor than parents, who merely gave them birth; for the latter provided mere life while the former ensure a good life. —Aristotle

Most teachers possess academic competence in their subject areas, but not all possess academic enthusiasm. —Tracey Bailey

Teaching is a timeless profession. It is the basis of all other professions. Good teachers plant the seeds that make good doctors, good accountants, good public servants, good statesmen, good taxi drivers, and good astronauts. When former students return to see me over the years, my heart fills up in the knowledge that I have been part of a wonderful accumulation of experiences that followed them through life. —Mary Bicouvaris

The failure to read good books both enfeebles the vision and strengthens our most fatal tendency—the belief that the here and now is all there is.
—Allan Bloom

If your plan is for a year, plant rice. If your plan is for a decade, plant trees. If your plan is for a lifetime, educate children. —Confucius

Failure is instructive. The person who really thinks learns quite as much from his failures as from his success. —John Dewey

I am a teacher because of teachers. They showed me that someone other than my mother could love me. —Guy Doud

Sixty years ago I knew everything; now I know nothing; education is a progressive discovery of our own ignorance. —Will Durant

The learner always begins by finding fault, but the scholar sees the positive merit in everything. —George Hegel

In a completely rational society, the best of us would be teachers and the rest of us would have to settle for something less. —Lee Iacocca

If the children . . . are untaught, their ignorance and vices will in future life cost us much dearer in their consequences, than it would have done, in their correction, by a good education. —Thomas Jefferson

Knowledge will forever govern ignorance, and a people who mean to be their own Governors must arm themselves with the power which knowledge gives.
—James Madison

Young people, especially those in college who should know better, frequently fail to realize that men and women who wish to accomplish anything, must apply themselves to tasks of tremendous magnitude.
—James Michener

What else is needed is something that teachers themselves are reluctant to talk about openly and it's our respect for them. It's what's missing in America, and it's what's been too long withheld from a profession so important to our national well being, as important as doctors or captains of industry or TV commentators. From sunup to sundown, the school teachers you have seen tonight work harder than you do—no matter what you do. No calling in our society is more demanding than teaching. No calling in our society is more selfless than teaching. No calling in our society is more central to the vitality of a democracy than teaching. —Roger Mudd

We can give students as many computers and cafeterias and curriculum administration as we want, but none of it will make any difference without the one thing that makes a classroom work—a dedicated and well-trained teacher. —Rod Paige

Principal leadership is the second most critical variable the school has for impacting student achievement, the first being the quality of instruction in the classroom. The principal has to be the teacher of teachers. —Thomas Payzant

To me the sole hope of human salvation lies in teaching.
—George Bernard Shaw

I am beginning to suspect all elaborate and special systems of education. They seem to me to be built up on the supposition that every child is a kid of idiot who must be taught to think. —Anne Sullivan

As Americans, the most formidable weapon we have in our arsenal is education. There is nothing more patriotic that one can do in his career or her career than become a teacher. —Chauncey Veatch

The mediocre teacher tells. The good teacher explains. The superior teacher demonstrates. The great teacher inspires. —Willliam Arthur Ward

I think I know about what most students think of somebody being a high school teacher, but it never has bothered me, and I've never tried to explain how mistaken they are. When you're a teacher and you see a child achieving something, when you see a child reach a new level of understanding about literature or history or . . . or . . . anything else, a level that child would have never reached without you, there's a satisfaction, a reward, that can't be expressed in words . . . In some way, no matter how small, you've helped create a new person. —Tom Wolfe from *I am Charlotte Simmons*

What Is a Great Teacher? The Student Perspective

A Great Teacher . . .

. . . is someone who makes good choices and talks to kids nicely.
—Tiffany, age 7

. . . is someone who respects his or her students, is passionate, and makes reading fun! —Jason, age 10

. . . respects the students. —Dante, age 9

. . . is someone who makes learning fun. She makes you feel like you are there!
—Jasmine, age 9

. . . is someone who explains things if you don't understand.
—Carlos, age 8

. . . is caring. —Deshonte, age 8

. . . remembers your birthday. —Christopher, age 6

. . . never embarrasses you in front of other people. —Raemond, age 12

. . . makes you never want to miss class. When the year is over, you hate it because you won't have this person teaching you again. —Robin, age 15

. . . doesn't do all the talking. He lets students talk as much as he does, and when they talk, he listens. —Melissa, age 16

. . . makes stuff stick in your head. —Tiffany, age 7

. . . is fun, surprising, respectful, thoughtful but is not a pushover.
—Andrea, age 16

. . . is the kind of teacher that you come back to later and say thanks for making me work hard. —Jason, age 17

. . . is someone who lets you work on a project until you get frustrated and then swoops in and saves the day—like superman. —Michael, age 18

. . . interacts with kids. He gets kids to understand what needs to be learned by interacting with them. —Bobby, age 16

. . . helps you get smarter. —Alicia, age 6

. . . makes a connection between what you learn in the classroom and what really goes on in life. A great teacher is someone who can explain and demonstrate why you really need to know algebra. —Liz, age 17

. . . makes you want to learn more. And a great teacher helps you do that. The really great teacher makes you want to grow up to be a teacher.
—Carlie, age 10

Appendix D

Must-See Movies for Teachers

1. *Mr. Holland's Opus* (145 minutes): Stars Richard Dreyfuss, Glenne Headly, William H. Macy, Olympia Dukakis—1995

This remarkable film traces the career of music teacher, Glenn Holland (Richard Dreyfuss), as he struggles and adjusts to the challenges of teaching during a career that spans four decades. He naively enters the profession in order to receive a steady pay check so that he can compose an original symphony during his "spare time." Holland quickly discovers that to be an effective teacher, it requires dedication and hard work. He slowly evolves into an inspirational and committed educator but his dreams of fame and fortune slowly fade as his students become his main priority. At the end of his long career, Holland learns of the profound impact he has had upon generations of his students.

Important Teacher Lesson: "Teachers sow seeds of harvest unseen."

2. *The Emperor's Club* (108 minutes): Stars Kevin Klein, Emile Hersch, Edward Hermann, Paul Dano—2002

The setting is an elite all boys prep school in New England. The film, *The Emperor's Club,* is the story of classics teacher, William Hundert (Kevin Klein). His love for his subject is infectious, and his lessons on ancient Rome are punctuated with important moral lessons and the need for living a purposeful, moral life. The highlight of each academic year is the Julius Caesar contest where toga-clad students compete before the entire student body testing their knowledge of the classical age. The winner is crowned with a laurel wreath, and his photograph is enshrined for posterity in the school's trophy case. Sedgewick Bell (Emile Hersch), the son of a powerful United States Senator, arrives at the school full of arrogance and attitude. He proves to be a constant source of frustration and despite Hundert's Herculean efforts, a major disappointment. Bell graduates from the school without ever grasping its important ethical lessons or accepting its core values. Still, he goes on to a life of wealth and fame but is ultimately a pathetic character. Hundert's cherished beliefs are confirmed instead by his other students whose own successes came honestly and without compromising their principles.

Important Teacher Lesson: "The unexamined life is not worth living."

3. *Stand and Deliver* (102 minutes): Stars Edward James Olmos, Lou Diamond Phillips—1988

Stand and Deliver is the inspirational story of math teacher, Jaime Escalante (Edward James Olmos), who teaches at Garfield High School in Los Angeles. Located in a high poverty district, its student body is almost exclusively of Latino descent. Escalante brokers no excuses for poor performance or mediocrity. He demands excellence from his students and works tirelessly to raise academic standards. Soon, his students are enrolled in AP Calculus. Escalante's innovative teaching techniques and his firm belief in the abilities of his students motivate the students to attend Saturday and summer classes in order to succeed.

Important Teacher Lesson: "All children can learn."

Read the Book: Jay Mathews. *Escalante: The Best Teacher in America.* ISBN 0-805-01195-1

4. *Conrack* (106 minutes): Stars John Voight, Paul Winfield, Hume Cronyn, Madge Sinclair—1974

John Voight stars in this poignant film about an idealistic, first year teacher (Pat Conroy/Conrack) who is assigned to a small school on the outer Sea Islands of South Carolina. Completely isolated from the mainland, the children are all but abandoned by a callous school administration. Consequently, they know little about the outside world and most were unable to read. Through Conrack's dedication and love, the students discover the joys and excitement of learning.

Important Teacher Lesson: "Teachers must be missionaries of learning and apostles of excellence."

Read the Book: Pat Conroy: *The Water is Wide.* ISBN 0-553-26893-7

A few other inspirational films for teachers:

In the film, Akeela and the Bee, *Dr. Larabee (Laurence Fishburne) tutors Akeela Anderson (Keke Palmer) in preparation for the National Spelling Bee competition in Washington, D.C.*

Akeela and the Bee (112 minutes): Stars Keke Palmer, Lawrence Fishburne, Angela Bassett, Curtis Armstrong—2006

Dead Poet's Society (128 minutes): Stars Robin Williams, Ethan Hawke, Robert Sean Leonard—1989

Finding Forrester (136 minutes): Stars Sean Connery, Rob Brown, F. Murray Abraham, Anna Paquin—2000

Lean on Me (104 minutes): Stars Morgan Freeman, Robert Guillaume, Beverly Todd, Alan North—1989

Important Resources for Teachers

Professional Teacher Organizations
(Most of the organizations listed below have local and state affiliates.)

American Federation of Teachers
555 New Jersey Ave. N.W.
Washington, DC 20001
www.aft.org
Association of American Educators
27405 Puerta Real, Suite 230
Mission Viejo, CA 92691
www.aaeteachers.org
National Education Association
1201 16th Street, NW
Washington, DC 20036-3290
www.nea.org

Selected Educational Websites
A to Z Teacher's Stuff: This website is designed to allow teachers to find online resources, including links to lesson plan ideas, teacher forums, and databases of leveled texts. www.atozteacherstuff.com
Animation Factory: For a small annual subscription fee, teachers and students have access to thousands of animated clip art, PowerPoint templates, and video files. This is a wonderful resource for presentations, webpages, and graphic design. www.animationfactory.com
Association for Supervision and Curriculum Development: This association is one of the most valuable assets to the education profession. www.ascd.org
EBooks: The University of Virginia maintains a large repository of online texts including many classic novels, primary source letters, and other materials. These are available at no cost but require Microsoft Reader which is available as a free download. etext.lib.virginia.edu/ebooks/
International Reading Association: This website offers a wealth of infor-

mation, ideas, and resources for teachers. www.reading.org

Marcopolo Education: This website offers ideas for lessons and professional development activities for teachers. www.marcopolo-education.org

National Council of Social Studies: The National Council of Social Studies is an umbrella organization for elementary, middle, and high school teachers of history, civics, economics, political science, etc. www.ncss.org

National Council of Teachers of English: This website offers information on educational issues, professional development, grants, and teacher resources. www.ncte.org

National Council of Teachers of Mathematics: This website offers numerous math resources for teachers. www.nctm.org

National Institute for Literacy: This website offers wonderful information for educators on literacy instruction with links to research and publications. www.nifl.gov

National Science Foundation: This website offers resources for science teachers, including ways to involve the community and grant opportunities. www.nsf.gov

Parent/Teacher Association: This is the national website for the PTA. It includes ideas on tutoring programs and tips for parents in regard to helping their children. www.pta.org

PBS Teacher's Source: PBS's website which offers ideas for lesson plans and integrating technology into instruction. www.pbs.org/teachersource

Poetry for Kids: This is Kenn Nesbitt's poetry site for kids. It contains information on writing poetry and samples of his hilarious poems. www.poetry4kids.com

Presenter's University: This outstanding website provides important advice and tips on how to enhance presentations. With free registration, users are given access to templates to use with PowerPoint. www.presentersuniversity.com/

ProTeacher: This website offers practical information and ideas for both teachers and parents on all kinds of subjects. www.proteacher.com

The Teacher Explorer Center: The Teacher Explorer Center is a website created by the University of New Orleans that provides a wealth of links to professional teacher resources. tec.uno.edu/

Software Recommendations

Accelerated Reader: This software program provides a way to motivate students to read independently. NOTE: This program should be used as motivation only, not as a reading program on its own. The quizzes that are a part of the program should never be given a grade. www.renlearn.com/ar/

A2ZSCDS: Low cost CDs and DVDs of old documentaries, educational films, maps, historical speeches, et al. It presents a wide variety of material to choose from for teachers and students, including photographic CDs on a variety of topics. www.a2zcds.com

Birthday Chronicle/Sands of Time: (Ken Kirkpatrick Software) This software allows teachers to print customized birthday certificates for students that highlight their day in the context of history. It is a wonderful motivational and recognition tool. www.kksoft.com/

EarthStation1.com: This site maintains an incredible selection of historic audio and video resources including old civil defense and World War II propaganda films. These materials are available on CD or DVD at very low prices and are of particular interest to history, social studies, and English teachers. www.earthstation1.com

Hotpotatoes: Free download program that allows teachers to prepare quizzes, crossword puzzles and other student assignments. These teacher designed activities can be then used by students online or printed for handouts. (Halfbaked Software) www.halfbakedsoftware.com/

Kidspiration: A software program for students in grades K-5 that allows them to build and use graphic organizers to improve learning. Inspiration allows older students to create outstanding visuals and diagrams for illustrations and multi-media presentation. (Inspiration Software, Inc.) www.inspiration.com

Microsoft Reader: A free download from Microsoft that allows students and teachers to read e-texts. etext.lib.virginia.edu/ebooks/

One Note: This commercial program makes note taking and studying easy. For use primarily with tablet-pcs, students can highlight text, write in different colors, and search their notes for key terms. www.microsoft.com

Photo Story: A free download from Microsoft, this program allows students and teachers to make Ken Burn's like films using still pictures. (Microsoft) www.microsoft.com/windowsxp/using/digitalphotography/photostory/default.mspx

Reading for Meaning: A reading comprehension program for students in grades 3-5 that develops skills in inferencing, sequencing, comparing and contrasting, and identifying cause and effect. (Tom Snyder Productions)

www.tomsnyder.com/

Tenth Planet Literacy: A word building software program for students in grades K-3 that focuses on the connection between consonant letters and sounds to provide a balanced approach to phonics instruction. (Sunburst) store.sunburst.com/

Selected Bibliographic Resources for Educators

Bernard, Sheila Curran and Sarah Mondale. *School: The Story of American Public Education*. Boston, MA: Beacon Press, 2001.

Bigler, Philip. National Teacher of the Year: Speech at Hollins College (Roanoke, Virginia). March 11, 1999.
Available: http://www.c-spanstore.org/shop/index.php?main_page=prod uct_video_info&products_id=121744-1

———. National Teacher of the Year: Rose Garden Ceremony. April 24, 1998. Videotape. C-SPAN. Available: http://www.c-spanstore.org/shop/index.php?main_page=product_video_info&products_i d=104422-1.

———. Press Release: 1998 National Teacher of the Year. 1998. Council of Chief State School Officers (CCSSO). Available: http://www.ccsso.org/ntoy98.html1998.

Blume, Judy. *Are You There, God, It's Me, Margaret*. Laurel Leaf Publishers, 1991.

Bolt, Robert. *A Man for All Seasons*. New York: Vintage Books, 1962.

Brown, Jeff. *Flat Stanley*. New York: Children's Books, 1992.

Caine, R. M. and G. Caine. *Making Connections: Teaching and the Human Brain*. Alexandria, VA: Association, 1991.

Clinton, President William Jefferson, Philip Bigler, and Sen. Chuck Robb. Remarks at the Rose Garden Ceremony Honoring the 1998 National Teacher of the Year. April 24, 1998. Available: http://www.ed.gov/PressReleases/04-1998/wh-0424.html1998.

Codell, Esmé Raji. *Educating Esmé: Diary of a Teacher's First Year*. Chapel Hill, NC: Algonquin Books, 2001.

Crosby, Brian. *The $100,000 Teacher: A Teacher's Solution to America's Declining Public School System*. Sterling, Virginia: Capital Books, Inc., 2002.

Crowther, Frank, Stephen S. Kaagan, et al. *Developing Teacher Leaders: How Teacher Leadership Enhances School Success.* Thousand Oaks, CA: Corwin Press, 2002.

Cuban, Larry. *Oversold & Underused: Computers in the Classroom.* Cambridge: Harvard University Press, 2001.

Dell, Diana J. ed. *Memorable Quotations: Famous Teachers of the Past.* Lincoln, NE: Writer's Club Press, 2001

Dill, David ed. *What Teachers Need to Know: The Knowledge, Skills and Values Essential to Good Teaching.* Jossey-Bass Inc., 1990. Hoboken, NJ.

Edelman, Marian Wright. *I'm Your Child, God: Prayer for Children and Teenagers.* New York: Hyperion for Children, 2002.

_____. *The Measure of Our Success: A Letter to My Children and Yours.* New York: HarperPerennial, 1992.

Fuery, Carol. *Are You Still Teaching? A Survival Guide to Keep You Sane.* Captiva Island, FL: Sanibel Sanddollar Publications, Inc., 1993.

Ginott, Haim. *Teacher and Child: A Book for Parents and Teachers.* New York: The Macmillian Company, 1972.

Goodlad, John I. *Romances with Schools: A Life of Education.* New York: McGraw Hill, 2004.

Goodnough, Abby. *Ms. Moffett's First Year: Becoming a Teacher in America.* New York: Public Affairs, 2006.

Greenspan, Elaine. *A Teacher's Survival Guide: Insight from the Classroom.* Portland, ME: J. Weston Welch, 1994.

Hendra, Tony. *Father Joe: The Man Who Saved My Soul.* New York: Random House, 2004.

Howe, Neil and William Strauss. *Millennials Rising: The Next Great Generation.* New York: Vintage Books, 2000.

I Teach . . . Because I Can. Virginia Department of Education. Video Tape. 2001.

Johnson, Susan Moore. *Finders and Keepers: Helping New Teachers Survive and Thrive in Our Schools.* San Francisco, CA: Josse-Bass, 2004.

Kane. Pearl Rock ed. *My First Year as a Teacher: Twenty-five Teachers Talk About Their Amazing First-Year Classroom Experiences.* New York: Signet Book, 1996.

Katzenmeyer, Marilyn and Gayle Moller. *Awakening the Sleeping Giant: Leadership Development for Teachers.* Thousand Oaks, CA: Corwin Press, Inc. 1996.

Mondale, Sarah and Sara B. Patton, ed. *School: The Story of American Public Education.* Boston: Beacon Press, 2001.

Mudd, Roger. "History and Teachers Matter," Occasional Paper. Westlake, OH: National Council for History Education. December, 2000.

O'Neal, John. "On Emotional Intelligence: A Conversation with David Goldman," *Educational Leadership.* vol. 54, #1, September 1996.

Page, Clarence. "White Kid, School Shooting, What Now?" *Houston Chronicle.* March 8, 2001.

Ruby K. Payne. *A Framework for Understanding Poverty.* Highlands, Texas: aha! Process, Inc. 2005.

Raskin, Jamin B. *We the Students: Supreme Courts Cases for and about Students.* Washington, DC: Congressional Quarterly Press, 2000.

Rubenstein, Grace. "Payzant on Principals." *Edutopia.* June 2006, pp. 54-55.

Santrock, John W. *A Topical Approach to Life-Span Development.* New York: McGraw Hill, 2007.

Shaara, Michael. *The Killer Angels: A Novel of the Civil War.* New York: Modern Library, 2004.

Schwarz, Eric and Ken Kay eds. *New Directions for Youth Development: The Case for Twenty-first Century Learning.* Danvers, MA: Wiley Periodicals, 2006.

Sennett, Frank. *Teacher of the Year: More than 400 Quotes of Insight, Inspiration, and Motivation from American's Greatest Teachers.* New York: McGraw-Hill, Inc., 2003.

Steffy, Betty E., Michael P. Wolfe, et al. ed. *Life Cycle of the Career Teacher.* Thousand Oaks, CA: Corwin Press, Inc., 2000.

Tolkin, Neil. *The Emperor's Club: The Shooting Script.* New York: New Market Press, 2002.

Trelease, Jim. *The Read-Aloud Handbook.* New York: Penguin Books, 1985.

"U.S. Schools: They Face a Crisis." *Life.* October 16, 1950.

U.S. Department of Education. "A Nation is at Risk" Available: www.ed.gov.

Weinig, Kenneth M. "The 10 Worst Educational Disasters of the 20th Century: A Traditionalist's List." *Education Week.* June 14, 2000, pp. 31 & 34.

Whitaker, Todd, Beth Whitaker and Dale Lumpa. *Motivating and Inspiring Teachers: The Educational Leader's Guide for Building Staff Morale.* Larchmont, NY: Eye of Education, 2000.

Whitaker, Todd. *What Great Teachers Do Differently: 14 Things That Matter Most.* Larchmont, NY: Eye on Education, 2004.

Endnotes

[1]Howard Gardner is the father of the theory of multiple intelligences. See John W. Santrock. *A Topical Approach to Life-Span Development.* New York: McGraw-Hill, 2007. p. 295.

[2] See www.wikipedia.com – Joseph Joubert.

[3] www.fablevision.com

[4] *Tucker Times* (Georgia). February, 1996.

[5] A selection from John H. Lounsbury, "As I See It." Published by the National Middle School Association. Columbus, Ohio, 1991, pp. 29-30, ISBN 1-566090-058-X. Available by calling 1-800-528-NMSA. Used with permission.

[6] Dr. Haim G. Ginott. *Teacher and Child: A Book for Parents and Teachers.* New York: The Macmillian Company, 1972, p.89.

[7] "U.S. Schools: They Face a Crisis." *Life.* October 16, 1950, p. 89.

[8] Rick Casey. *Houston Chronicle.* January 23, 2004, Section A, p. 25.

[9] "Class of '57" written by Harold Reid and Don Reid. © 1972, 2000 (renewed) House of Cash, Inc. (BMI) Administered by Bug. All rights reserved. Used by permission.

[10] Jim Trelease. *The Read-Aloud Handbook.* New York: Penguin Books, 1985, p. 54.

[11] John O'Neal. "On Emotional Intelligence: A Conversation with David Goldman," *Educational Leadership.* vol. 54, #1, September 1996, p. 10.

[12] Clarence Page. "White Kid, School Shooting, What Now?" *Houston Chronicle.* March 8, 2001.

[13] Walker Percy quoted in Marian Wright Edelman. *The Measure of Our Success: A Letter to My Children and Yours.* New York: Harper Perennial, 1992, p. 8.

[14] Keynote address by Ernest Boyer transcribed from audio tape, 94th Annual Meeting of the Southern Association of Colleges and Schools, Atlanta, Georgia, 1989.

[15] Nancy Larsen. "The Lesson" (October 15, 1999) adapted from Edgar Guest's "Sermon's We See." Available at www.appleseeds.com. Nancy Larsen teaches English at the American School of El Salvador.

[16] See http://www.quotegarden.com/teachers.html.

[17] See http://www.newmanstecher.com/html/quotes.htm.

[18] Ted Sizer. Keynote address. "Partnership for Excellence." Ernie Boyer. Keynote address. "New Answers to Old Questions." 94th Annual Meeting of the Southern Association of Colleges and Schools, 1989.

[19] Ruby K. Payne. *A Framework for Understanding Poverty.* Highlands, Texas: aha! Process, Inc. 2005.

[20] Haim Ginott. *Teacher and Child.* New York: Touchstone Press, 1998, p. 15.

[21] John I. Goodlad. *Romances with Schools: A Life of Education.* New York: McGraw Hill, 2004, p. 41.

[22] Theodore Roethke. "My Poppa's Waltz." Available at http://gawow.com/roethke/poems/43.html.

[23] See Judy Blume's wonderful book *Are You There God, It's Me, Margaret.* Laurel Leaf Publishers, 1991.

[24] David Dill ed. *What Teachers Need to Know: The Knowledge, Skills and Values Essential to Good Teaching.* Jossey-Bass Inc., Hoboken, NJ, 1990.

[25] The Entire "A Nation is at Risk" Report is available at the U.S. Department of Education website: www.ed.gov.

[26] Keynote address by Dean Birkley transcribed from audio tape, "It Ain't All Bad," delivered at a meeting of community administrators and teachers, St. Petersburg, Florida, 1981.

[27] Tony Hendra. *Father Joe: The Man Who Saved My Soul.* New York: Random House, 2004. p. 238.

[28] Michael Shaara. *The Killer Angels: A Novel of the Civil War.* New York: Modern Library, 2004.

[29] Philip Bigler. *In Honored Glory: Arlington National Cemetary: The Final Post.* St. Petersburg, FL: Vandamere Press, Fourth Edition, 2006 and *Hostile Fire: The Life and Death of Lt. Sharon Ann Lane.* St. Petersburg, FL: Vandamere Press, 1994. Available at www.vandamere.com.

[30] Henry Littlefield. *The Wizard of Oz: Parable on Populism.* 1964. Available at http://www.amphigory.com/oz.htm. Also see The Wizard of Allegory. 1992. Available at http://www.ozclub.org/reference/littlefield.html.

[31] R.N. Caine and G. Caine. *Making Connections: Teaching and the Human Brain.* ASCD: Alexandria, VA, 1991.

[32] See the Comer School Development Program at Yale University: www.med.yale.edu/comer.

[33] Marian Wright Edelman. *I'm Your Child, God: Prayer for Children and Teenagers.* New York: Hyperion for Children, 2002. Hyperion Books.

[34] "According to the U.S. Department of Education Congress enacted the *Education for All Handicapped Children Act* (Public Law 94-142), in 1975, to support states and localities in protecting the rights of, meeting the individual needs of, and improving the results for Hector and other infants, toddlers, children, and youth with disabilities and their families. This landmark law . . . is currently enacted as the *Individuals with Disabilities Education Act* (IDEA), as amended in 1997." See U.S. Department of Education: http://www.ed.gov.

[35] Donna Winchester. "Many Teachers Buy Supplies for Students." *St. Petersburg Times.* May 22, 2006. <www.sptimes.com>.

[36] See <www.thinkexist.com>. Search John Mayer.

[37] Thomas L. Friedman. *The World is Flat: A Brief History of the Twenty-First Century.* New York: Farrar, Straus and Giroux, 2005, p. 469.

[38] Each summer, the wild ponies are herded across Assateague Channel to thin out their numbers to preserve grazing. See <www.chincoteague.com> and Marguerite Henry's novels including *Sea Star: Orphan of Chincoteague* and *Misty of Chincoteague.* These books are excellent readings for younger audiences.

Index